BYRON GRAVES MGR. OF THE FORD MOTOR CO. LEADING THE FORD PRO-CESSION DOWN SPRING STREET — PUZZLE, "WHY IS A FORD LIKE A NOSE" ANS. BECAUSE EVERY-BODY'S BLOWING ONE" HAVE YOU GOT A COLD?

"BILL" LA CASSE, SALES MGR. STUDEBAKER CORPO-RATION OF AMERICA. BILL IS A JOLLY GOOD SCOUT AND HAS SOLD MORE CARS IN LAST 6 MO'S. THAN ANY OTHER FOR THE FIRM IN THE WEST.

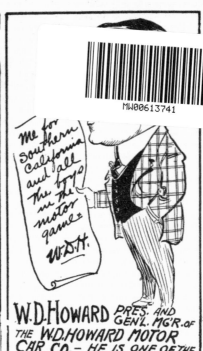

Me for Southern California and all the boys in the motor game. W.D.H.

W. D. HOWARD PRES. AND GEN'L MG'R OF THE W.D. HOWARD MOTOR CAR CO. — HE IS ONE OF THE LIVE DEALERS, SELLS THE PIONEER EXCLUSIVE SIX CYLINDER, AND ORIGINAL SELF-CRANKING "WINTON"

DAILY LETTER TO PAIGE MOTOR CAR CO. DETROIT MICHIGAN. Why Don't You Ship more Cars? A.M. Young

A. M. YOUNG PRESIDENT OF THE THOMAS MOTOR CAR CO. AND THE CARPENTER MOTOR SALES CO. HE MANAGED THE 2 LAST SANTA MONICA ROAD RACES OUTLAWED BY A.A.A — DON'T CARE.

The solid west for good roads. E.E.H.

IT'S "TEDDY"

FIAT

THE WORLD'S RECORD.

E. E. HEWLETT, PRES. OF THE FIAT MOTOR SALES COMPANY.

THE STEVENS-DURYEA COVERS THE GROUND REGARDLESS OF ROAD CONDITIONS BUT — MORE GOOD ROADS MEANS GREATER SUCCESS TO EVERY ENTERPRISE C.A.E.

CLARENCE A. ENGLISH. — GEN. MGR. ENGLISH MOTOR CAR CO. DEALERS FOR THE STEVENS DURYEA & BROC ELECTRIC. CLARENCE JUST SAWS WOOD BUT BOOSTS EVERY DAY

A big asset to the Truck industry is our good roads. R.J. Chandler

R. J. CHANDLER OF THE LOS ANGELES ALCO MOTOR SALES CO. DISTRIBUTORS OF THE "ALCO" MOTOR TRUCKS AND PLEASURE CARS

SAN DIEGO ROAD RACE 1913 MERCER 2ND PLACE.

NEVER STOP BOOSTING GOOD ROADS, BOYS.

AL G. FAULKNER MGR. LOS ANGELES BRANCH "SIMPLEX" AND "MERCER" PACIFIC COAST AGENCY. "AL" IS AN OLD TIMER IN THE GAME. HE MADE TRIP TO N.Y. CITY IN BEST TOURING TIME 17 DAYS ACROSS THE CONTINENT

DRIVING
FORCE

TOURING TOPICS

July 1925

R.F. Hackmon/25

Touring Topics Has a Larger Circulation Than Any Other Motoring Magazine in the United States

DRIVING

AUTOMOBILES AND THE NEW AMERICAN CITY, 1900–1930

FORCE

ANGEL CITY PRESS

DARRYL HOLTER WITH STEPHEN GEE

FOREWORD BY JAY LENO

FOR
CAROLE SHAMMAS

▶ A proud motorist sits behind the wheel of a new Franklin. Note the car's dynamic styling, easy-to-open doors and low body. Women played a critical role in the design and marketing of early automobiles.

CONTENTS

◀ J. Philip Erie outside his Boyle Heights home in the first car in Los Angeles.

Great Scott! How He Has Grown.
Original cartoon by John T. McCutcheon—*The Chicago Tribune.*

Ever since I can remember, I have always been fascinated by anything that rolls, explodes, and makes noise. The history of transportation in America at least for most people is about individuals and their accomplishments. Henry Ford, Alfred Sloan, David Dunbar Buick, the Dodge brothers, and Fred and August Duesenberg to name just a few. Like most enthusiasts I enjoyed reading the exploits of how engines were developed, raced, and how that technology eventually made its way to the cars we drive every day. Like most people, I just assumed that manufacturers set up showrooms and sold their cars—case closed. But like everything else in America, the real story is a lot more complicated than that.

Darryl Holter's new book *Driving Force* fills this gap in automobile history with his story about how the earliest dealers brought cars from factories in the East to car buyers in Los Angeles. Some of the story was a total surprise to me. While the car manufacturers were making cars, local dealers were providing the capital for the manufacturers to assemble cars. They repaired customers' cars when there was no such thing as a factory warranty. They offered credit to customers because banks would not. Dealers organized car races and started the first auto show in Los Angeles. Holter's incredible research shows that auto retailing, like manufacturing, was a brand-new start-up industry, and dealers—largely through trial and error—had to teach themselves how to sell people new and used cars.

With archival material from the dealers' association and other sources, Holter brings to life important innovators like Ralph Hamlin, the bicycle repairman who became the most successful Franklin dealer in America, Les Kelley, who founded the famous *Kelley Blue Book*, and Paul G. Hoffman, the car salesmen who rose to become president of the Studebaker Corporation and was named by President Harry Truman to head the Marshall Plan.

Holter also uncovers largely unknown members of the early automobile community. We meet Tommy Pillow Jr., a fourteen-year-old African-American youngster who built a car in 1902 and went on to an outstanding career as a race car driver and car salesman. We learn the fascinating story of Sybil C. Geary, the most important woman in the early years of the Automobile Club, who led the placement of the original road signs in Southern California and spearheaded the first rules for automobiles for the state of California. Until I read this book, I didn't realize that women were so important to the auto industry as designers, salespeople, and by encouraging necessary reforms that impacted every driver.

Darryl Holter shows how auto retailers connected manufacturers to buyers, changing America and shaping the history, economy, and culture of Los Angeles.

◀ When this editorial cartoon was reproduced in *Out West* in February 1913, the journal noted the car was now a "necessity and not a luxury."

PREFACE
DARRYL HOLTER

Before I was an automobile dealer, I was a historian. An unusual set of circumstances—including the civil uprisings in Los Angeles in 1992, the destruction of most businesses on and around Figueroa Street (the city's historic Auto Row) and the declining health of my father-in-law, a longtime automobile dealer—pulled me from the ivory towers of UCLA into the oldest automobile dealership in Los Angeles, Felix Chevrolet, located at the corner of Figueroa and Jefferson Boulevard.

One day in 2017, I received a call from the California New Car Dealers Association (CNCDA) in Sacramento. "We were clearing out old boxes from our offices and we were going to discard several of them with a lot of stuff about old meetings and a bunch of photos. But someone said, 'Darryl is a historian, so maybe he should look at these before we throw them out.' Maybe you should take a look."

A few weeks later, when I arrived in Sacramento for a CNCDA board meeting, I looked over the materials. What I found was amazing: three bound volumes of minutes from meetings of the Motor Car Dealers Association of Los Angeles beginning with its founding meeting in 1905 and continuing into the 1920s. There were also several large boxes full of reports from the first auto shows in Los Angeles, beginning in 1907, along with a wonderful set of photos of shows that extended into the 1950s.

This set of primary materials is the kind of documents that historians love to discover because they open the door to new research based on previously unknown material. This incredible find plunged me into a research project that has culminated in this book.

A century's worth of historical research has produced a large inventory of material on the early advocates of the automobile, trends in automotive technology

$5000.00 Washington Sweepstakes 100 miles
Ascot Park, Los Angeles, Cal. March 5, 1916.

Photograph by
Prince, 939 S. Hill St.

mechanics and design, and the impact of the automobile on American cities, culture, literature, and art. However, I found that much less is known about how these early machines moved from a small factory in Detroit or Cleveland to the streets and garages of Los Angeles or San Diego. Automobile retailers only rarely appear in the academic literature.[1]

As Steven M. Gelber wrote in 2008, "Despite its importance for household and national economics, the dealer-customer relationship has remained almost invisible in automotive research."[2] In his history of salesmanship as a profession, Walter Friedman omits any discussion of the relationship between salespeople and customers.[3] Perhaps the best book on the subject, James Rubenstein's *Making and Selling Cars: Innovation and Change in the US Automotive Industry*, devotes a mere nine pages to the role of auto dealers prior to 1920.[4] His treatment of dealers opens with information from a 1914 study prepared by Charles Coolidge Parlin and Henry Sherwood Youker, and produced by Curtis Publishing Company, a leading publisher of popular magazines such as the *Saturday Evening Post*. Although the purpose of the Curtis study was to convince automakers and retailers to increase their spending in magazine advertising, because it was the first exploration of auto retailing, it became the starting point for the small number of scholars who have examined the retail side of the industry.[5]

More than sixty years have passed since my father-in-law, Nickolas Shammas, erected the giant three-sided Felix the Cat sign on the roof of Felix Chevrolet. Over the years, hundreds of Angelenos, as well as tourists from all over the world, have photographed that iconic Cat. And nearly everyone I have met since I began working at Felix Chevrolet in 1995 always asks me to explain the connection between the dealership and the Cat.

Now that Felix Chevrolet is more than a century old (and the oldest dealership in Los Angeles), it seems like an excellent time to produce a book that explores the early days of auto retailing in this always-modern city. Focusing on the critical role of dealers in the rise of the automobile and the growth of Los Angeles adds to our understanding of how the automobile developed from a fleeting fad to a necessity of modern life for millions of Americans, rich and poor, urban and rural, men and women.

▼ Drivers line up for a photo before a 100-mile race at Ascot Park, 1916.

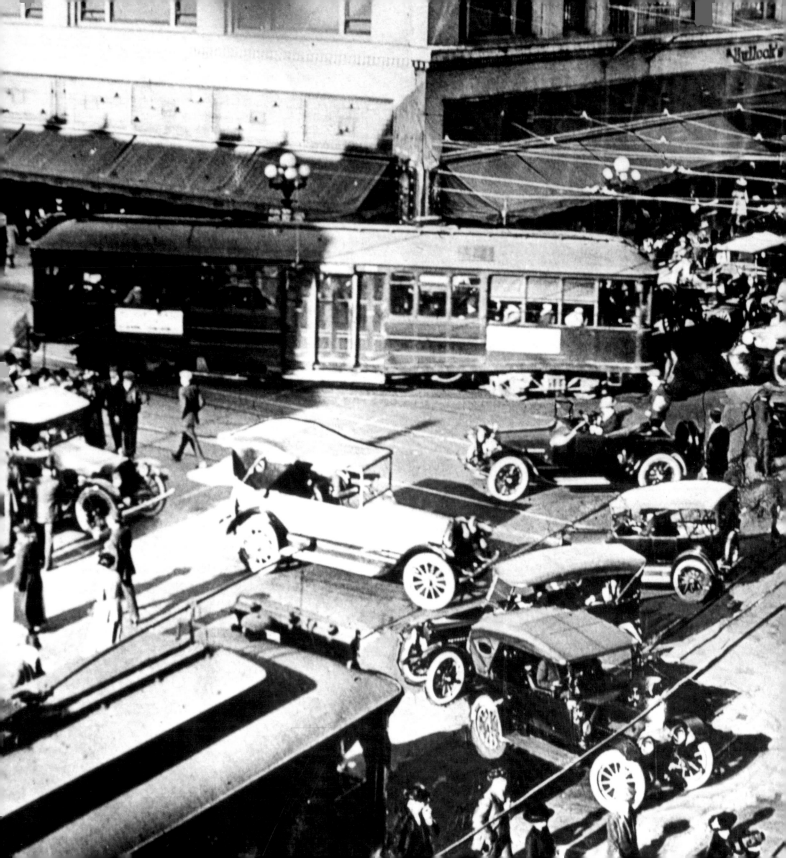

INTRODUCTION

"Thousands of employees are required to cater for the wants of Los Angeles autodom, which has grown to such proportions that numerous garages, both private and public, are involved in the great innovation that now ranks among the highest commercial possibilities of the present."

—*Los Angeles Herald*, July 29, 1906[1]

"There is perhaps no other one thing which is such an integral part of the twentieth century mode of life as the 'automobile,'" Los Angeles-based Packard distributor Earle C. Anthony argued in 1927. "Modern men and women depend upon it to such an extent that, if all motorists were suddenly deprived of their cars and manufacturers ceased to produce them, progress in every field would suffer a serious setback, and we would soon find ourselves living according to the standards of the nineteenth century."[2]

The automobile was introduced to Los Angeles not by carmakers in the Midwest or in the East, but by pioneer auto dealers who seized the opportunity to be involved in a start-up industry that would reinvent the city. The fledgling automobile business succeeded because dealers, largely on their own, found ways to sell cars to Los Angeles citizens.

"The auto makers didn't see much hope in factory-owned outlets for their vehicles," Joseph Crown, the publisher of *Automotive Age*, wrote. "It is an irrefutable

◀ Traffic jam at 7th Street and Broadway.

fact that the automobile industry would have taken years longer to flourish had it not been for the introduction of automobile dealers."[3]

The first automobile was sold in Los Angeles in 1899 when it was the thirty-sixth largest city in the United States with a population approaching 100,000. "The only stable thing about the automobile industry of that day was the insatiable interest in automobiles," the *Los Angeles Times* noted in 1916 looking back at the birth of automobile retailing in the city.[4]

Local dealers carried the burden of providing facilities to sell cars, and as no factory warranties existed on early automobiles, they would also come to assume most of the responsibility for providing service and repairs.

"Up-to-date and progressive in every feature of its life and development, Los Angeles is predominantly the home of the automobile enthusiast," the editors of *Greater Los Angeles Illustrated* enthused in 1907. "To supply the constantly increasing demand for the newest models of motor vehicles of various classes, agencies for all the most popular machines have been established in Los Angeles."[5]

By 1910, Los Angeles had a population of close to 320,000 and was now the seventeenth largest city in the nation. Some seventy local dealers represented 105 different automobile brands. Los Angeles embraced cars so fervently that the city soon ranked second to New York

▲ Bicycle parade at 9th and Main Streets, 1904.

in the number of cars on its streets. Although more people wanted to own cars, manufacturers lacked the capital to offer customer financing and most of them opposed selling on credit. It was left to dealers to fill the gap and experiment with credit sales by accepting down payments and deferred payments.

"There was a time when the horse was in a majority but conditions are such on the coast today that in one city at least, Los Angeles, the horse is all but shooed off the street," *Out West* observed in February 1913. "There is not more than one horse drawn vehicle to every twenty motors and the horses delay traffic frightfully in that rapidly moving city."[6]

The automobile business had completed a transformation "from a universal joke to a universal joy" by 1914, according to James S. Conwell, who was both an automobile dealer and a member of the Los Angeles City Council.[7] "The motor car manufacturer who comes here finds plenty of evidence that his work has been appreciated," proclaimed Hugh Chalmers, president of the Chalmers Motor Company, during a visit to Los Angeles the following year. "I thought there was a remarkable number of automobiles on the streets of Los Angeles when I was here two years ago, but it was nothing compared to what I find here now."[8]

By 1920, the population of Los Angeles was approaching 600,000 and the city had surpassed San Francisco to become the largest metropolis on the West Coast and the tenth largest city in the nation. In 1923, there were 358,000 automobiles in Los Angeles County and more cars per capita in Southern California than any other part of the country. So many cars had been sold in the United States, there were now fears that with unchecked mass production the auto industry had reached a saturation point.

"Because a start was made from nothing the business has been beset with more difficult problems than any other in history," Earle C. Anthony opined. "At first the major question was to perfect the motor car. It was answered so successfully that it carried the business into the second era when everyone wanted to buy a car, but only the wealthy could buy. The great problem then was to develop processes, methods and machinery by which automobiles could be built so well and cheaply and in such number that everyone could own one. Successful solution of this has resulted in the third stage of the industry, the period of necessity. The greatest problem of this third era is…the question of the used car."[9]

Los Angeles dealers not only changed the way automobiles were sold, they also influenced their design. Ralph Hamlin, Franklin's most successful dealer, threatened to quit selling the popular car if its manufacturer refused to make the styling changes he demanded, while Ygnacio R. del Valle lobbied the Brush Runabout Company for two years to build an automobile to his specifications. "This nifty little machine looks like the real goods and at the low price should appeal to many," the *Times* raved after the first models arrived in the city.[10]

Although many early retailers would eventually see the brands they represented go out of business, some distributors of popular cars grew wealthy and powerful. Earle C. Anthony, Cadillac distributor Don Lee and Studebaker distributor Paul G. Hoffman invested their riches into influential, pioneer radio stations. Hoffman was so pro-

▲ Los Angeles's first automobile dealer, William K. Cowan in a Waverley Electric on Spring Street.

ficient at selling Studebaker automobiles in Los Angeles, the carmaker put him in charge of their national sales operation. He would later serve as the company's President.

"Although geographically separated by more than 2000 miles, Detroit and Los Angeles are perhaps more closely related than any other two cities of the country, for Los Angeles is the greatest per capita consumer of the product of Detroit, the motor car capital of the world," the *Los Angeles Times* declared in 1926.[11]

By 1930, Los Angeles had a population of more than 1.2 million and was the fifth largest metropolis in the United States. Approximately 500,000 automobiles were registered in the city, 1.2 automobiles to each of the 392,598 homes, based on building permits.[12] It had become a new kind of American city that relied almost entirely on motorized transportation to function. "Modern automobiles…have been so perfected that motorists know practically nothing about their cars except how to drive them, but this permits them to turn their attention to other things," Earle C. Anthony reflected.[13]

This book explores the birth of the automobile in Los Angeles and the remarkable pioneers who were the driving force in putting its citizens behind the wheel.

Barney Oldfield races his Christie automobile against a Curtis biplane at Ascot Park.

1 CITY OF CARS

"Blessed with sublime weather, a seemingly endless variety of scenery from semi-tropical to snowclad and a network of boulevards unsurpassed in the United States, if not the world, Los Angeles rightfully is entitled to the distinction of being a motorists Mecca."

Los Angeles Evening Express, February 29, 1924[1]

The story of the automobile and that of Los Angeles have been intertwined for more than a century. As the city transformed from an outpost to a metropolis at the dawn of the twentieth century, so too did the fledgling automobile simultaneously come of age.

While both captured the nation's imagination, Angelenos came to recognize this exciting transportation was so much more than a replacement for a horse or bicycle, it would forever change the way they lived, traveled, worked, and even shopped.

Although the automobile was first introduced, built, and sold in the Midwest and eastern United States, it would become king in Los Angeles, connecting communities with a convenient substitute for public transit. Today, you only have to examine a map of the city's labyrinth of freeways to comprehend the scale and durability of that connection.

The explosive growth of the city's passion for automobiles was ignited by an unlikely, visionary mix of entrepreneurs and risk-takers. It owed its inception to the bicycle shop owners who began repairing and selling cars, carriage retailers, and automobile aficionados who ventured into unknown territory to sell a product regarded by nearly all banks and most businesses as a fad at best.

These early adopters learned how to broaden the market for automobiles and convince the public the car was no longer a luxury but a necessity. They promoted

◀ Motorists drive past the headquarters of the Automobile Club of Southern California on Figueroa Street, which opened its doors January 27, 1923.

▲ Ralph Hamlin's South Main Street Franklin dealership, 1905.

cars through racing and auto shows and advocated for better roads and safe-driving rules.

As the market for automobiles grew, so too did the need for space to sell them. While early cars in the city were often sold in modest facilities where other products were offered, it wasn't long before dedicated dealerships emerged and the city's first auto row took shape.

By 1906, the city had become "one of the greatest automobile centers of the country," according to the *Los Angeles Herald,* "with three thousand machines flying about the streets."[2] The automobile was no longer "only a toy for the rich," the newspaper told readers the follow-

ing year. "The wealthy have paid for the experimental stage of the game and the general public has begun to reap the benefit."[3]

In the years that followed, public interest would skyrocket. Membership in the Automobile Club of Southern California exploded from 300 in 1908 to 136,000 in 1929. Automobile registrations in Los Angeles County ballooned 550 percent between 1919 and 1929, hitting a high of 777,000.[4]

The story of the automobile in Los Angeles is in-

terwoven with the region's unique topography and sun-drenched climate in which motorists were rarely inconve-nienced by the rain, snow, and ice that made dirt roads in the East impassable.

There, automobiles without hard roofs (which was most cars until 1920) were often stored in garages during the winter months, as opposed to sunny Southern Cali-fornia, where cars could be driven almost every day of the year.[5] "The auto owner can enter his car and run hither and thither at will, while his brother of frozen places must walk, cling to a trolley strap or use unkind language dur-ing the thaw outs," the *Herald* bragged.[6]

Automobiles could also be sold year-round in L.A., unlike the normal four-month selling season in other parts of the country. Local dealers were able to retain their sales staff, while their counterparts laid off employees during the winter months, recruiting new personnel in the spring.

The independence and convenience of an automo-bile, for those Angelenos who could afford one, was ir-resistible. Although the local streetcar system boasted over twelve hundred carts on more than one thousand miles of track in 1911, it would fail to keep pace with suburban expansion.

Formed in 1898 by Henry E. Huntington, with

▲ Crowds line the streets for the 1910 Santa Monica road race.

the expansion of the Los Angeles Railway electric line and supplemented by the Pacific Electric Railway Company in 1901, the network connected Los Angeles to San Bernardino and Newport Beach. Its creation was directly linked to land speculation, subdivision, and residential development at the outer edges of the city.

"The railways and the interurbans had already played a crucial role by establishing a pattern of suburbs and satellite towns, but typically these were sited in flat areas of the coastal plain or inland valleys," author Christopher Finch explained in his book, *Highways to Heaven*.[7] The automobile allowed developers to reimagine terrain unsuitable for streetcars and exploit spectacular, previously untouched areas of the city.

The possibilities of the automobile inspired a broad coalition of Los Angeles enthusiasts, including elected officials, local clubs such as the Southern California Automobile Club, and the city's chamber of commerce, to mobilize and advocate for good roads. While bicycle riders initiated a good roads movement in the 1880s, the automobile community gave it new life.

"Decent roads are the crying need of the present time," Rambler dealer William K. Cowan told the *Los Angeles Herald* in 1906. "Any number of would-be tourists of Southern California are cutting Los Angeles out of their route and all because they cannot enjoy themselves in and around the city."[8]

DRIVING FORCE

Geo. Kussmann, Driver.

Ralph Hamlin, Driver.

100 Mile Race at Agricultural Park, Los Angeles
May 31st, 1908.

"Neck and Neck" Race between a 40 H.P. Tourist Roadster $2500.00
— and 6 Cylinder Franklin $4200.00

Running Mile after Mile in from 1:01½ to 1:05

Photo timed at 1/1000 part of second.

▲ Ralph Hamlin races at Agricultural Park, 1908.

When Ralph Hamlin, a local Franklin automobile distributor, joined the Chamber of Commerce Committee on Boulevards, Parks, and Roads, he successfully lobbied the state legislature to establish a highway commission to dramatically expand the permanent roadways in Los Angeles County.

"The building of 300 miles of permanent road in this county will mean more for the advancement of Southern California than could result from any other improvement," a 1908 chamber of commerce report concluded. "It will furnish the farmer with better means to market his crops; it will add much to the pleasure of our people, and

it will attract to our country thousands of tourists who now seek the good roads of Europe on which to enjoy themselves with their automobiles."[9]

Hamlin was chairman of the committee when a $40 million state highway bond issue was approved by voters in 1920. Two years later, Paul G. Hoffman, a Studebaker dealer (who later was elevated to the presidency of the Studebaker Corporation), took over as chair and reorganized the committee to focus solely on city and county highways.[10]

Los Angeles's pleasant weather and varied landscape gave it an advantage in another, more adventurous pastime: car racing. As advertising revenue for automobiles, parts, and services grew, newspapers feverishly documented the dozens of drivers who raced from Los

Barney Oldfield, in "Old No. 5," leads Bill Bramlett at the Cactus Derby, 1914.

Angeles to Yosemite or competed in the Cactus Derby a grueling 450-mile trek through mountains and desert from Los Angeles to Phoenix.

Editors also assigned reporters to cover hill climbs, which challenged contestants to race against the clock to reach the top of Mount Wilson or a similar peak, and endurance runs between Los Angeles and Santa Barbara, San Bernardino, or San Diego.

Local dealers took full advantage of the publicity by entering their own cars in competitions. Hamlin, who drove a Franklin, Leon T. Shettler, a Reo, and P.A. Renton, a Rambler, all got behind their respective wheels to demonstrate complete confidence in their own products.

The mile-long dirt track at Agricultural Park (now Exposition Park in Los Angeles) became synonymous with glamor, speed, and danger when in 1903, America's most famous race car driver, Barney Oldfield, produced a record-setting circuit in fifty-five seconds in his world-renowned "Bullet" race car.

"The public reads of these races and doubtless marvels at the craze of driving at what seems a pace that kills," he told the *Los Angeles Times* shortly before the event. "But to ride faster than any man ever rode before, to feel that space is being cut down 'til man is master and speed his slave—these things are worth feeling and there is an

▼ Racers compete at the Los Angeles Motordrome, 1910.

ecstasy in the drive that tingles through every fiber of your being."[11]

Los Angeles automobile retailers capitalized on the excitement of local track races by entering cars. "The efficacy of publicity obtained through having a car that is entered in the races of note at Ascot Park or elsewhere cannot be better exemplified than in the results obtained by the C.S. Slaughter Motor Company distributors for the Stearns cars," the *Herald* reported in December 1909. "As is well known the Stearns handled faultlessly by Charles Soules last Sunday on the Ascot track, made all sorts of new records which will probably stand for a long period of time and since that date the selling force of the Slaughter company have booked a sale of more than a car a day since Sunday."[12]

The first Los Angeles Auto Show was held in 1907 at Morley's skating rink and billed as "the biggest west of Chicago."[13] Even the *San Francisco Chronicle* admitted, "it excelled some of the larger and more pretentious shows of the East."[14] In the coming years, the event would come to be regarded as the best auto show in the country.

When a committee from the Motor Car Dealers' Association of Los Angeles, featuring Hamlin, Shettler, and William R. Reuss, organized a 1909 street race in Santa Monica, they were left stunned when more than 50,000 people showed up to watch.

"Nothing has done more to interest the manufacturers in the chances for the automobile trade expansion on the coast than the numerous race meets and road races held during the past three years by the dealers and automobile organizations in Oregon and California," the *San Francisco Chronicle* remarked in April, 1910. "These contests, especially in California, have proved to Eastern makers of automobiles that we have the best roads and climate anywhere in the country."[15]

Excitement surrounding the automobile reached new heights when the new Los Angeles Motordrome opened the same year. The first board racetrack in the world made of wooden two-by-fours, it was designed by Jack Prince, who gained fame creating similar "bicycle saucers."[16] A mile-long oval with all-around banking at twenty degrees, the distance from the ground up to the top wooden railing was twenty-five feet.

"Expert engineers as well as pilots of cars endorse it strongly," the *Baltimore Sun* marveled from the other side of the country, "chiefly because of the slight heating effect the surface will have on tires, the coefficient of friction between wood and rubber being much better than between rubber and any other surface. They declare that on such a banked course there will be no skidding."[17]

The story of the automobile in Los Angeles is also interwoven with a new era of women's rights and a growing female influence on the design of automobiles. By 1920, California led the nation in the number of women drivers who made up twenty percent of the drivers in Los Angeles.[18] However, the history books have forgotten how women championed the regulation of automobiles in California or drove many innovations we now take for granted, such as electric ignition switches, windshields, glove compartments, and upholstered seating.

▶ The Los Angeles Willys Overland factory employed nine hundred people and produced one hundred cars daily in 1929.

"Los Angeles will be one of the leading motor car manufacturing centers of the country in the near future," predicted Ygnacio R. del Valle, a prominent local Touraine automobile dealer, in 1914. "This is the most ideal market in the world for pleasure cars and there is no reason why they cannot be manufactured here as well as in the East."[19]

The Auto Vehicle Company began producing Tourist automobiles in 1902 in a small factory on North Main Street. By 1909, the firm employed 250 workers and completed three cars a day.[20] In 1907, the Durocar Manufacturing Co., based on South Los Angeles Street, was building five Durocars a week and employed seventy-one people.[21]

Henry Ford recognized the city's potential and spent a half-million dollars to erect a five-story car factory at 7th Street and Santa Fe Avenue in 1913. It was predicted the new facility, designed by Los Angeles architects Parkinson & Bergstrom, would produce as many as ten thousand automobiles per year.[22]

When in 1919 the Leach Biltwell Motor Company acquired a new factory on Santa Fe Avenue, the *Los Angeles Evening Express* called it "an epochal event in the industrial life of Los Angeles." The plant, originally built for the Republic Motor Truck Company, would have the capacity to produce one thousand luxury cars a year.[23]

"The latest of the great Eastern manufacturers to recognize and take advantage of the natural and strategic value of locating a production plant in this center of an immensely rich and swiftly growing market is Willys-Overland, Inc.," the *Express* noted in 1929. Some eight hundred Los Angeles workers would be recruited to pro-

▲ ◀ Durocar Manufacturing Company was based on South Los Angeles Street.
▲ The Los Angeles Ford factory at the corner of 7th Street and Santa Fe Avenue.

ing many motors, carburetors, pistons, and piston rings developed by local inventor, Harry A. Miller, that were now being produced by major east coast manufacturers.[25]

The story of the automobile is also inextricably linked to the growth of the Southern California film industry. Private cars provided unprecedented convenience when films were shot on location. Previously, having to use public transportation forced actors to wear their full costumes and make-up on the trolley on the way to and from filming. Production crews which had to haul props, extra costumes, cameras, and lights, also now had a fast and efficient way of getting to work.[26]

"There are tens of thousands of natural 'back-drops' near Los Angeles, which enable the director to find almost any type of scenery he may wish. But he must know them all and be able to pick from them, " Keystone Film Company director E.A. Frazee explained in 1916. "This is where the automobile is such a tremendous help to the director. I spend much of the time when I'm not actually directing in search of new locations in my Reo Six."[27]

Packard distributor, Earle C. Anthony, claimed in 1927 the modern motor cars he sold were as important to the movie business as "the camera, Klieg Lights, and the director and actors," themselves. "These cars, of course carry the cameras, cameraman, and director and are used for filming all sorts of action from the deliberate slow-moving wagon or the prairie schooner to chariot races, automobile chases and speeding trains," he explained.[28]

Film stars drove interest in automobiles and fueled a fascination with customizing them.

Celebrities looked to dealers such as Don Lee and automotive designer, Harley J. Earl (who later imagined the Chevrolet Corvette), to adapt cars to better express their individuality. Clara Bow had her Kissel Car painted flaming red; Rudolph Valentino preferred a cream-colored Mercedes; Gloria Swanson drove a Lancia with leopard-skin upholstery; and Fatty Arbuckle's Pierce-Arrow came with a cocktail bar and a toilet.[29]

Away from Hollywood, a much larger group of less affluent enthusiasts were "tinkering" with cars and prefig-

duce 30,000 cars annually.[24]

By 1916, more than one thousand Angelenos were employed making parts or accessories for automobiles. "These goods vary from 25-cent cans of polish to $4000 motors—from devices for scraping carbon from pistons to standard makes of tires—from auto locks to carburetors used by the world's speediest and most daring drivers," wrote the *Los Angeles Times*.

In the previous five years, 350 automobile related patents had been granted in Los Angeles County, includ-

uring a cultural revolution for American youth. When a car broke down, which was often, the only remedy was to take it apart, identify a broken or worn part or component, either fix it or replace it, then put it back together and see if it works.

No one proved to be a better representative of the early automobile "tinkerers" than Carl Breer, the son of a blacksmith from South San Pedro Street, who had built a steam-powered automobile as a teenager in 1901 and drove it around the streets of Los Angeles. He showed his hand-built car to the head of the service department at the Auto Vehicle Company, which was developing its Tourist automobile, and was hired instantly.

When the engineering department at Stanford University turned down his application, informing him four years of science courses were required, Breer visited a math and engineering professor at the Throop Polytechnic Institute in Pasadena (later the California Institute of Technology). After the Institute's president and other professors rode in his steamer chariot, he was granted admission to the school and after graduating, was accepted for further graduate studies at Stanford.

Breer gained valuable experience at various automobile companies in Los Angeles before joining the ranks of Studebaker in Detroit where he enjoyed a half-century career as the lead engineer at Chrysler, developing innovations such as hydraulic brakes and the famous streamlined 1930s Chrysler Airflow.[30]

Henry Ford's mass-produced, bare-bones 1908 Model T was sturdy, reliable, and cheap. As the market for used Model T's advanced, a new generation of drivers emerged, many of whom had the technical skills to repair and recondition used cars. Among them was Glendale native, Ed Winfield, who learned to rebuild the car as a teenager and would go on to become one of the pioneers of hot rodding. He participated in informal racing in the Los Angeles region and went on to teach younger drivers

◀ Traffic on Figueroa Street looking north from Adams Boulevard.

how to customize old cars and improve their performance in speed shops in California and Las Vegas.[31]

The city's automobile obsession inspired numerous local businesses to offer after-market automobile accessories, including headlights, electric ignition switches, turn signals, mud guards, interior heaters, and gas gauges, but also items that altered the look of the car, such as steel fenders, tops for open cars, and even entirely new bodies that personalized vehicles.[32]

By 1924, it was estimated there were 186,000 passenger cars in the city of Los Angeles. "Should every man, woman, and child in Los Angeles decide today to take a motoring trip there would be sufficient automobiles to completely depopulate the city," the *Los Angeles Evening Express* boasted.[33]

"That Detroit is the king of the automobile producing world is admitted," Earle C. Anthony reflected, "but we in California believe that our State will be crowned the queen of the motoring field at the end of 1926. Primarily the automobile is built and sold for transportation, which presupposes, first, some place to go and second a pleasant means of getting there.

"Where the Eastern purchaser buys his car to make his business day more efficient, the California motorist buys not only that service but hundreds of hours of wonderful scenic driving, every one of which is an extra dividend on his investment in automobile technology."[34]

Of the 1,638,345 vehicles in use in California in 1927, some 941,829 were in Southern California, representing an estimated investment of $753,000,000.[35] In 1930, Los Angeles City Planner Gordon Whitnall suggested, "So prevalent is the use of the motor vehicle that it might be said that Southern Californians have added wheels to their anatomy."[36]

▶ Looking west from the Los Angeles Chamber of Commerce Building at 12th Street and Broadway, toward a burgeoning strip of auto repair shops and supply stores, 1926.

2

DEALERS AND MANUFACTURERS

"Practically every manufacturer of steam, gasoline and electric vehicles is represented in Los Angeles, which has become one of the great automobile centers of the United States."

Los Angeles Times, August 28, 1904[1]

American manufacturers would transform the automobile from an experimental luxury into affordable mass-produced transportation. However, to sell them as far west as Los Angeles, the burgeoning auto industry with roots in Detroit, Cleveland, and other Midwest and Eastern cities needed a distribution system. Not many buyers would travel cross-country to purchase a car, and although some automakers solicited customers by mail, few would invest in such an expensive item without first driving it.

Early manufacturers lacked the capital to find, build, and maintain facilities for sales or repairs and while some used a branch system, hiring managers to oversee key towns and cities, others experimented with middlemen, agents, and traveling salesmen who worked on commission. Increasingly, they relied on local independent businessmen who paid freight costs, provided their own sales facilities, and hired their own employees. These independent dealers were granted a franchise by the manufacturer to represent its brand.[2]

"Los Angeles justly can be claimed to be the banner automobile city in the country," the *Los Angeles Express* opined in 1903. "According to leading dealers in the city there are about 300 automobiles of all kinds in use in this city, and this goes ahead of any city of its size in the United States."[3] The following year, the *Los Angeles Times* noted, "practically every successful eastern manufacturer of electric, steam and

◄ Ralph Hamlin's Franklin dealership at 11th and Olive Streets, 1907.

gasoline machines" was represented locally. Of the 1,500 automobiles on the streets of Los Angeles and Pasadena, the newspaper estimated forty percent were Oldsmobiles.[4] The company's cars were sold locally through Pioneer Motor Company, which was also the agent for Winton Motor Carriage Company.

Other prominent early local dealers included the Los Angeles Automobile Company which proudly sold eighty-four Ford Motor Company cars in the first eight months of 1904; Lee Automobile Company, which handled Buick and would soon incorporate as Lee Motor Company to become the local agency for Cadillac; and Norman W. Church's dealership on East 3rd where oil baron, Edward L. Doheny, spent $4,750 on a 1905 four-cylinder Peerless.

They would soon be joined by a host of others, including Success Automobile Company, Southern California agents for Locomobile, promoted as "The King of American Cars"; Superior Auto Company, which represented the popular Haynes brand; Parley A. Lord of Lord Motor Company, whose devout religious beliefs meant he refused to sell Studebakers and E.M.F. automobiles on Sundays; and Harry O. Harrison, who rose to prominence as a race car driver before selling Everitt and Peerless cars.[5][6]

Peerless Motor Car Company used a franchise agreement in 1903 that was typical of early contracts between manufacturers and dealers. It authorized retailers as exclusive agents for one year with the expectation they maintain a "suitable" salesroom, repair shop and spare parts; stock one demonstrator (a vehicle used to show customers how it operates) and at least one car that could be purchased immediately. In addition to giving their "best energies" to selling the brand's products, dealers were required to buy a specified number of cars and pay a ten percent deposit on all orders and the balance upon delivery.

By contrast, the automakers' only legal responsibility was to provide occasional advertising material and replace defective parts under weak warranty standards. Peerless was not required to ship the number of automo-

biles the dealer agreed to purchase and maintained the exclusive right to cancel the agreement if dealers failed to meet sales objectives.

"Under present conditions agents in the more important cities must invest considerable money if they expect to do a fair amount of business; and, besides, they must stake their time and efforts selling cars without any guarantee that they will be able to get the cars when the delivery dates arrive," *The Horseless Age* observed in October 1906. "Some of the best known manufacturers have absolutely failed to keep delivery dates."[7]

The journal informed motor enthusiasts earlier the same year that while "some agencies handling popular makes of cars in good territories" had done well, the majority of agencies had "led a precarious existence." It recommended dealers, instead of handling a single car as was common practice, should sell a range of different vehicles, including trucks and delivery wagons.[8]

To secure the coveted Los Angeles area franchise for Franklin Automobile Company, local bicycle dealer Ralph Hamlin, working with his neighbor and investor, Albert R. Maines, sent a wire to the carmaker's headquarters in Syracuse, New York.

Franklin's range of 1904 automobiles included a four-seater touring car with its signature air-cooled (as opposed to water-cooled) engine, which performed well

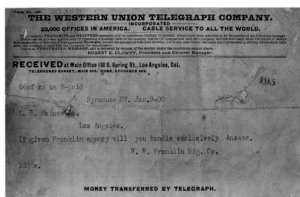

▲ Ralph Hamlin sold bicycles before he and his business partner A. R. Maines received a telegram securing their new franchise to sell Franklins, 1905

in hot, arid climates, and Hamlin, an avid automobile racer, had enthusiastically followed reports of the record-setting Franklin driven cross-country by Lester L. Whitman.

The company's president, Herbert H. Franklin, was keen to exploit Southern California's expanding market, and Hamlin and Maines' correspondence proved well-timed. "They came back with a wire," Hamlin remembered. "They said Mr. Earle Anthony has ordered one and he wants to take it on, but we don't want to make the deal unless it is a carload. So, Maines wired right back. He says, 'We want two carloads.' And that was the start of the Franklin account."[8]

Hamlin's Los Angeles Franklin dealership would soon expand from its original space on Main Street to a much larger facility on Flower Street. He then became a distributor and set up additional dealerships in Hollywood, Glendale, and San Diego.

Hamlin hired sub-dealers to run their dealerships, oversaw all their operations, and made sure their financial practices adhered to Franklin's regulations. He also signed the same one-page franchise agreement as the sub-dealers he selected.

The distributor model was popular with automakers who sought to keep up with Southern California's expansion without the hassle of signing new dealers. Among the best-known local dealers who were also distributors were Don Lee for Cadillac; Earle C. Anthony for Packard; Walter M. Brown for Stutz; Nate Cordish for Dover; J.M. Sterling for Page and Jewitt; William E. Bush for Pierce-Arrow; J.A. Wilcox for Maxwell; William K. Cowan for Jeffrey, Mitchell, and Stearns-Knight; Roger H. Miller for Pullman; Harold L. Arnold for Hudson; C.F. Smith for Stearns; and L.E. Crowe for Marion.

In 1905, Los Angeles dealers consolidated their regional influence to form the Motor Car Dealers' Association of Los Angeles. "They claim they have banded together to remedy certain evils, which have grown up in what is practically a new business the country over, and that they are merely following the example of dealers in other large cities," the *Los Angeles Herald* reported.

William K. Cowan was elected president, and Earle C. Anthony was voted in as secretary of the organization. "There is no intention to raise prices on machines or on repairing," Cowan stated. "Machines are sold by the agents at the prices set by the manufacturers. Repair work which hitherto has been on a scale depending on how good a friend you were of the repairer, and where the stranger paid for what was knocked off on the bill of the other

fellow, will be made just to all and posted in every shop. I estimate that the prices paid machinists will be cut by nearly thirty percent by the organization."[9]

The group soon expanded its activities to include organizing races and auto shows, and lobbying for legislation favorable to motorists. By 1909, Motor Car Dealers' Association of Los Angeles was the largest dealers' association in the world with forty members.[10]

Oakland Motor Company, established in 1907 by Pontiac Buggy Company, the nation's largest producer of horse-drawn vehicles, began selling automobiles in Los Angeles the following year through Woodhill Auto Com-

pany based in the Pacific Electric Building.

The franchise agreement Gilbert Woodhill signed with Oakland reflected the power of early manufacturers. While the automaker granted dealers an exclusive right to sell their vehicles in a specific territory, they simultaneously forced retailers to hold the company without liability if another dealer sold the same cars in the same territory. Oakland agreed to sell automobiles at a 25 percent discount from the list price, provided all orders came with a deposit of 20 percent and the dealers paid the balance. Only when

▲ Ralph Hamlin's South Main Street dealership.

full payment had been made was the title released to the dealer.

Oakland's responsibility for loss or damage ended when they delivered the goods. Dealers had to report defective parts within sixty days of delivery and pay for their return to the automaker. The parts would be replaced for free if Oakland agreed the parts were defective. The agreement was for one year and could be terminated by either party within thirty days. Any violations of the terms or conditions of the agreement could be considered sufficient cause for termination.[11]

Prior to 1908, most Ford Motor Company vehicles were sold by independent dealers commonly referred to as "agents." While most automakers were moving from the branch system to the franchise system, relying on independent dealers to retail their vehicles, Ford moved in the opposite direction, selling cars directly to customers through Ford-owned branches run by Ford employees. "We had plenty of money," Henry Ford later explained. "Since the first year we have always had plenty of money. We sold for cash. We did not borrow money. And we sold directly to the purchaser."[12]

Ford made the switch as it unleashed the Model T into the market. The new system was primarily orchestrated by Norbal A. Hawkins, an auditor who had overseen the company's finances since 1904 and was elevated to general sales manager in 1907. Hawkins argued independent dealers would not have the same loyalty to the company as branch managers they hired, and selling cars directly to the public lowered costs and raised profit that would not have to be shared with outside dealers. Transportation costs would also be reduced by shipping large quantities of cars to big cities.[13] Under Hawkins's guidance, between 1907 and 1908, Ford established new branch stores in eleven major cities in the East and Midwest and added fourteen more by 1910.

RETURN IN FIVE DAYS TO

Ralph C. Hamlin

ORIENT AUTOMOBILES AND
MOTOR BUCK-BOARDS
1806 SOUTH MAIN STREET
LOS ANGELES, CAL.

▲ Before selling Franklin cars, Ralph Hamlin experimented with buckboards.

Ford executives sought to install a service regime that mirrored the assembly-line efficiency of their automobile production, with consistent training, a broad inventory of parts, daily telegrams for replacement parts, and unannounced inspections of branch facilities by company staff. Ford produced 10,600 Model T's in 1909 and priced them at $950. By 1913, they produced 265,000 and sold them at $550.[14] The company could not open new facilities and train staff quick enough to keep pace with increased demand.[15] However, as its production and market share rose, Ford abandoned the branch system, converted branches into distribution centers, and returned to the reliance on local dealers who had their own money invested in the business. Branch sales offices became local factory offices where Ford representatives supervised regional dealers to increase sales and monitor service operations to ensure proper equipment, parts, and Ford-approved signage and advertising.

There were 895 car dealers in California in 1915, more than half of which were located in the southernmost counties. There were also 50,000 automobile owners in Los Angeles County and 30,000 in the city of Los Angeles. "The most urgent need of the automobile industry in Southern California today is the full recognition by the general public that the automobile industry is a legitimate and enormous business ranking well up among the largest industries in this and every other State in the Union," Earle C. Anthony insisted. "So rapid have been the strides by which the automobile industry has attained this commanding position that the public at large does not begin to realize what 'a place in the sun' the automobile trade is entitled to. Consider for a moment that $40,000,000 worth of automobiles were purchased in Southern California last year."[16]

When F.C. Chandler, president of the Chandler

Motor Company, arrived in Los Angeles in October 1915, he confidently predicted sales in the coming year would be "the best in the history of the automobile industry." Production at his Cleveland, Ohio, plant had doubled to more than a hundred cars a day.[17] "I am glad to know that in California such rapid strides have been made, and that the state is more than holding its own with the big Eastern states in the number of machines," Chandler told the *Los Angeles Evening Express*. "Here the motor market has reached its highest development in my opinion, and I look to the enterprising Western dealers for many instructive hints on selling cars."[18]

The first Chandler car arrived in Los Angeles in 1914. The vehicles were distributed in Southern California by Earl V. Armstrong, who would soon move into a "palatial" new facility on South Hope Street. "It is doubtful that there is another concern in the United States engaged in a similar enterprise that has shown such progress while representing a single make of cars exclusively," the *Los Angeles Times* declared in 1917. "It is an organization of young men, as there is no one identified with it in any capacity, who is more than 35 years of age."[19]

The extensive 1916 agreement Chandler required dealers to sign formally recognized a dealer's territory, however, it also made it clear the company would not be held liable for any sales made by unauthorized sellers in the area. The company agreed to ship a certain number of cars per month for one year, but reserved the right to change models and alter list prices, net prices, and rebates at any time and without notice; and Chandler also tightened the policy for the replacement of defective parts by adding strict time limits and stipulated no credit would be granted unless the set conditions were met.

While Chandler agreed to four very loose commitments to dealers, dealers were obliged to agree to twenty potentially expensive demands. They were left with no choice but to accept the number of cars allotted and the price they could be sold for. Payment was expected in full, either cash or certified check, on or before shipment, and the dealer was expected to "advertise vigorously" and to inform the company in advance of any intention to take on another brand that could be viewed as a competitor.

Dealers were also expected to make speedy payment for parts and were prohibited from working with sub-dealers to lower prices. In the event of a dispute, Chandler or a committee of three dealers it selected would make a binding decision. The company would also be held legally protected in the event it failed to deliver goods for any reason beyond its control. Additionally, it was the dealer's responsibility to collect from a shipper if a vehicle was damaged in transit.[20]

Although the terms of agreements were stacked in favor of automakers, the franchise system provided dealers some territorial protection and allowed them to become financially stronger, attract higher-quality managers and employees, and retain customers.

Manufacturers benefited from having a small number of stable, profitable, and well-run dealerships. The franchise system also made it easier for them to plan production and deliveries, reduce shipping costs, ensure quality sales and service facilities, store more inventory, purchase more equipment, and spend more on advertising.[21]

"While a few of the weaker firms will probably cease to exist, those who have made remarkable successes will continue to greater rewards," F.C. Chandler predicted during his visit to Los Angeles. "The motor car will be more than ever a commodity for all the people."[22]

Although nearly five hundred companies were formed to produce automobiles before 1910, an estimated 40 percent of them soon failed.[23] Only those that managed to produce a significant number of vehicles to offset the costs of mass production survived.[24]

"The conditions arising from the war have merely hastened a tendency that has been evident for some time in the automobile industry, namely, the concentration of the bulk of automobile manufacture in the hands of a comparatively few large companies," Earle C. Anthony explained.

◀ William K. Cowan's Rambler dealership at 5th and Spring Streets sold both bicycles and cars, 1905.

"All but the most solidly founded firms are bound to be eliminated in the fierce competition which the next few years are bound to witness in the automobile industry."[25]

As weaker companies fell by the wayside, a smaller group gained stronger market share. They succeeded by erecting large factories with assembly-line production and built large volumes of durable and reliable cars that were distributed throughout the country. The ten largest car manufacturers in 1917 produced 75 percent of the total production. These included Ford, General Motors, Studebaker, Willys-Overland, Maxwell, Dodge, Hudson, Packard, Nash, and REO—all of which were represented in the Los Angeles market.

"A number of firms dropped out of the business, while others came in, but the chief changes in motordom's directory were in transfer of agencies for cars from one firm to another," Frederick Wagner, automobile editor of the *Los Angeles Sunday Express,* opined in 1918, reflecting on how the First World War had impacted the local automobile business.[26]

While the automobile industry endured a period of uncertainty during and following the war, the competition to represent popular models remained fierce. When it was announced in 1919 that William P. Herbert Company would be the new Southern California distributor for Cleveland Six, the firm was inundated with applications from prospective local representatives.

"From one town there have been 18 applications for the Cleveland Six representations; from another 12; another 9 and so forth," the *Long Beach Daily Telegram* recorded. "There is hardly a town in Southern California [in] which an application has not been filed in person or writing." Enthusiasm for the light, popular-priced cars caused many to apply without ever seeing one in person.[27]

In 1920, the population of the United States was 106 million, and there were 7,602,000 automobiles, one for every fourteen people.[28] There was a growing concern among major manufacturers that the automobile market had reached a saturation point as national sales declined for the first time. In May 1921, one by one, carmakers began lowering prices to catch up with the market as they confronted deficits that pushed many of them into insolvency.

In Southern California, however, sales initially remained robust. In the first four months of 1921, 13,879 passenger cars, representing $25 million, were sold in the region, more than the entire national production of automobiles in 1903.

T.G. Kress, statistician for Los Angeles-based Automobile Publishing Company, publishers of *Motor Fax* and other car-related publications, told the *Los Angeles Evening Express*:

> In no other section of the United States has this volume of business been transacted. The ability of the dealers to choose the time for campaigns in the face of discouraging conditions and to make these campaigns successful proves the pick of the automobile sales force in the United States has gathered in Southern California and shows that this section not only is the most beautiful playground of the country, but a place where business is always at the top notch regardless of conditions in other parts of the country.[29]

Eventually, nationwide price-cutting caught up with Los Angeles, although industry executives, including P.W. Wisdom, western manager for Moon Motor Car Company of St. Louis, insisted the city remained "the bright spot on the business map of the country."[30]

Harold L. Arnold, Los Angeles distributor for Hudson and Essex argued:

> One of the main reasons for the recent depression in the motor car industry can be traced directly to the attitude of some manufacturers and dealers. These men clung to the worn out theory that the manufacture and sale of automobiles constituted a new and different type of commodity with new and different methods of selling … This theory did not bring disaster so long as the

▲ Hamlin's Graham dealership on Flower Street.

public demand for cars exceeded the supply. But just the moment that this demand fell off, these dealers and manufacturers were faced with the serious problem of changing their policy during a time when their organizations should have been showing their greatest efficiency. The result was inevitable… The older and wiser factories had long since realized that automobiles must be merchandised in the same manner as any other piece of goods. Motor cars are nothing more than goods to be sold the public on their merits.[31]

Into the 1920s, the most important change in the dynamic of power between manufacturers and dealers was the demand by automakers for an increased volume of sales, especially for more affordable models. In response, dealers competed by discounting prices on new cars and accepting over-allowances on trades in order to sell more vehicles, which drove down dealer profits. Carmakers increasingly demanded exclusive representation and canceled agree-

ments when franchise holders took on competing brands. Many manufacturers also abandoned the distributor arrangement. Studebaker executive Paul G. Hoffman wrote that the shift from using the distributor system to "direct dealer" marketing lowered costs and improved control over dealers.[32]

Prior to World War I, the more cars the factories delivered, the more profits the dealers earned, but this changed dramatically as capacity overcame demand. Production increased, but dealer profits collapsed, and dealers started complaining they were being forced to accept more orders than they could sell. A few industry insiders began to assert that the earlier mutual interest in ever-increasing production had come to an end.[33]

A comprehensive study published by the Federal Trade Commission in 1939 detailed that while new-car sales volume in 1926 was up 9.3 percent over 1925, average dealer profitability fell by 73 percent.[36] Franchise

dealers were increasingly compelled to invest in larger and more luxurious facilities, special tools and equipment, and hire a wider range of dealership personnel.[34]

"Never before in the history of the automobile business has there been greater buying activity than during the last several months, due to the presentation of a large number of beautiful and improved models at exceptionally low prices," the *Los Angeles Evening Express* reported in 1928.[35] Sales of new automobiles in Southern California in 1928 totaled 111,709, an increase of 13,163 over the previous year. "Los Angeles and suburbs recorded the lion's share of the increased volume of new automobile sales over the previous year," noted the *Express*. "This 40-mile area having accounted for 10,154 of the 13,163 sales increase."[36]

The newspaper observed the trend toward "two or more cars per family" was keeping pace. Los Angeles now had "many thousands more automobiles" than there were families. However, the Great Depression beginning in 1929 would have a devastating impact, diminish production, and forever change the automobile industry. Among the popular brands which would go out of business were Peerless, De Vaux, Marmon, Franklin, Auburn-Cord-Duesenberg, Durant, Pierce-Arrow, Stutz, and Hupmobile.

WILLIAM K. COWAN

William Keen Cowan was the first Los Angeles automobile dealer, the first president of the Motor Car Dealers' Association of Los Angeles, and a founding member of the Automobile Club of Southern California. He also had the unfortunate distinction of being the first motorist to receive a speeding ticket in Pasadena.

Born in a log cabin in Greenfield, Missouri, in 1863, his grandfather encouraged his education, and as a young five-year-old, he walked three miles to school. He went on to study at Baker University in Kansas, where his roommate, Joseph L. Bristow, would become a future United States senator who introduced the resolution that led to the Seventeenth Amendment to the US Constitution, allowing voters rather than state legislatures, to elect senators.

Cowan also graduated from Park College at Parkville and the Chicago Horological School before moving west and beginning his working life in Los Ange-

▲ William K. Cowan and his South Hope Street Rambler dealership.

les as a jeweler in 1887.[1,2] His journey to selling cars began with a passion for bicycles.

He competed in races from Riverside to Temecula and Los Angeles to San Diego in 1892.[3] The following year, he helped form a bicycle club called Argonaut Wheelmen. He then managed Rambler Bicycle Shop at 427 South Spring Street in 1894, renting bicycles and selling them for both cash and on installments.[4] When he became owner of the business, he moved it to 207–209 West 5th Street.[5]

"If I can ever get hold of any of those things, I'm going to sell them here in Los Angeles," Cowan told his family after spotting the first horseless carriages on the city's streets. In April 1899, after three weeks of negotiation, he made good on his word, selling a Waverley Runabout, an electric car, to Los Angeles resident, Stephen G. Hall.[6]

In the next four years, he sold about a hundred more Waverleys from his bicycle shop[7] before receiving a sample model of the new Rambler Gasoline automobile. In 1902, he sold five Ramblers, then thirty in 1903, eighty-five in 1904, and 125 in 1905.

"Ever since Mr. Cowan introduced the Rambler to Southern California several years ago, it has become one of the most popular cars on the market," the *Los Angeles Times* wrote in February 1905. "Each year he has been unable to get enough cars of this make to fill the demand, even though the output of the factory at Kenosha has been multiplied many times."[8]

"According to Mr. Cowan, the chief difficulty in selling the cars in the pioneer days was in convincing a doubting public that the things would actually run, and would really take them, say, to San Bernardino and back without relying on services of a crew of expert mechanics," *Motor West* reported.[10]

When Cowan moved to a new facility at 830–834 South Broadway, the *Los Angeles Herald* described the modern showroom, office, garage, and storerooms as "the finest place of its kind in the city."[9]

It was no surprise when in 1905, local automobile dealers formed an organization and elected Cowan as

▲ A February 1909 advertisement in *Touring Topics*.

the founding president.[11] Leading the Motor Car Dealers' Association of Los Angeles, Cowan began organizing a Great Endurance Run from Los Angeles to Santa Barbara along a 110-mile route through the steep Casitas Pass over unpaved, rock-strewn roads.

The race was conceived as a way of demonstrating dealer confidence in the automobiles they sold. Some sixty drivers took part, however, when the award committee announced four cars had tied for first place, including Cowan and his Rambler and Leon T. Shettler in a REO, Shettler challenged Cowan to race back to Los Angeles.

He accepted, and it was agreed the winner would be determined by three factors: speed (how long it took to finish), reliability (any problems that required repairs or adjustments), and economy (how much gas was required). In the end, Cowan won because his Rambler used two or three pints less than Shettler's REO.

Cowan differed from many early Los Angeles dealers in his fascination with selling "commercial cars" or what later came to be called "trucks." His first truck sale was an electric vehicle purchased by a liquor dealer in San Bernardino. He later sold an electric car with a top speed of 20 miles per hour to the City of Los Angeles to be used as a patrol wagon. In 1907, the Long Beach Fire Department purchased Southern California's first horseless fire wagon from Cowan, a specially built Rambler.[12]

Cowan's wife, Martha, who served as president of the local Women's Twentieth Century Club, shared her husband's passion for automobiles and documented the family's ten-day adventure to San Francisco in an article for the *Rambler Magazine*, a national publication produced to promote brand loyalty. "I am glad to say," she wrote, "that except for one hour's delay, our Ramblers never faltered, and when you consider that we drove 1,270 miles through nine mountain passes and that one of the machines was an old one that had already traveled 17,000 miles, I have only to ask, 'How much more could anyone want?'"[13]

The Cowans' motoring experience was not always so pleasant. They were arrested in Pasadena in 1907 by two "irate speed cops" on bicycles when at 14 or 15 miles per hour, they violated the city's 12-mile an hour speed limit.[14]

By 1908, Cowan was the Southern California distributor for Rambler cars and he built a new facility at 1140 South Hope Street.[15] The following year, he organized a hill-climbing road race event in Altadena in which stock (as opposed to modified) vehicles competed against runabouts, roadsters, touring cars, and other categories.[16]

Cowan was a founding member of the Automobile Club of Southern California formed in 1900.[17] He also served as a member of the first board of trustees of the city of Eagle Rock in 1911. "Mr. Cowan has lived in the valley nearly six years, and may really be said to be a pioneer, having come here before there was either car or water service," the *Eagle Rock Sentinel* told readers.[18] He helped organize the Congregational Church of Eagle Rock and was among the early subscribers for stock in the Bank of Eagle Rock.[19]

The Rambler Company was acquired by the Jeffery brand and in 1915, Cowan sold his interests in Jeffery. After a six-month period of retirement, he signed up to represent the Grant brand in Pasadena, Eagle Rock, and Altadena.[20][21] He joined the sales department of Harris M. Hanshue's dealership selling Apperson cars in 1917, prompting the *Los Angeles Times* to report, "Back on the row again and, so he says, glad to be back. W.K. Cowan is now greeting old and new friends alike."[22]

Cowan retired from the business in 1931 after thirty-two years of selling automobiles and launched an unsuccessful campaign to become the Los Angeles City Council member for the fourteenth district. He died of a heart attack in 1952. "When you get exasperated with Los Angeles traffic, blame William K. Cowan," the *Los Angeles Times* wrote. "He started the whole thing."[23]

▶ The Pacific Bicycle factory on Broadway where Hamlin worked.

RALPH HAMLIN

▲ Ralph Hamlin and navigator Guy K. Erwin drive past his Franklin dealership.

Ralph Cunningham Hamlin personified the glamor and excitement of early Los Angeles motoring. Not only was he the top Franklin dealer in the nation, whose clients included luminaries such as Harry Chandler and William Mulholland, he was also a successful car racer himself.

Born on October 17, 1880 in San Francisco, Hamlin arrived in Los Angeles when he was six years old. He was suspended from school when he was fifteen after refusing to identify a classmate who placed matches on stairs as a prank. He ignored his parents' pleas to return and instead took a job as a bicycle messenger before being hired by Pacific Cycle Company. [1][2]

"They manufactured Pacific Bicycles on Broadway directly across from the Bullock's Department Store in Los Angeles," he recalled. "I got a job as an apprentice and was there for about a year and a half … This was a wonderful experience because I got the full idea of building a bicycle. It included brazing, bending handlebars, stringing wheels or anything else."[3]

With the support of a neighbor, Albert R. Maines, who manufactured and sold furniture, Hamlin started a South Main Street bicycle shop in 1896 in a space that also operated as a blacksmith shop. He paid no rent, but instead he helped the owner use his forge.[4]

Hamlin began bicycle racing after purchasing a badly damaged bike that had been run over by a buggy. He repaired it and rode it in the Fourth Annual Road Race from Los Angeles to Santa Monica in 1895. "I was entered in a field of 75 riders with a ten-limit handicap and I won," he reflected. "I won a Cleveland bicycle worth $155. That was the beginning. With that Cleveland bicycle I was in every race that I could get in."[5] He quickly generated enough publicity and new business that he was able to move into his own store.[6]

Hamlin brought the first motorcycle to Los Angeles, an Orient. "The motorcycle had an Astor 4-cycle engine which was completely foreign to me," he noted. "I took that engine apart to learn about the four-cycle principle and what the timing meant on it."[7]

He won the first motorcycle race on the Pacific Coast at Agricultural Park on May 7, 1901 and sold Orient motorcycles in his store until he began selling the Orient

◄ Hamlin celebrates with the Howdy Band after winning the grueling Los Angeles to Phoenix Desert Race in 1912.

Buckboard, a very basic motorized buggy.

An expert mechanic, Hamlin made extra money repairing two-cylinder motors and in 1902, used bicycle wheels and scrap parts to assemble what the *Los Angeles Times* claimed was the city's first bicycle car, which he later sold for $450.[8]

Hamlin soon began buying non-operating, cheap used cars from frustrated owners. "On the old cars that came into his possession, Hamlin worked ceaselessly, until he made them run and then, after selling them, he kept them running," *Motor Age* explained. "That was his earliest conception of service, and it was many years before the term became common usage."[9]

He was fascinated with the Franklin which, unlike other gas-powered cars, used an air-cooled engine. He applied to become a dealer and traveled to the Franklin factory in Syracuse, New York. With the financial backing of his friend Maines, Hamlin received a franchise agreement to sell Franklin automobiles in 1905.[10] He later became a distributor for the automaker and hired managers to run dealerships in Hollywood, Glendale, and San Diego.

"It was not easy to sell air cooling," he wrote. "My competitors, all of whom sold water-cooled cars, would tell my prospects that if air cooling was so good, the rest of the cars would be using it."[11]

To promote the vehicles he sold, Hamlin entered and won races, endurances tests, and long-distance competitions. He showcased the Franklin's air-cooled engine in blistering deserts and on rock-filled mountain roads, and in June 1905, teamed up with endurance driver, Lester L. Whitman, to attempt a record-breaking drive from Los Angeles to San Francisco. Whitman had recently driven a 10-horsepower Franklin from San Francisco to New York in an unmatched 32 days, 17 hours, 20 minutes.

Together, they navigated through mountains, farmland, and dry riverbeds to reach Market and Third Streets in San Francisco in 37 hours, 53 minutes, smashing the previous record by sixteen hours. However, when they returned to Los Angeles, they discovered a competitor, driving a Rambler, had made the reverse journey six hours quicker. They attempted to recapture their short-lived record the following month but were hampered by a coastal storm that bogged them down in the mudflats around the Ventura River.[12]

"All my early day racing—bicycle, motorcycle, speed boat and automobile—was strictly amateur," Hamlin explained. "I enjoyed the thrill of winning, but the most important of all was the publicity I gained for the merchandise I was selling. In those days a win was a great boost for sales."[13]

Hamlin was instrumental in the formation of the Motor Car Dealers' Association of Los Angeles in 1905. He would later serve as the organization's president and as a board member, and he regularly helped organize the Los Angeles Auto Show.

He became adept at generating publicity and earned headlines driving the first automobile up Mount Wilson in 1907, navigating the route on the Altadena side in a 10-horsepower vehicle.[14] More attention followed when he took on Barney Oldfield and Ralph DePalma in the 1909 Santa Monica race—on a course he designed. Although he didn't win, he was awarded a prize for being the "most consistent" with speeds between 60 to 70

► Hamlin kept a 1902, 1904 and 1907 Franklin in a museum at his home.

m.p.h.[15] When President William Howard Taft visited Los Angeles the same year, Hamlin drove the Franklin that Taft and Los Angeles Mayor George Alexander rode in during a celebratory parade.

His passion for speed and modern transportation led him in 1911 to invest in a Farman biplane which he stored at Dominguez Field in Rancho Dominguez. "Mr. Hamlin, it is believed, will have no difficulty in mastering the art of flying," the *Los Angeles Evening Express* enthused. "The principal requirement of a birdman is a cool head and a thorough knowledge of mechanics."[16]

Hamlin was victorious in the grueling Cactus Derby from Los Angeles to Phoenix in 1912. He achieved a re-cord-breaking time of 18 hours and 22 minutes in what the *Times* called a "nerve-wrecking, muscle-straining race" as five of the twelve competitors broke down.[17] At the fin-ish line, he had a 43-minute advantage over his nearest rival, Charles Soules, in a Cadillac. "When he brushed the tears away and mopped his red eyes … he showed himself as a man who could appreciate the right kind of welcome," read the *Los Angeles Times*.[18]

"After winning that Phoenix race our sales jumped very fast," Hamlin recalled. "My competitors couldn't knock it. I think I had the only air-cooled car in the race."

Hamlin hired a professional writer to produce the *Franklin Camel News*, a monthly magazine with details on new models and services. He emphasized customer ser-vice and responded to every customer criticism with posi-tive action. He also forbade staff from accepting cash tips.

"It is evident from the Hamlin layout that cleanli-ness may be made akin to Godliness even in the auto busi-ness. The walls and floor of the salesroom are absolutely immaculate," *Motor Age* noted after a 1920 visit to Ham-lin's facility. "The janitor is furnished uniforms—blue for winter service, white for summer—and he is always busy with a brush, broom or cloth in hand."[19]

At Franklin Automobile Company meetings

in New York, founder Herbert H. Franklin made sure Hamlin was placed at his table. Hamlin had made several recommendations on improvements to vehicles that were, in fact, implemented. However, in 1923, he threatened to switch to another franchise if the company refused to make styling changes to the front end of the vehicles, and shocked by his protest, Franklin agreed.[20]

The same year, Hamlin's sense of adventure led him to travel to Egypt and pay a visit to King Tutankha-mun's newly discovered tomb. He became the Southern California distributor for De Vaux automobiles in 1932.[21] During his 45-year career selling automobiles he also rep-resented Lozier, K-R-I-T, and Scripps-Booth. Like many of the smaller brands that were not part of the "Big Three" (Ford, General Motors, and Chrysler), Franklin did not survive the Depression and filed for bankruptcy in 1934.

Hamlin later acquired a Graham dealership and drove the Graham Supercharger in the final three Yosem-ite Economy Runs beginning in 1936. He retired from racing after winning the 1938 contest and would retire completely in 1950. He moved into a Bel-Air house once owned by Bessie Lasky, the wife of the famed film pro-ducer Jesse L. Lasky, where he kept three old Franklins in a personal museum. He died on July 5, 1974 at age 93.

3

AUTO ROWS AND RETAIL FACILITIES

"The automobile with all its comfort, simplicity, cheapness and speed will soon be as familiar a sight to the residents of Los Angeles as they are now to the citizens of New York, London and Paris."

Los Angeles Times, June 16, 1899[1]

The first automobiles sold in Los Angeles were purchased in bicycle and carriage shops, livery stables, blacksmith and machine shops, and occasionally, in hardware and department stores. However, as interest and sales accelerated, dedicated dealerships emerged and soon the city's finest architects competed to design structures that paid homage to the glamor and excitement of motoring.

Liveries were obvious trading venues, as owners of cars often already owned carriages and stored them in livery stables within a short distance of their home. Many liveries would transition not only to storing and selling cars but also offering rentals and service.

For local blacksmiths, who survived replacing horseshoes, wagon wheels, and axle bearings, motorists brought new sales and service opportunities. Existing tools were often enough to repair, replace, or modify faulty parts. However, the arrival of the assembly system, producing cars with interchangeable parts, would herald a dramatic decline in business.

Los Angeles machine shops benefited from repairing, selling, and in some cases building automobiles. Samuel D. Sturgis who, along with his brother, William, operated a machine shop at 208–210 West 5th St., was the co-inventor with J. Philip Erie of what was proclaimed on May 30, 1897 to be the first automobile driven in Los Angeles. Fearing they would be overwhelmed by curious spectators if they test drove

◀ Auto Row on Olive Street, 1916.

their creation during the day, they waited until 3 a.m. before taking to the streets. The *Los Angeles Herald* described the vehicle as "a handsome coach, capable of seating nine persons … propelled by a gasoline engine concealed in the body between the running gear." Although it moved slower than expected, it still managed to complete a journey of "several blocks."[2]

Bicycle shops were also natural venues to segue to selling cars in Los Angeles. Like automobiles, bicycles offered both an alternative to a horse and the freedom of individual mobility. The city's first automobile dealer, William K. Cowan, was a bicycle enthusiast who managed and later owned the Rambler Bicycle Shop on Spring Street. Cowan entered the automobile business in April 1899 and soon afterward completed his and the city's first automobile sale, a Waverley Electric runabout.

Others who followed his example included Charles A. Redmond who formed Central Auto Garage and Bicycle Shop on Central Avenue in 1905 and William F. Pipher who came to be regarded as "the dean of brokers" in early used and second-hand automobiles.[3] Pipher's brothers, Roy and Frederick, also transitioned from selling bicycles to automobiles.

John Wheeler Leavitt's road to becoming a Los Angeles automobile dealer began in Cleveland, Ohio, where he teamed up with Alexander Winton in 1890 to build bicycles. In the aftermath of the 1893 financial panic, he headed west, setting up a bicycle shop on 9th Street. He initially sold REO before moving onto Overland, Oldsmobile, Peerless, and Falcon-Knight.[4]

"Twenty years ago the bicycle represented the highest ideal of an outing machine, the latest word in fresh air and luxury, and today that place has been filled by the automobile," the *Los Angeles Herald* observed in a 1916 editorial.[5]

Owners of Los Angeles carriage shops also came to understand the automobile would forever change their business. Kentucky native Charles E. Capito established Capito Carriage Company on 12th and Main Street for carriage sales, however, by 1906, most of the space was used to sell automobiles.[6] Although carriage and wagon makers enjoyed strong demand for their products near the turn of the century, several of the nation's most important carriage makers such as Studebaker entered the automobile business as a hedge against the challenge of the horseless carriage.[5]

The car had such an impact on Los Angeles that even hardware and department stores experimented with selling them, but the space they took up and the difficulty getting them to the street for a test drive was often impractical.

As the market for automobiles grew, the pressure to provide larger facilities became compelling; however, the first dedicated automobile dealerships in Los Angeles had little in common with the modern showrooms of today. Frequently located in two-story buildings beneath apartments or offices, they offered enough space to display a single demonstrator. Poorly lit, reeking with the stench of automotive products, they often had a small, partitioned space or a desk in the corner of the room to serve as an office and an area at the back for gasoline, oil, and tools to make minor repairs or adjustments to the demonstrator.

▲ J. Philip Erie and William H. Workman enjoy a ride in Los Angeles's first car, in Boyle Heights, 1897.
▶ Main Street, home to Los Angeles's first Auto Row.

Many dealers began to take on second or third brands and hence needed additional space and demonstrators. When manufacturers started producing a wider variety of models, even more demonstrators were required, so the need for floor space intensified.

As more cars were sold, more customers returned to the dealership for repairs; dealers had to expand service facilities adjacent to the showroom. More repair work necessitated storage space for parts and additional parking for cars waiting to be serviced and others waiting to be picked up by owners.

Dealers were forced to create new rooms for customers and sales managers to finalize deals, as well as offices and employee facilities. As automobiles became more commonplace, customers were no longer willing to place orders and wait weeks or months for delivery. Instead, dealers ordered cars in advance and expanded their facilities to store the increased inventory. As the industry matured, a new generation of "second-hand cars" began to flood the market, forcing dealers to create additional space to recondition, store, and display them.

In the first decade of the twentieth century, automobile facilities were initially scattered across Los Angeles. However, leaders who were driving sales and putting the city's citizens on four wheels began to group together downtown on Main Street to form the first "Gasoline Street."

Among the enterprises congregating on the busy thoroughfare were the Auto Vehicle Company, manufacturers of the Tourist car; Heineman and Pierson Company selling Moline cars; the Bennet Auto Company featuring Wayne, Peerless, and Maxwell; Don Lee selling Cadillac; and William K. Cowan's Waverley agency.

"Every appliance and convenience known to the modern mechanic and architect has been called to the aid of the local trade," the *Los Angeles Herald* stated in 1906. "Prospective purchasers realize without investigation the fact that the finest machines of American make are to be secured in Los Angeles."[7]

In the years that followed, there would be dramatic advances in facilities, fixtures, and furnishings as dark, uninviting dealerships were replaced by purpose-built automobile palaces.

Typical of this transformation was Don Lee, who

▼ Figueroa Street became Los Angeles's new Auto Row.

had established a modest Buick dealership at 1032 S. Main St. in the early months of 1905. A year later when he took on Cadillac, which was rebranding from an economy car into a higher-end vehicle, he relocated two blocks south to a well equipped facility at 1218–20 S. Main St.

His new dealership, a refined Mission-style building, boasted large, arched windows that teased the merchandise to passing traffic and impressive double doors that led to an elegant showroom.

Other dealers followed suit illuminating display vehicles day and night, replacing concrete or wooden floors with tile, and adding furniture for customer comfort. Another common addition was a separate office space where customers could sit with the dealer or sales manager to complete the financial arrangements that closed the sale.

Main Street's mantle as the city's Auto Row would be short-lived as Olive Street, four blocks west, quickly took over. Western Motor Car Company was the first automobile business to build on Olive Street, followed by the Fisk Tire Company.[8] In 1907, there were twenty-three dealerships on Main Street and one on Olive. Just three years later, there were twenty on Main Street and thirty-two on Olive. "Automobile Row is now no longer a 'row,'" the *Los Angeles Herald* emphasized in August 1908. "It is becoming more and more divided weekly; of late there has been a mild stampede to get to a location on Olive, Hope, or Grand."[9]

Ralph Hamlin moved his Franklin dealership to a new facility on South Olive near 12th Street. "We are not looking for the tourist trade, and I do not feel that an automobile dealer needs a busy location like Main Street, where the traffic is so heavy that a purchaser is somewhat timid about starting out with his car," he told the *Los Angeles Evening Express*. "Olive Street is broad and improved and a fine place to show cars."[10]

Hamlin reserved services at his Hamlin Garage exclusively for clients of his Franklin dealership. Only Franklin parts were stocked, and patrons were not charged for storage. The garage had a storage capacity of forty cars. The building, with a yellow pressed-brick exterior, was designed in an L-shape that extended around a neighboring house. The showroom and the service area were separated by a fireproof wall. Yet, Hamlin did not separate the workshop from the main body of the garage because experience had proven, "owners of cars in the repair shop… could not be kept away from their machines either by partitions or 'keep out' signs."[11]

By 1910, the Automobile Club's Los Angeles Dealer Directory listed seventy dealerships selling 105 different brands, all of which were located in the city's central district.[12]

As automobiles became more reliable and affordable, dealers expanded sales to the professional classes. Mass production steadily reduced prices, and soon the old system of displaying a demonstrator became outdated. Customers expected to see and test drive the exact car they would be purchasing, and dealers were compelled to stock new vehicles for sale, requiring even more space to store inventory.

As auto retailing evolved, so too did the relationship between dealers and their clients. Selling a car was only the first step in building a relationship; providing repairs and service would become key to customer retention. As a result, garages began to expand services, not only by storing more cars, but also by washing, polishing, and making repairs to vehicles.

Dealers, especially those representing top-selling brands, saw the benefit of maintaining a dedicated space for service and repair work operated by full-time mechanics, and soon the majority of garages on or around Olive Street were connected to a dealership.[13]

"Many of them will make repairs at reduced prices on machines bought through them, often replacing parts free of charge if the buyer becomes obstreperous," the *Horseless Age* reported in a 1909 article examining the city's garage business.[14]

Garage owners commonly added well-stocked service departments to reduce time storing "dead" cars while parts were shipped in from faraway factories. In 1909, of the more than five thousand cars in daily use in Los Angeles, 75 percent were estimated to be housed in private garages and the remainder in public facilities which charged on average $5 a month.[15]

White Garage on South Olive Street was one of the largest and most impressive new facilities in Los Angeles. Previously located on South Broadway in the heart of the business district, it moved in 1909 to a residential area.

To add significance to the name, the two-story brick structure was clad with glazed white tile and had two white enameled ornamental lamp posts flanking the entrance. The garage's moniker was displayed on an elec-

tric sign that stretched the width of the building.

The lower story, behind a row of plate glass windows, included office space for the president, secretary, treasurer, publicist, bookkeepers, and a superintendent; an information bureau and lobby; as well as a showroom large enough to accommodate four cars. Directly behind was 14,000 square feet of floor space with a capacity for one hundred cars. The building's iron support columns

▼ The Lord Motor Car Company located at 1240 S. Figueroa Street.

were arranged where "not a single post interferes with the movement of machines."[16] The second floor was reserved for repairs and the stockroom. A platform with wheels was used to raise cars four feet from the ground as a substitute for the below-grade "pit" system used in most ground floor garages.

The facility was managed by Harmon David Ryus, who represented Pope-Hartford and Pope-Tribune cars, as well as the White Steam Car, produced by White Sewing Machine Company of Cleveland, Ohio.[17]

When the prominent local dealer Leon T. Shettler began selling cars in 1902, his showroom was on 6th Street between Spring and Broadway. He later moved to Grand Avenue as he considered the previous location too far south and the $75-a-month rent excessive. In 1912, as a sales agent for REO and Apperson cars, Shettler announced plans to open a new garage on Pico Street between Main and Hill Streets. The 10,000 square foot, fire-proof building would be dedicated to the sale, service,

and repairing of machines he sold.[18] [19]

"Leon T. Shettler is one of the oldest dealers in the business," the *Los Angeles Times* declared. "When automobiles were hard to introduce and were few and far between on the streets of Los Angeles, Shettler was agent for the two-cylinder Reo, and he sold a large number. He is now agent for the Apperson line and recently has taken a partner into the business."[20]

The second decade of the twentieth century witnessed a spectacular growth of auto retailing in Los Angeles and the emergence of the city's third Auto Row. The same desire for space that drove early dealers from Main Street to Olive Street pushed them further west and south to Figueroa Street and adjacent Flower Street, and then to Jefferson Boulevard.

Figueroa Street offered dealers important visibility to the public. It was a major north-south thoroughfare extending nearly thirty miles long from Wilmington all the way to what is now La Cañada Flintridge.[21]

Unlike dealerships built in the 1950s, fronted by a large expanse of customer parking and rows of new and used cars for sale, customer parking was less of an issue

▼ Ralph Hamlin's Franklin dealership on Flower Street.

The fleet of Dodge Brothers touring cars the Los Angeles Police Department ordered from the Albertson Motor Car Company on Figueroa Street in 1921 came equipped with a "penetrating siren."

▲ The salesroom at Earle C. Anthony's Los Angeles Packard dealership, circa 1915.

in the 1910s, since most people still used street cars. The early facilities took full advantage of every inch of their real estate, extending the footprint of the building right up to the sidewalk. Customer parking was less of an issue then, when most people still used street cars.

The first floor typically housed the showroom and offices while the second and higher floors were occupied by garage and service activities. Dealers regularly used the roof as a parking level for new cars or to store repaired vehicles waiting for pick up.

Among the most extravagant new facilities in the area was the Packard dealership built in 1911 for Earle C. Anthony's California Motor Car Company which would be described as "the most completely equipped automobile salesroom and service building west of Chicago."[22] Anthony moved his enterprise from South Olive Street to the corner of 10th and Hope Streets and into a new facility designed by Los Angeles architects Parkinson & Bergstrom and decorated and furnished by the Pasadena firm of Greene & Greene. Two East Coast research trips resulted in a simple but elegant design that provided the maximum floor space and "the most convenient interior arrangements."[23] The first floor showroom faced Hope Street while the two service entrances were on 10th Street. The second floor included a mezzanine overlooking offices and a large stockroom. The third was reserved for used cars, and the fourth housed a machine shop.

When Hartwell Motor Company, the representatives for Jeffrey cars and trucks, opened a new building in 1916 at the intersection of 12th and Flower Streets, the *Los Angeles Times* proclaimed it to be one of the "prettiest salesrooms on the Pacific Coast."[24] "Some might call it a salesroom, and it is, but when the furnishings and lighting system, and decorations, and fixtures suggest the interior of a mansion, why not call it a parlor?"[25]

The first floor was devoted to a "beautifully harmonious" showroom with walls and ceiling adorned with frescos by artist John B. Holtzclaw, complimented by a color scheme of orange, black, and soft gray, continuing throughout. The floors were decorated with "a charming lighting system" accented by "expensive furniture." The *Los Angeles Herald* gushed the interior decorations were, "wonderfully luxurious, refreshing, appealing and artistic."[26]

▼ The salesroom at the Greer Robbins Company Chrysler dealership on South Figueroa, 1925.

Behind the salesroom were offices, as well as "an exceedingly attractive ladies' restroom" and "a special room with telephones and easy chairs for closing deals." The second floor, reached via a large freight elevator, included what was billed as "probably the best lighted" machine shop in the west, as well as a stockroom. The mezzanine also housed a stockroom.

"We feel that more and more the public will demand service, but to give good service, one must be equipped for it," General Manager F.H. Hartwell explained. "Service doesn't mean standing back of a guarantee, and repairing or replacing anything that goes wrong—although that in itself is important—but also in providing a well-furnished and attractive showroom in which to receive old and new friends."[27]

In 1917, real estate investor Amanda Salter erected a lavish new home for Speers Motor Company, representing Haynes and Grant cars, at the nearby intersection with 11th Street.[28][29][30] Salter's pharmacist father, John R. Vogel,

amassed a fortune investing in local property, including a prime lot on the corner of Broadway and 7th Streets he purchased in 1892 for $33,000 and sold fourteen years later for $650,000. Four years after his death in 1913, she used part of her inheritance to recruit architect William S. Garrett to design a two-story brick building offering more than 32,000 square feet of floor space.

Speers Motor Company, the successor to Bekins-Speers Motor Company which had operated in the city since 1911, would occupy the building for only a year before it was taken over by Troy Motor Sales Company, distributors of Nash cars and trucks.[31]

Other prominent new businesses in the area included a 45,000 square foot Chandler facility operated by Earl V. Armstrong on Hope Street near 10th Street. In just four years, Chandler sales nationwide had risen from 500 to 25,000 cars.

"Our rapidly increasing business, particularly in the last six months, made this move imperative," Armstrong explained. "In March (1917) we sold more cars than any of our competitors in the $1200 to $2500 class—again and again we have been at the top of the honor roll in Chandler sales throughout the country."[32]

"That section of Los Angeles known as 'automobile row,' in reality has not been a row for several years," observed the *Los Angeles Times*. "If one were to see from an airplane how many blocks are taken up with buildings devoted exclusively to the marketing of motor cars, it would be apparent that 'automobile town' would be a far more appropriate name."

The newspaper estimated almost four thousand people were employed in the roughly two hundred automobile and accessory showrooms in the area "bounded by Los Angeles Street on the east, Figueroa Street on the west, 7th Street on the north, and 16th Street on the south." The number did not include the "innumerable" independent repair shops.[33]

Architect Albert C. Martin's reputation for innovative design made him an obvious choice to imagine a new home for Stutz Automobile Company in 1917 at the intersection of Washington Boulevard and Figueroa. He had made headlines for his work on Million Dollar Theatre on Broadway and would later be part of a trio of architects to design Los Angeles City Hall.

Martin was recruited by dealer Walter M. Brown who wanted a new building worthy of housing Stutz's celebrated sixteen-valve speedsters. The architect responded by adding double-door entrances on both Washington and Figueroa and a pair of eighteen foot driveways. The main entrance on Figueroa led to a service room for minor repairs while the main machine shop included 125 feet of pit space.

The showroom with ample space for six cars was described as "one of the largest, lightest, and most pleasing" to be unveiled in the city that year and was decorated in an old ivory enamel color scheme accented by "several clusters of lamps" that furnished "a semi-inverted light."[34] The facility also included a "large" waiting room, offices, and restrooms.

Martin's skill designing automobile facilities would be put to use again in 1931 when he designed the Auburn-Cord dealership on Wilshire Boulevard.

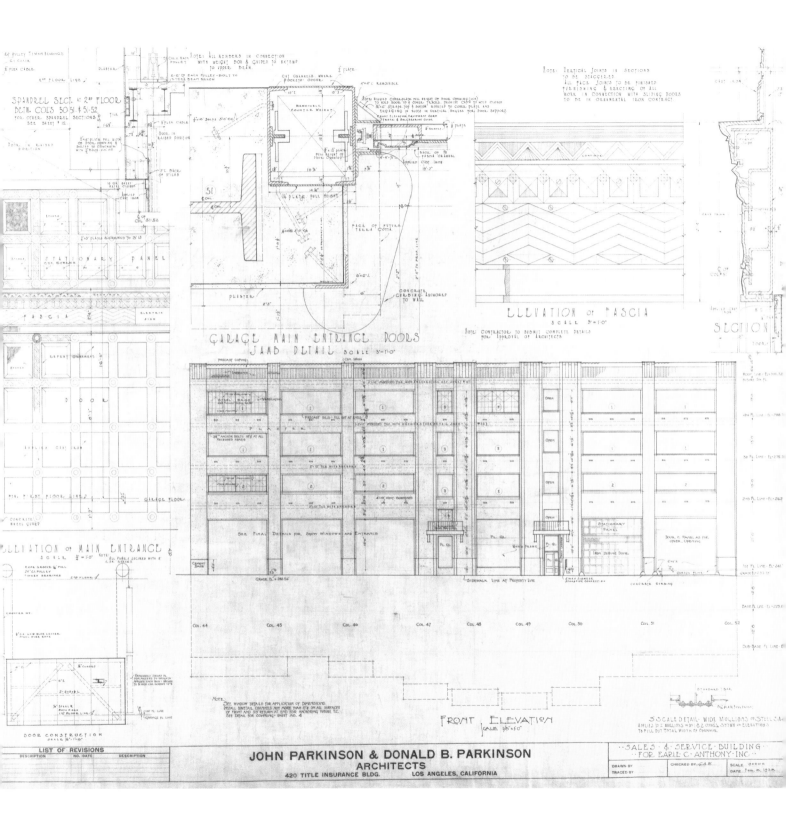

GARAGE MAIN ENTRANCE DOORS

ELEVATION of FASCIA

FRONT ELEVATION

JOHN PARKINSON & DONALD B. PARKINSON
ARCHITECTS
420 TITLE INSURANCE BLDG.   LOS ANGELES, CALIFORNIA

SALES & SERVICE BUILDING
FOR EARLE C. ANTHONY INC.

Tupman Ford Company erected a new building in 1920 at the corner of Figueroa Street and Jefferson Boulevard which extended Auto Row. The company would become one of the first in the region to establish a department exclusively for Lincoln cars.[35 36]

When William P. Herbert became the Southern California distributor for Cleveland Six in 1919, he set up a temporary location on South Olive Street before building the "largest" and most "modern" building "devoted to motor car merchandising and service in the city" at 11th and Flower Streets.

Herbert, a former director of Chandler Motor Company, expanded his ambitions for the structure after receiving reassurances from Cleveland Six management of the availability of inventory. Plans for the Renaissance-style structure included a 6,000 square foot showroom with a 27-foot high ceiling and a mezzanine with sales offices below.[37]

"Every modern convenience that can be thought of for providing top-notch service to owners of Cleveland cars has been included in the specifications of the building," the *Los Angeles Times* enthused.

Herbert later also represented Chandler at the same facility. Although the company went out of business during the Great Depression, the building survived and in the early 1990s became the home for the Palm Restaurant, a New York–based chain of steakhouses. The original showroom was left largely intact with two-story high ceilings, elaborate ceiling moldings, and a large mezzanine overlooking what had been the showroom.

Albert C. Martin's close friend and occasional collaborator, architect John Parkinson, and his son Donald, had a passion for automobiles that translated into the 1926 design of a Maddux-Lincoln Figueroa sales and service facility described as "the biggest and best Lincoln home in America."[38]

Widely regarded as the dean of Southland archi-

◄ Earle C. Anthony's expanded sales-and-service building under construction.

Crowds fill the showroom at the opening of Earle C. Anthony's expanded Los Angeles facility.

tects, John Parkinson had a fascination with all things automotive and held a patent for an automobile speedometer; he had designed a Los Angeles factory for Henry Ford; a dealership for Earle C. Anthony; and imagined a structure for Firestone Tire and Rubber Company. Along with his son, he would design the 1929 Douglas M. Longyear Packard dealership at the intersection of Sunset Boulevard and Cherokee Avenue in Hollywood.

The three-story Spanish structure the Parkinsons created for Jack Maddux, president of the Los Angeles Lincoln agency that bore his name, cost $400,000 and occupied a full city block between 21st and 22nd Streets. It offered clients what Maddux referred to as "hotel service," including "a system of pigeon holes for the filing of customer's service charge bills"; a clerk to "assign cars to certain stalls; a speed elevator operating to all four floors; a luxurious lobby; a reading and retiring room for guests; bell-boys that may be summoned for errands; even a check room where customers may, without charge, leave in safety anything they do not wish to be encumbered with."[39] It also included an employee lounge with soft chairs, showers, and lockers. The high-ceilinged showroom featured a mezzanine for offices. A second and third floor was used for service, and the roof could store more than a hundred cars.[40 41]

Maddux, who also owned local Ford dealerships, had a passion for both cars and airplanes and established Maddux Air Lines in 1927. He began by offering flights from Los Angeles to San Diego, but soon expanded to other destinations such as San Francisco, Phoenix, and El Paso. The airline merged in 1929 with Transcontinental Air Transport (whose investors included Charles Lindbergh and Mary Pickford), to become TAT-Maddux. When the business joined forces in 1930 with Western Airlines, it was rebranded as Transcontinental and Western Airlines, which later became known simply as Trans-

▲◀ Earle C. Anthony's sales-and-service building with KFI radio antennas.
◀ Ramps to reach the service department.
▶ Anthony's showroom.

World Airlines (TWA).

In 1928, Earle C. Anthony returned to John Parkinson with a request for a new four-story facility on Hope Street adjacent to the 1911 building the architect designed while in partnership with G. Edwin Bergstrom. This time, responsibility for the interior was handed to the renowned San Francisco Bay Area architect, Bernard R. Maybeck, who Anthony enticed to join the project by offering him a specially made black-and-silver 1929 Packard Phaeton as part of his payment.[42]

Unlike many newly constructed dealerships, the project began below grade with the excavation of 35,000 cubic feet to create a basement and sub-basement for storage. The structure included a system of ramps to move cars between floors and a "Work-Lite" system of lighting that "illuminated the service repair areas so that no shadows were possible."

A 1929 book published to celebrate the grand opening paid tribute to Maybeck's work in the showroom:

> His well-known freedom from architectural dogma and conventional design is seen to splendid advantage in, for example, his daring conjunction of tremendous Byzantine columns of black marble with travertine capitals and corbels which contain elements from several architectural epochs.[43]

▲◀ John Parkinson's 1920 concept for a sales-and-service building for the Troy Motor Car Company (unbuilt).
▲ The Maddux-Lincoln Figueroa sales-and-service facility John and Donald B. Parkinson designed.

By 1927, of the 126 new-car dealerships and used-car operations located in Los Angeles, only three were located outside of the downtown area. Of these, seventy-six were new-car franchise dealerships while fifty were selling used cars, reflecting the rise in used-cars sales in the region and throughout the country. Some fifty-four auto sales operations were located on Figueroa and Flower Streets (thirty-two new and twenty-one used) while the remainder occupied other streets in the downtown area.[44]

Auto Row became the prime district for the growing used-car market. While new-car franchise dealers preferred to build at major intersections for greater visibility and to provide multiple points of entry, in 1927, twenty-one used-car dealers had established operations near the new-car dealerships, often in the middle of the block or at minor intersections.

The huge investments in large and elaborate auto facilities on Figueroa Street created an Auto Row in Los Angeles that rivaled Broadway in Manhattan, South Michigan Avenue in Chicago, North Broad Street in Philadelphia, and East Jefferson Street in Detroit.[45]

DON LEE

Don Musgrave Lee's name would become inseparably linked with Cadillac Motor Car Company for whom he was the California distributor. Lee was recognized as "one of the outstanding merchandisers of motor cars in the country."[1] He was also a broadcast pioneer who owned influential radio stations in both Los Angeles and San Francisco and an early Los Angeles television station.

Born in Lansing, Michigan, on August 12, 1880, he attended school in Chicago and graduated from the city's Northwestern Military Academy. He immediately moved to Detroit, Michigan, where he was employed as a clerk in a wholesale dry goods business. After ten months on the job, he moved west in 1898 to Seattle.

Lee went into the lumber business and took over the management of a shingle mill and also became the director of a logging camp. He sold his interest in the enterprise in 1902 and entered the automobile business as the Oregon and Washington agent for Cadillac Manufacturing Company, in charge of branch agencies in Tacoma and Portland.[2]

In 1904, he moved to Los Angeles seeking another brand and a bigger market. He signed on with Buick and established a dealership on South Main Street. The following year when Cadillac transitioned from selling economy cars to luxury vehicles, Lee was rehired as a dealer and the Southern California distributor.

He recruited Joel E. Brown from Cadillac's Detroit headquarters in 1906 to become his Los Angeles service manager. Brown had expert knowledge of the company's vehicles and would become a vital influence on his enterprise. In 1907, Lee also took on the Royal Tourist brand and in 1908 opened a branch office in Pasadena. He became the Cadillac distributor for the entire state of California in 1911, with new branches in San Francisco and Oakland.[3]

Lee became renowned for selling custom cars in new colors to movie stars and business leaders. In 1918, Motor West reported that in the parking lot of the Famous Players-Lasky Corporation, there were twenty-two Cadillacs belonging to the film company's executives and stars, including Cecil B. De Mille, Mary Pickford, Sessue Hayakawa, Jack Holt, John Fairbanks, Edna Mayo, Olga

▲ Don Lee and his Main Street Cadillac dealership.

Petrova, Henry Walthal, and Julian Eltinge. Lee also built a custom $25,000 "ultra-modern" automobile for Roscoe "Fatty" Arbuckle.[4]

He purchased Earl Automobile Works in 1919 and changed the name to Don Lee Coach and Body Works, and promoted it as the "largest builders of high grade custom bodies in the west and one of the six largest in the United States."[5]

The *Los Angeles Evening Express* called the deal, "the most important move of the last five years in Los Angeles automobile circles."[6] Lee convinced J.W. Earl, head of the business since 1899, to remain as manager and hired his son, Harley, as chief designer. He immediately announced the output of custom bodies would be increased and within days, the new business received "several large orders from dealers."[7]

"We build just as good bodies, and in most cases more modern and distinctive, than are built anywhere in the East," Harley Earl told the *Express* after returning from a tour of factories in the East and Midwest. "Our stationary tops are far ahead of anything I saw, and I was surprised to learn that throughout the factories the special tops which are so popular in California are known as 'California tops.' It would be proper to call these 'Los Angeles tops,' as they originated here."[8]

Earl claimed to have received more than a thousand inquiries about their custom tops from eastern motorists in the twelve months. In the following year, the new business built three hundred custom bodies, mostly on a Cadillac chassis, but also on Locomobile, Packard, and Crane-Simplex chassis. They would be purchased by numerous celebrities, including Anne May, Tom Mix, and Blanche Sweet.[9] Harley Earl went on to enjoy a successful career with General Motors where he designed the Corvette in the 1950s.

Lee was recognized in 1923 for selling more Cadillacs wholesale and retail in Los Angeles than were sold in Chicago. He would have sold more than the Cadillac dealer in New York had the sales in Newark, New Jersey, not been included in the New York territory.[10]

"Don Lee has been a progressive businessman, an organizer and a leader, and today has one of the largest and finest organizations known to the motor industry, with branches in Los Angeles, San Francisco, Oakland, Pasadena, San Diego, Fresno, Sacramento and Burlingame and sub-dealers throughout the state," the *Los Angeles Evening Express* reported in 1930."[11]

Like other dealers, he invested heavily in newspaper advertising, but was fascinated by the possibilities of radio. In 1925, he bought the KFRC station in San Francisco and a year later, KHJ in Los Angeles, formerly owned by the *Los Angeles Times*.[12]

His stations featured live music and actors and actresses who pitched Cadillac and GM's new, racy La Salle model, which would make its world premiere at the fourteenth annual Los Angeles Automobile Show in 1927. Lee also connected his radio stations to telephone service so customers could call in for information.

In 1931, he started a television studio—one of the first of its kind—at Don Lee Cadillac/LaSalle in downtown Los Angeles. The Federal Radio Commission granted a license to station W6XAO which took to the air in December, sending images to five receiving sets in Los Angeles, broadcasting one hour a day, six days a week.[13] It was claimed the footage the station broadcast of the 1933 Long Beach earthquake were the first scenes of a major disaster to ever be shown on television.

Although he made a significant contribution to California's automobile and broadcast industries, the negative publicity from his personal life tarnished his stellar reputation. Lee divorced his first wife Etta, mother of their son Thomas Lee, in 1915. He married Anabelle Torker the same year, and when they split a decade later, she filed a lawsuit that included claims of cruelty, which he denied. They later settled out of court.[14]

He was sued by 22-year-old Joy McLaughlin in 1934 for $500,000 for breach of promise. She claimed after

◄ Don Lee's Cadillac/LaSalle dealership at 7th and Bixel Streets.

they met in 1927, she agreed to an intimate relationship based on his promise to marry her. Lee reportedly gave McLaughlin three cars and an expensive diamond ring and took her on many trips aboard his yacht during their engagement.[15]

In August 1934, three months before he died at the age of 53, he married 24-year-old Texas socialite Geraldine May Jeffers Timmons. When it was discovered Lee had left almost his entire million-dollar fortune to his son, his young widow launched a lawsuit.

At a highly publicized trial, Geraldine May Lee testified her late husband lost a large part of his fortune due to love affairs, including a $11,500 settlement with Joy McLaughlin. Judge Walton J. Wood ordered her husband's estate to pay her a $500 monthly allowance, despite Thomas Lee's insistence that his father had made sure she signed a prenuptial agreement.[416]

In 1950, Lee's 45-year-old son, Thomas, died when he plunged to his death from the twelfth floor of the Pellissier Building on Wilshire Boulevard. His family later alleged he had been given an unprescribed lethal dose of morphine and insulin.[17] While many of the businesses Don Lee started would continue to carry his name, the television station he nurtured is now KCBS-TV in Los Angeles.

◀ Don Lee built a radio-and-television empire.
▼ Geraldine May Lee.

EARLE C. ANTHONY

Earle C. Anthony was a titan of the early Los Angeles automobile business whose name became synonymous with the luxury and prestige of the Packard automobile. He was also a master communicator who owned influential radio stations and used his political clout to champion better roads and the construction of bridges across the San Francisco Bay.

His long list of achievements includes building his own automobile, the first service station in Los Angeles, and installing one of the city's first neon signs. "Anthony's accomplishments are no accident," Lynn Rogers, the *Los Angeles Times* Automobile Editor, wrote in 1949. "Behind them stand years of pioneering plus a foresighted character into which fate blended such components of success as spirit, leadership, a keen sense of humor, understanding and sympathy."[1]

Born in Washington, Illinois, in 1880, he first arrived in Los Angeles in 1890 where he attended Los Angeles High School. As a 17-year-old student, his interest in electrical engineering led him to design and build an electric horseless carriage. "The car was propelled by a one-half horsepower motor," the *Los Angeles Times* detailed. "The body was an old buckboard and the transmission was taken from a wheelchair. With Earle at the wheel, the Anthony Special met an abrupt end when it struck a chuck hole on the old Beaudry Street hill."[2] The incident was one of the city's first automobile accidents on record.

Anthony went on to major in mechanical engineering at the University of California in Berkeley where he also edited *Blue and Gold*, the class yearbook; launched a humor magazine called *Pelican*; and served as an associate editor of the *Daily Californian*, a student newspaper. He also co-wrote the musical *Doraflora* which was performed at San Francisco's Fisher's Theatre.[3][4][5]

After completing his studies, he returned to Los Angeles where he formed Western Motor Company with his father, Charles. In a modest one-story building at 720 South Spring Street, the cars they sold included Thomas, Pope-Toledo, and Northern, whose slogan, "Silent as the stars" was, as the *Times* wrote, "considerably more poetic than accurate."[6]

"Mechanically the cars of 1904 were a joke," the

▲ Earle C. Anthony was still a student when he built his first electric horseless carriage.

◀ Anthony behind the wheel of the 1908 "Purple Pup" Packard runabout.

newspaper observed in 1916. "The financial status of the makers was a thing to keep the automobile dealer lying awake at night. But people wanted automobiles, and the Anthony organization of 1904 set about satisfying the demand."[7]

As the Anthony business grew, it took over Norman W. Church's dealership and with it, the right to sell Peerless, Knox trucks, and Stevens-Duryea. In 1905, the firm was awarded the prestigious Packard franchise. "This superb car has never before been represented in this territory as the eastern demand has taken the entire output of the factory. We have, however, secured ten cars … and, of these, three have already been sold," Anthony trumpeted.[8]

According to the *Times*, there was, "no better agency in Los Angeles than the Packard. The cars sell themselves. They have a name that means a ready sale."[9] Anthony would eventually become the Packard distributor for all of California as well as representing other brands, including Chalmers, Dort, Sheridan, Yale, Reo, and Scripps-Booth.

As a founding member of the Motor Car Dealers' Association of Los Angeles, Earle C. Anthony helped shape the organization's mission, as well as the city's automobile show. He displayed cars in every show for a half century until 1957 when Packard failed to deliver cars on time.[10]

Like other members of the association, Anthony entered cars into endurance runs and hill climbs, often with custom paint jobs. He was a major promoter of the audacious 1908 New York to Paris Race which began in New York City, journeyed to California, then Alaska, across the Bering Strait to Siberia, through Russia and central Europe, and finished in Paris.[11]

He also generated newspaper copy with "Cactus Kate" and "Cactus Kate II," Packard stunt cars used to demonstrate the power, endurance, and ability of the brand and to set record-breaking times on numerous cross-country journeys.[12]

Believing the old method of driving into a garage and having a vehicle refueled from a portable gas container was outdated, Anthony joined forces in 1913 with Cadillac dealer, Don Lee, and his brother, Cuyler Lee, along with Lee's San Francisco manager, P.T. Prather, and the Hudson distributor, Harold L. Arnold, to form National Supply Station Company.

They opened the first service station in Los Angeles at Washington Boulevard and Grand Avenue, and soon expanded with a network of thirty outlets selling Standard Oil Company's Red Crown gasoline. "The advent of the new organization has caused a howl of protest from garage men who have been dependent on the sale of gasoline for a large part of their profits, and from small refiners as well," *National Petroleum News* reported.[12] The journal expressed suspicion the oil company was secretly backing the business since its own recent application to start a similar chain of stations had been refused by city officials.

The following year, Anthony and Arnold bought out the other partners and opened new stations in Pasadena and four hundred miles north in Oakland.[3] There were 259 stations when the Standard Oil Company took official control of the enterprise in 1914.

"There are many innovations in automobile methods for which Anthony is responsible," the *Los Angeles Times* declared in 1916. "The purchase form of contract, which is used by practically every dealer in Los Angeles,

▼ Aviator Col. Charles A. Lindbergh rides in a 1927 parade through downtown Los Angeles in a Packard Straight Eight Phaeton supplied by Earle C. Anthony.

was originated by the Anthony organization. The word "service" was first used in connection with the Packard cars years ago." [14]

His interest in electrical engineering and his marketing instincts also led to a fascination with new radio technology. After experimenting at home, he considered using radio to communicate with California Packard dealers. After building a transmitter and installing an antenna on top of his Packard dealership at 10th and Olive Streets, he decided to expand his reach and broadcast to the general public.

In April 1922, station KFI went on the air with the message: "This is K-F-I Earle C. Anthony, Incorporated,

California distributor of Packard motor cars." Before long, Anthony built a new 5,000-watt transmitter making KFI one of the most powerful radio stations in the country. In 1926, he was elected president of the National Association of Broadcasters, and in 1929, he purchased another radio station in Los Angeles, KECA.

With a flair for publicity, Anthony installed one of the earliest neon signs in the city in the mid-1920s. "Packard" in bright electric neon letters could be seen blazing atop a building opposite Barker Bros. at 7th and Flower Streets. He also installed a similar sign at his San Francisco showroom.[15]

When famed aviator, Col. Charles A. Lindbergh, arrived in Los Angeles in 1927 for a hero's parade celebrating his non-stop solo flight across the Atlantic, Anthony made sure he rode alongside Mayor George E. Cryer in a seven-passenger Packard Straight Eight Phaeton. The hundreds of thousands of spectators who crowded the parade route also saw forty-four other Packards in the procession. Anthony also arranged for Packards to be used for a similar event in San Francisco.[16]

Anthony sold eleven Packards early on in 1906 and 3,511 in 1928.[17] He marked the twenty-fifth anniversary of his involvement in the automobile business in 1929 by opening a new million-dollar dealership at the corner of 10th and Hope Streets in downtown Los Angeles. It was the final structure in a trio of lavish Packard facilities that included a San Francisco dealership which opened on April 2, 1927 and an Oakland location that began business on November 17, 1928.[18] For each unique structure, Anthony worked with architect, Bernard Maybeck, who also designed Anthony's Los Feliz home.

Anthony was an early champion of bridges across the San Francisco Bay. He believed the city lacked the roads and infrastructure to be competitive and set out to do something about it. He rallied other northern California automobile dealers, including Don Lee and his general manager, Fred Pabst, to sponsor newspaper advertisements calling for action. Ten local dealers contributed one thousand dollars each to begin the effort.[19] Ultimately, San Francisco Dealers' Association contributed more than $100,000 to the bridge-the-bay movement.[20]

Local automobile retailers paid famed bridge engineer, Ralph Modjeski, to draw plans and make estimates for the Oakland Bay Bridge. When it eventually opened in November 1936, it was Anthony who drove the first car, a Packard limousine, with California Governor Frank Merriam and former President Herbert Hoover to the other side.

"More than 125,000 automobiles have been sold by the organization since the inception of the company and I feel that the friendship and support of the owners of these cars have been the contributing factor in the growth and success of this organization," Anthony said proudly in 1939.[21]

"He still has his visionary look in his eyes that seems to pierce the future and fathom out the significant from the nonessential," the Times noted the same year. "His temperament is highly strung like that of a fine race horse. He is one of the easiest men to talk to if you have something worthwhile to say. If not, you are dismissed rather abruptly."[23]

In the early 1940s Anthony built an experimental television station, W6XEA, and in 1948 he launched KFI-TV, which offered local television viewers "programs for the entire family."[22] His refusal to recognize the Television Authority (TVA) as the bargaining union for the station's employees led to a five-month strike in 1951 that ended when he sold the business to Thomas S. Lee Enterprises, a subsidiary of the General Tire and Rubber Company. The station is known today as KCAL-TV.

With the demise of the Packard brand in the late 1950s, Anthony began to withdraw from automobile retailing and he died in 1961 at age 80. His philosophy was simple: "Don't waste time dreaming about it! If it's worth thinking about, do it! If not, forget it!"[24]

▶ Anthony launched KFI radio in April 1922.

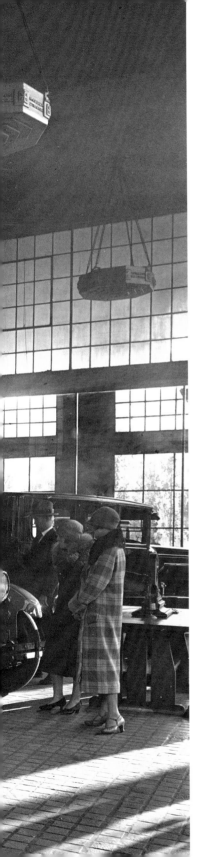

4

SELLING CARS ON CREDIT

"A good many embryo economists and a large proportion of the rather numerous authors of thrift lessons, take the position that the person who buys an automobile on the installment plan is a reckless extravagant person likely to spend his declining days in the poorhouse."

Automotive Industries, August, 1923[1]

For more Los Angeles citizens to buy automobiles, the city's dealers recognized they had to change the way they were sold. While early "pleasure cars" were reserved for a privileged few, assembly-line production allowed manufacturers to produce more affordable machines that, with credit, were within reach of the professional classes. As the market for expensive models tightened, dealers turned to doctors, lawyers, and tradespeople who they knew were interested in buying cars but often lacked the cash to complete an outright purchase.

Critics, however, forecasted allowing the customers to pay in installments would spell doom for the fledgling automobile industry. Much of the blame for the collapse of the bicycle craze had been directed at careless retailers who provided credit to customers who then defaulted and failed to return their bicycles. And it was feared automobile dealers, without experience determining a good from a bad credit risk, would make the same mistakes and flood the market with repossessions.

"There is no excess of cars, and customers are to be found for all of the reputable makes that are produced," *Motor World* wrote in 1905, "To deviate from the cash system now in universal use is to invite disaster…No sane businessman will bring himself to this."[2]

The early automobile industry was characterized by instability, as nearly two hundred companies entered and exited the market between 1903 and 1926.[3] Most

◄ A salesman shows off the latest Packard cars at Earle C. Anthony's Los Angeles showroom.

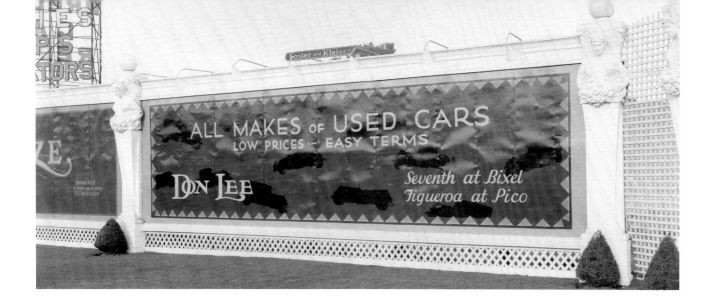

banks refused loans to carmakers and regarded early automobiles as luxury items. Banks also turned away dealers because they were concerned by a clause in franchise agreements that allowed carmakers to cancel arrangements in as little as ten days if a retailer appeared to be financially unstable. A canceled dealer could not compel the manufacturer to buy back any autos in the dealer's inventory.[4]

Automobile dealers sold cars on a cash basis because manufacturers demanded large deposits for wholesale purchases and full payment prior to delivery. Manufacturers relied on dealers to provide the deposits for working capital and for credit from parts suppliers so they could continue assembling their cars without major disruption.

Around 1905, dealers began to experiment with what was referred to as "time sales" or "time payments" by accepting a substantial deposit, as much as 70 percent, and then allowing the customer to pay two promissory notes within sixty days to cover the balance.

Among the local retailers who began to see time sales as a necessity was Ralph Hamlin, the Franklin dealer, who had sold bicycles on credit and adapted a contract used by his business partner, investor Albert R. Maines, to sell automobiles on installments.

"My friend Mr. Maines … had quite an interest in a big furniture set-up in town and they had a furniture contract," he remembered. "So, we took this furniture contract and put [in] automobiles instead of furniture. I sold bicycles on that. That was the first I knew of any installment plan.

"My deal with Maines when he first consigned to me he consigned bicycles to me. The papers would come in, I would settle up with him the payments and the last payment was mine. That was the way it worked. In other words, when the deal was closed I got my commission."

As a result of the arrangement, Hamlin saw an uptick in sales and other local dealers soon followed his lead. "They finally got on to it," he recalled. "They had to."[5]

Hamlin's arrangement reflected a national trend. The small town nature of the city also meant local dealers often sold cars to people they already knew and trusted.

As manufacturers produced better and cheaper cars, the demand for time sales grew, and dealers found themselves competing with their peers, not only based on the sale price of the car, but also on the terms of the deferred payments, many of which were extended to a year or longer. But, under pressure to meet sales quotas, dealers who relaxed their standards for down payments and promissory note payments soon found themselves forced into bankruptcy by numerous defaults and re-possessions of damaged cars.

"As a rule, dealers had far too little capital for any extensive undertaking, nor had they an organization capable of keeping close watch on payments; and the establishment of such a force was obviously more of a burden than the profit to be derived," author William Grimes observed in an early study of automobile retailing.[6]

In 1907, when the Los Angeles-based Auto Vehicle Company, which produced the Tourist automobile, ran into financial difficulty, *Pacific Motoring* questioned whether the firm's financial problems stemmed from offering too much credit.[7]

Morris Plan Banks, established by Arthur J. Morris to provide loans that were not available to the middle class through traditional banks, began offering limited automobile financing as early as 1910. The very next year, Studebaker Corporation announced it would accept notes endorsed by its dealers on purchases.

"We have in view the future rather than the immediate present," declared Studebaker General Manager Walter Flanders. "We have considered the advent of credit in this business as inevitable and our move is but the consummation of a plan long since laid."[8]

However, just two weeks after making the announcement, Flanders and his associate, E. Leroy Pelletier, felt compelled to offer what was described as a "fresh interpretation."

"Despite the general belief to the contrary, Pelletier,

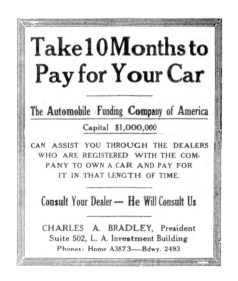

Take 10 Months to Pay for Your Car

The Automobile Funding Company of America

Capital $1,000,000

CAN ASSIST YOU THROUGH THE DEALERS WHO ARE REGISTERED WITH THE COMPANY TO OWN A CAR AND PAY FOR IT IN THAT LENGTH OF TIME.

Consult Your Dealer — He Will Consult Us

CHARLES A. BRADLEY, President
Suite 502, L. A. Investment Building
Phones: Home A3873—Bdwy. 2493

▲ Advertisement for the Automobile Funding Company of America.

▼ General Motors began financing cars in 1919 when it formed the General Motors Acceptance Corporation (GMAC).

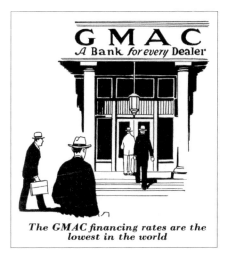

GMAC
A Bank for every Dealer

The GMAC financing rates are the lowest in the world

without a smile, stated that it never was the intention to accept notes from farmers, doctors, etc. and that the plan has to do exclusively with dealers whose notes are the only ones that will be accepted and then only when they are financially responsible or the security offered is ample and beyond question," *Motor World* reported.[9]

Apparently, this new plan was not designed to assist retail car buyers seeking credit, but rather to make it easier for dealers to consent to purchase wholesale units throughout the year and to store them until the selling season started up again.

Access to credit for automobile purchases in Los Angeles expanded in 1913 with the formation of the Automobile Funding Company of America. "Right in Los Angeles there are business houses, with capital tied up, for whom one or more trucks would prove a boon," Charles A. Bradley, president and general manager, told the *Los Angeles Times*. "There are professional men, salesmen and others who could use a motor car to their advantage. We expect to reach these."[10]

The enterprise, backed by prominent local dealer, James S. Conwell, who served as the group's secretary, was quickly overwhelmed by credit applications, as it announced plans to open a San Francisco branch. "Even while the proposition was so attractive from the standpoint of buying stock in the company, the demands for money have far exceeded, up to the present time, the ability of the company to fully meet them," *Out West* reported. "This can only be accounted for by the stringency in the money

Workers install a Packard billboard at the intersection of Wilshire Boulevard and Western Avenue in 1926 opposite Bank of America.

market ever since the commencement of the operation of this company."[11]

In 1914, there were 123,000 automobiles in California, one for every eighteen residents. The state in proportion to its population had three times as many automobiles as New York and two and a half times the number in Illinois.[12] Angelenos spent ten million dollars on automobiles in the first seven months of 1915 alone, an increase of 115 percent from the previous year. Harold L. Arnold, local distributor for Dodge Brothers, reported selling 586 cars in the same period, while Don Lee's Cadillac sales jumped 37 percent, representing a $280,000 year-on-year gain.

"The increase in the sale of pleasure cars has been largely due to bettered conditions since the beginning of the year; but the increase in population had a share in bringing the figures of the Los Angeles dealers up to the 115 percent gain," according to the *Los Angeles Times*. "The lowering of the price increased sales of many makes, placing cars within the reach of those who heretofore were unable to purchase a car."[13]

By working with finance companies, automobile dealers avoided the time-consuming task of qualifying customers' credit and chasing them down in case of a default. They also received cash for every sale which freed up capital for other uses.

The Guaranty Securities Company was formed in 1915 in Toledo, Ohio, to provide deferred payment services to Willys and Overland dealers. It was reorganized a year later as the Guarantee Securities Corporation of New York City with the intention of providing time sales for twenty-one makes of vehicles, including all General Motors models.[14]

The corporation established a San Francisco branch in 1916 to offer its Guaranty Plan to West Coast dealers and automobile buyers.[15] The business promoted what they described as a "dignified, confidential and standardized system of credit, absolutely safe and fully safeguarding the banking properties." *Motor West* described the plan as "sensational" and predicted it would "virtually revolu-

tionize the marketing of motor cars."[16]

Still, the National Automobile Chamber of Commerce and major automobile executives continued to oppose selling on credit. Henry Ford told a convention of the Wisconsin Bankers' Association in 1915 that Ford Motor Company was "not interested in promulgating any plan which extends credit for motor cars or for anything else."[17] Franchise agreements between Ford and its dealers prohibited credit sales.

In 1916, Cadillac Motor Car Company issued a statement to *Motor West*, making it clear it had "made no arrangements with, or through any financing concern for the sale of Cadillac cars." And senior management at Buick and Oldsmobile argued deferred payment plans would lead to "a period of financial stringency" that would straddle dealers with "a quantity of half-sold cars … of second-hand value, little cash and no credit at the bank."[18]

Attempts at automobile financing for retail sales were slow to develop but accelerated after World War I. In anticipation of a post-war boom, manufacturers invested in new factories and increased production. However, sales were still seasonal, and roughly half of all cars were purchased between March 1 and June 30. Production though had to be fixed on a year-round basis which left manufacturers with the dilemma of where to locate tens of thousands of cars during the remaining months. It was predicted the storage cost was enough to make some of them unprofitable. Hence, manufacturers looked to dealers to take the cars, but dealers were no more financially capable than the automakers.[19]

Rather than removing the cancellation clause in their agreement with dealers (which prohibited them from securing loans from banks), manufacturers began to work with finance companies that would take on a dealer's inventory loans and purchase their retail installment contracts. As Martha L. Olney explains in her book, *Buy Now, Pay Later: Advertising, Credit, and Consumer Durables in the 1920s*, "Auto sales finance companies were first established therefore not to market cars nor in response to buyer demand for convenient payment schemes, but to preserve manufacturer power over dealers while simultaneously solving the problem of inadequate wholesale inventory financing."[20]

General Motors became the first automaker to finance all of its products when it formed General Motors Acceptance Corporation (GMAC) in 1919, using time sales as part of its successful strategy to carve deeply into Ford's market share.

GMAC's success paved the way for the entrance of a host of specialized finance firms into the auto retail arena. "Conservatism of banks and money interests generally, toward the automotive field, is fading fast," *Motor West* assessed in its February 1920 edition. It cited as evidence the establishment in Los Angeles of Pacific Finance Corporation capitalized at four million dollars "to provide better credit facilities for automobile dealers."[21]

By 1921, there were more than 110 automobile finance companies in the United States.[22] In addition to qualifying customer credit, auto finance companies began to fill the role that bankers would not, by helping dealers to buy their vehicles from the factories with wholesale financing, which soon came to be called "floorplan assistance" or "flooring." This provided a bridge between dealers and commercial banks and allowed dealers to improve their cash flow and partially overcome their own problems with the seasonal nature of the business.

In 1922, the average price of a car in the United States was $900. The value of cars sold in that year was estimated to be $2,070,000,000. Of these vehicles, 75 per cent, or $1,552,500,000, were purchased on installments. Of the 252,000 trucks sold, 90 percent were bought on installments.[23]

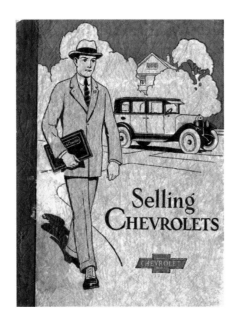

▲ *Selling Chevrolets* was subtitled "A Book of General Information for Chevrolet Retail Salesmen," circa 1926.

"The percentage of passenger car purchasers who fail to complete their payments is surprisingly small and their paper is uniformly good," *Automotive Industries* reported. "The paper given by truck buyers, on the other hand, is considered the poorest in the market."

The forty-eight members of the Automobile Finance Credit Men's Association, offering automobile financing "from Boston to the western boundary of Ohio and south to New Orleans" was responsible for funding $1,000,000,000 of the nation's auto sales. GMAC handled $200,000,000.[24]

In 1924, the nation's drivers operated an estimated 15 million motor vehicles, 88 percent of the world's total. "I don't believe there is a business in the world which shows a more favorable record in regard to bad debts than the automobile industry," Alfred H. Swayne, vice president of the General Motors Corporation, told the *Los Angeles Times*. "Our total loss for our own company last year (1923) through bad debts was only two-hundredths of 1 percent."[25]

By 1925, 3.5 million cars or nearly 70 per cent of new and used cars in the US were sold on the installment plans. In Southern California, eighty-five percent of cars were purchased on deferred payment plans.[25] The same year, the leading fifty automobile finance companies reported losses of less than one-fifth of one percent.[26] Encouraged by the success of time sales, dealers began to reduce required down payments from the original 66 percent to 60 percent to 50 percent, dropping to 33 percent to 20 percent and sometimes as low as 10 percent, while extending payment deadlines up to as much as two years.[27]

However, as the terms became more competitive, the number of customers who defaulted increased. After several dealerships and finance companies went out of business, the National Automobile Dealers Association and the National Association of Finance Companies reached agreement on a recommended formula of 33 percent down payment and no more than twelve months to complete payment.[28]

Even though this was more of a recommendation than a requirement, it prompted more dealers and finance companies to be more cautious in qualifying customers for time sales.

"The average automobile buyer does not take the trouble to ask just how much money he is paying for interest, insurance and carrying charges," Los Angeles Chevrolet dealer Winslow B. Felix put forth in making the case for short-term contracts in October 1927.

"In one typical case a customer of mine who was considering the purchase of a car found out, after investigation, that in order to buy a moderate priced car on a two-year payment plan he would be required to pay more than 25 percent of the balance as the charges for buying on deferred payments.

"The mushroom growth of dozens of private finance companies in the past few months bears witness to the fact that motorists are fattening the bank rolls of hundreds of men who take advantage of the fact that long-term purchase contracts mean fat profits for the finance company."[29]

Although some lenders had critics, the evolution from early dealer-managed credit programs to more sophisticated auto finance companies provided a workable balance of interests among manufacturers, dealers, banks, and customers that continues to this day.

▶ James S. Conwell (right) grew up in Winona, Minnesota.

JAMES S. CONWELL

▲ James S. Conwell was president of the Indiana Bicycle Company when they introduced the first Waverley electric car.

James Simpson Conwell was hailed as the dean of early Los Angeles automobile dealers. Before selling cars, he managed some of the pioneer factories that produced them. He would also wield considerable political influence as president of the Los Angeles City Council.

Born in Winona, Minnesota, on July 4, 1857, he graduated from Lake View High School in Chicago and earned a bachelor of science degree from Northwestern University in 1882. Conwell served as the Evanston, Illinois, town clerk before heading to Los Angeles with his wife, Mae, where he was hired to work at a men's furnishing company on Main Street. The business was renamed Evans and Conwell after he became a partner in 1885.[1]

He later moved to San Francisco where he worked for umbrella manufacturer, Folmer, Clogg & Company, from 1889 to 1894 before entering the bicycle business as a manager for the Indiana Bicycle Company.[2]

Early evidence of his leadership skills came with his participation, as a founding member, in the San Francisco Cycle Board of Trade in 1896. The group, made up of twenty-nine local dealers, would lobby for better city streets, improved lighting in parks, and stronger laws to prevent bicycle thefts.[3] "We have been joining in the slogan of 'Repave Market Street.' We know that before this can happen we must reform the City Government," he told the *San Francisco Call*, shortly before being elected president of the board.[4]

As head of the organization, Conwell formed an alliance with the National League for Good Roads and rallied a coalition of like-minded business and political leaders, including the city's mayor, James D. Phelan, to attend the board's first meeting of 1897.[5]

Later the same year, he was summoned to Indianapolis to meet with owners of Indiana Bicycle Company who invited him to become their president. "Cycle Trade Loses An Earnest Worker" was the headline in the *San Francisco Examiner* as Conwell departed the city.[6] Like other bicycle companies, Indiana entered the fledgling automobile manufacturing business and Conwell helped debut the Waverley electric car in 1899.[7][8] He would later invent a Hydro-Thermal Distillate-Gasifier for automobiles.[9]

MISS CONWELL

Age 3 years—the Youngest Cyclist in the World

She rides a *Waverley* and recommends it as the most rigid, lightest and easiest running wheel she has ever mounted.

SAN FRANCISCO, July 22, 1895

◀ James S. Conwell's daughter, Larooka, appeared in this 1895 advertisement for Waverley bicycles.

After leaving Indiana Bicycle, Conwell became president of Wilke Manufacturing Company, which made refrigerators, before being tapped to manage Marion Auto Company in Indianapolis in 1905. He returned to California in 1907 to be head of the Los Angeles-based Auto Vehicle Company, which manufactured Tourist automobiles. The company regularly entered cars into races and hill climbs to earn brand recognition. His biggest publicity coup was the "Tour of the Tourist," a run from Los Angeles to San Francisco limited to Tourist automobiles and their owners. Thousands witnessed twenty-six vehicles navigate the thousand-mile route.[10][11] Conwell was joined on the journey by his wife and daughter, Larooka.

"A tour from Los Angeles to San Francisco has always been a pet idea of his and when he failed to interest others in the idea, he went to work and successfully carried it out," the *Los Angeles Herald* wrote.[12]

Tourist sales improved as the company introduced more powerful models, but Conwell would soon move on to another position. He was hired in November 1908 to take charge of the local branch of the Maxwell-Briscoe Company. [13] "I regard the Maxwell-Briscoe factory as one of the greatest automobile plants in the world and I am proud to be connected with them," he told the *Times*.[14] Conwell sold Maxwell automobiles from

his United Motor-Los Angeles Company showroom on South Olive Street.

"J.S. Conwell, secretary pro tem of the Automobile Dealers' association of Southern California and local representative of the Maxwell car, is not only the admitted dean of the dealers of this city, so far as age of service in the automobile trade goes, but he undoubtedly is the 'dean of ideas'," proclaimed the *Los Angeles Herald* in 1909.[15]

Conwell's latest musing was for an outdoor automobile show where cars could be exhibited underneath large tents. He also contemplated an obstacle race with dummies on the track, including a "a deaf man with his speaking trumpet, a street gamin" and "a portly old gentleman with an aldermanic paunch." He then suggested, "Let the fellow who thinks he is the best driver, or that his car is best governed work his way through." He predicted it would be more fun for the audience than going to the circus.[16]

Although his obstacle course concept didn't materialize, for many years holding automobile shows underneath tents became standard practice. The Motor Car Dealers' Association of Los Angeles, which elected Conwell president in 1911 and 1912, would rely on him to help organize auto shows and other events.

Under his stewardship, the organization became more involved in city politics; challenged speed limits; lobbied for lower city taxes on cars; and urged Los Angeles police to patrol the city's Auto Row to mitigate speeding and the irritation of noisy mufflers.[17][18][19]

He served as the secretary of the Ocean to Ocean Highway Association from 1911 to 1912. The organization championed a national highway from the Pacific to the Atlantic. "He has been obliged to give his time and money gratis," the *Los Angeles Times* wrote. "He has never complained, however, and has done great things for the national highway cause."[20][21]

Conwell was also a pioneer of automobile financing. He recognized there were many people interested in

▶ In 1917 during his third term as a member of the Los Angeles City Council, James S. Conwell was elected president.

buying cars who lacked the funds to make an outright purchase and in 1913, he served as secretary of the Automobile Funding Company of America. The business offered buyers the means, previously unavailable, to finance an automobile purchase.

The same year, he announced a run for Los Angeles City Council. His successful campaign was endorsed by the Automobile Club of Southern California, energized by the idea of having "the motoring industry represented in the municipal government."[22]

Conwell had been away from Auto Row for all of one month when it was announced he would combine his civic duties with the management of the local branch of Haynes Automobile Company. "I have been familiar with the Haynes car for a very long time," he told the *Los Angeles Express*. "Ever since, in fact, the first automobile show held in this country."[23]

Conwell was the only member of the Los Angeles City Council of 1915-1916 to be re-elected. In 1917, during his third term, he was voted president. "Mr. Conwell has a cool head; he is disposed to be fair with everyone; he never permits his personal feelings to sway his decisions in matters of public interest, and his experience as a parliamentarian fits him as the leader of the city's most important official body," read the *Times*.[24]

Conwell, who timed his vacation to allow for his continued involvement in the Los Angeles Auto Show, was a member of both the city council's efficiency and supply committees. He led the fight for an ordinance to restrict billboards in residential neighborhoods; made sure the City and County used the same methodology when assessing the valuation of vehicles; and established new standards for gasoline sold in the city.[25][26] He also championed an ordinance ensuring utility companies that tore up paved streets for excavation would replace the pavement at their own cost.

Away from city hall, he was affiliated with the Uni-

versity Clubs of Los Angeles and Indianapolis, the Los Angeles Athletic Club, Society of Automobile Engineers of America, the Phi Kappa Sigma Fraternity, Automobile Club of Southern California, and Gamut Club and various lodges.

When his physician determined that his many responsibilities were taking a toll on his health and recommended that he rest and spend at least two weeks in the hospital, Conwell instead decided his recovery would speed up with an automobile tour to Phoenix and back. He died of heart failure in Blythe, California, during the return leg of his journey.

When news of his passing reached Los Angeles, city flags were immediately lowered to half mast. Prior to his funeral, his body would lie in state in the city hall's Council Chamber.

Newspapers speculated as to who would replace Conwell as council president, leaving Acting Mayor Frank L. Cleaveland to respond, "We do not expect to act for a week or two, possibly a month. We owe that much respect to the man we loved and admired for his sterling, manly qualities."[27]

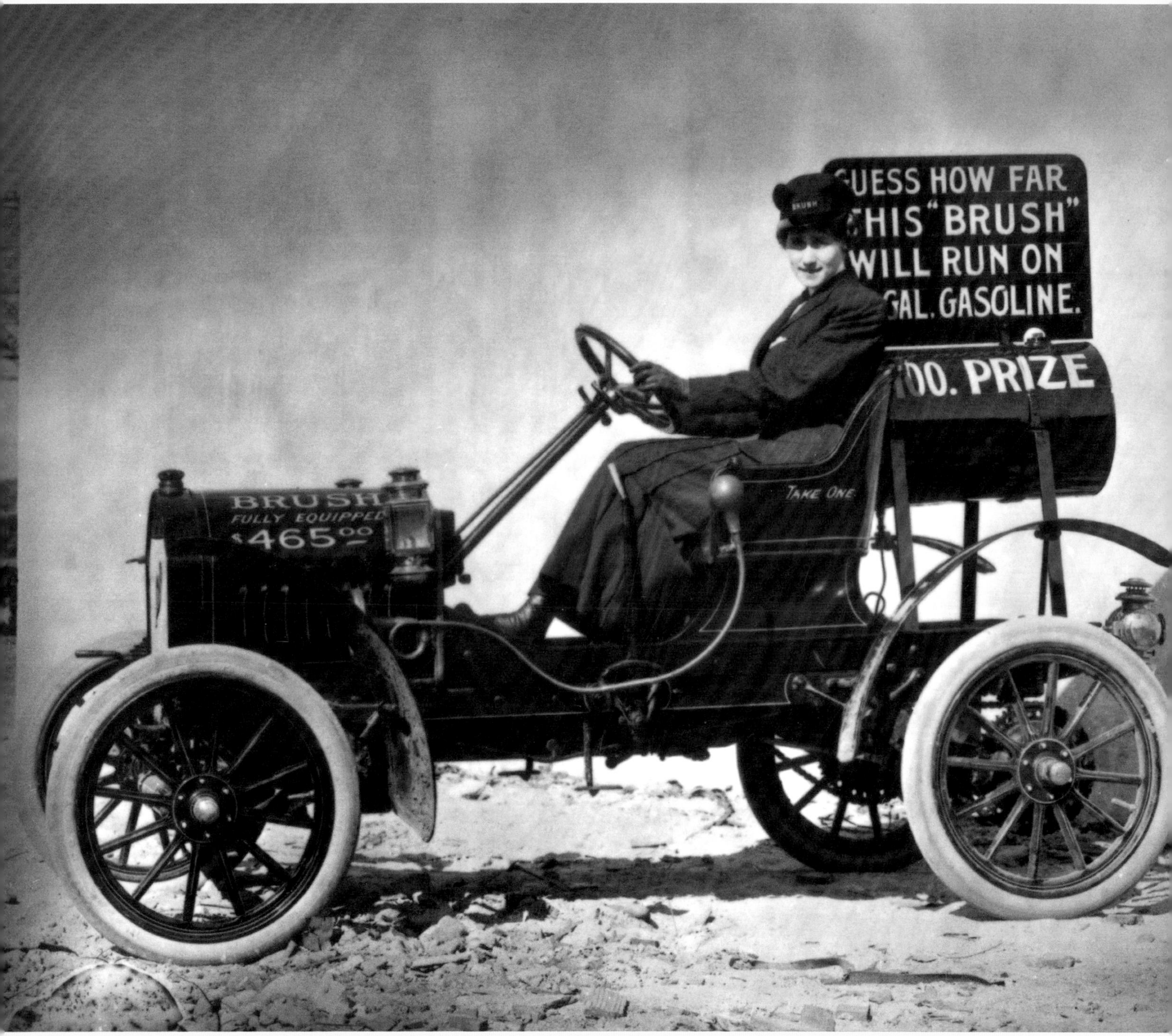
GUESS HOW FAR
THIS "BRUSH"
WILL RUN ON
GAL. GASOLINE.
00. PRIZE
BRUSH
FULLY EQUIPPED
$465.00
TAKE ONE

YGNACIO R. DEL VALLE

Los Angeles automobile dealer, Ygnacio R. del Valle, came from one of California's most prominent pioneer families. He was also renowned for representing Brush cars, advertised as selling for "less money than it costs to keep a horse." He set records for mileage and efficiency in competitions driving the vehicles he sold and became an early advocate of trucks.[1]

Del Valle was born in 1870 on the family's Camulos Ranch in Ventura County, made famous as the fictional Moreno Rancho in Helen Hunt Jackson's 1884 novel *Ramona*. In the last years of Mexican rule and early years of California statehood, the del Valle family was among the most influential families in Southern California.

He graduated from Santa Clara College in 1890.[2] Fluent in English, Spanish, and French, he worked as a customs inspector in 1894.[3] After a brief career selling insurance and real estate, del Valle entered the automobile business in 1909. He was a dealer for Brush which sold "the simplest, most economical and easiest riding runabout made," as well as a delivery or commercial car built on the same chassis.[4][5]

"The Brush has made rapid headway in Los Angeles and Southern California during the past year," the *Los Angeles Express* reported in 1911. "Early in the season Mr. del Valle placed an order for 750 cars. He expects to have the allotment increased by 50 cars."[6]

Del Valle was behind the wheel of a Brush automobile that drove a record breaking forty-eight miles on a single gallon of gasoline earlier the same year.[7]

While most dealers focused on selling "pleasure cars," del Valle promoted the Brush commercial car to small businesses willing to replace a horse and wagon with a small truck. Although used car dealers were already repurposing damaged automobiles as trucks, Brush was one of the first makers of pleasure and commercial cars.

◀ Brush cars were marketed for their low cost and efficiency.

As his business grew, del Valle moved from his modest showroom on 9th Street to a new, larger facility on the corner of Grand and Pico.[8] "Del Valle's process of reasoning in choosing cars to represent is unique and somewhat derogatory to his qualifications as a salesman," the *Express* noted in 1912. "He claims that life is too short to work, except along the lines of least resistance, and that in order to make up for his shortcomings as a salesman he must handle cars that sell."[9]

His success selling Brush vehicles led to his becoming the Southern California distributor for another economy automobile, the new Detroiter, which had made its debut at various East Coast auto shows the previous winter. Speculation was rampant as to which Los Angeles dealer would be recognized as the local agent.

"Though there were 192 automobile manufacturers in the field when the first Detroiter was built a little over a year ago, the Briggs-Detroiter company today ranks eleventh in point of production among the automobile companies of the United States and will turn out 5000 cars during the coming season," the *Express* reported in 1913.[10]

When Claude S. Briggs, president and general manager of the company, visited Los Angeles for the first

▲ Del Valle family group portrait at Rancho Camulos, Ventura County, circa 1888.

time, he was eager to exploit a growing market. "It has proven one of our best territories, I know, and now that the work of the organization of a system of sub-agencies has been so successfully completed by Mr. del Valle, I am confident that it will prove to be even better than it has in the year just past," he enthused.[11]

Del Valle's interest in commercial vehicles also led to him being selected to represent the Koehler truck, a 1,600-pound capacity vehicle described as "the simplest, strongest, most economical and foolproof delivery car in the market."[12][13]

A functional, uncovered wagon-on-wheels, the truck lacked the graceful lines of a pleasure car, and the driver's seat was very close to the front to maximize the space for transporting goods. It was created by L.E. Schlotterback of Newark, New Jersey, who wanted to reach "the middleman, the tradesman who needs a light delivery truck at a low price." The truck was priced at a prudent $850.[14]

Del Valle later added the Touraine Six, a six-cylinder high-power, but moderately priced pleasure car to his showroom. Built by Nance Motor Company of Philadelphia, it offered clean, attractive lines and a "beauty and symmetry of design, elegance of finish, and superior qual-

ity of construction."[15] In 1914, when Nance introduced the Vim, a light delivery truck, del Valle enthusiastically added it to his growing stable of trucks. Unlike the Koehler truck, the Vim was covered. Covered vehicles were generally more expensive than those without roofs, however, the new Vim sold for only $685.[16]

The same year, del Valle, who had done business as Mission Motor Car Company, sold his interest in the enterprise. Although he would no longer represent Koehler and Detroiter, he continued to be the local representative for Touraine and the Vim, and he moved into a new facility on Olive Street.[17] In a local newspaper interview, he made a compelling argument about the contribution light delivery vehicles had made to the nation:

> The truck has enabled the big stores to grow, covering larger areas, and in this way increasing the markets for all kinds of goods. The farmer also is using the light truck extensively, and this has brought many new things into use on the farms—new types of plows and all kinds of implements drawn by motor

▲ Ygnacio R. del Valle entered the automobile business in 1909, selling Brush cars. By 1913 he became a representative for Detroiter.

power—and the farmer is also able to get his goods to markets, in turn enabling him to buy better things for himself and family. No matter what industry or business you may select, you will find that trucks are a big factor in its success."[18]

After receiving suggestions from Vim owners that the delivery truck could be converted into a pleasure car, del Valle hired a truck designer, James Fouch, to come up with a plan that would allow the owner to "make the little truck suitable for use as a business or pleasure car at a moment's notice."[19]

Eventually, del Valle would abandon the automobile business, because the brands he represented either went out of business or limited their production. During World War I, he put his language skills to work for the US Immigration Department before returning home in 1919 to manage the Camulos Ranch. The del Valle family sold the property in 1924. Ygnacio del Valle died suddenly in February 1930 at the age of 59.

SELLING CARS ON CREDIT

"Automobiles don't eat hay or rolled barley, but, gee-whiz! gold coin of the realm is their steady diet. Buzz wagon doctors are expensive!"

Los Angeles Times, October 3, 1906[1]

Pioneer Los Angeles automobile dealers not only needed to convince people to buy cars, they also required a reliable and affordable means of keeping them on the road. The city's army of bicycle salesmen understood maintenance and repairs were key to customer retention, and car dealers also quickly came to recognize the critical importance of a reliable service department.

However, many of the city's trailblazing retailers lacked the space and funds to establish service facilities or pay for skilled mechanics and tools. And while they received little or no support from the automakers, they understood referring customers to a nearby mechanic or blacksmith could damage their reputation if repair costs escalated.

"Naturally no machinist outside of the factory is familiar with an automobile, and even the simplest adjustments and repairs take a great amount of time, because the operation and construction are not understood," a frustrated reader of the *Horseless Age* wrote to the editor in 1901. "As a rule, a job that should take an hour will consume a day, for it takes about eight hours to find out what needs to be done and how to do it. In many cases when one part is duly fixed something else is thrown out of adjustment, and then comes a puzzling search, sometimes taking several days…the owner just sits down and trembles until the job is finished."[2]

Early automobiles were assembled with parts that were neither standardized or

◀ Ralph Hamlin's new dealership on Flower Street included a large service department.

interchangeable, and since no manuals existed, mechanics relied on trial and error to fix problems resulting in repairs that could result in exorbitant charges. As more cars were sold, a new cottage industry of self-professed "auto mechanics" emerged.[3]

"The most distressing feature of the business ... was the prodigal waste of time," the editors of *Motor World* opined in 1911 looking back at the birth of the automobile service business. "With no definite program for determining what work should be done on a given car, how it should be done or when it should be completed, it seldom happened that the labor charge was anywhere near reasonable."[4] And the owner of the car was often miserably surprised and angry.

While some industry leaders called for more uniform parts to reduce costs, others championed new regulations and education for vehicle owners. First-time automobile owners often damaged cars by shifting gears incorrectly, overloading them, or driving off road and over rocks. "The majority of people who own cars know less about them than anyone else," Barney Oldfield complained to the *Los Angeles Times*. "In case of an accident, even of a trifling nature, they simply have to send for someone to fix the machine. Everyone who owns an automobile should learn how the machine is put together."[5]

Early motorists routinely deferred basic mainte-nance until a serious problem occurred. "The large expense that is borne by many drivers is due almost entirely to the lack of proper care of the machine or foolish neglect," wrote the *Los Angeles Herald*.[6]

The *Times* reported many delivery businesses who experimented with automobiles went back to using horse-drawn vehicles again. "In every case poor automobiles or poor drivers or both has been the cause. It stands to reason that a small boy cannot care for a piece of machinery like an automobile, and that abuse when kept up means ruin."[7]

Between 1903 and 1904, the number of automobiles produced in the United States increased by 30 percent.[8] The rise in Los Angeles motorists and the subsequent need for service meant, by 1904, most city agencies now included a repair department. The number of local repair shops, the *Times* noted, was becoming "numerous and still increasing."[9]

Local retailers had obvious advantages over their counterparts in other areas of the country for providing service. Southern California's enviable climate ensured that engines and batteries were not damaged by snow, ice, and freezing temperatures. Good weather also allowed repair shops to stay open through the winter months and employ full-time mechanics.

Don Lee added a "very reliable and complete" service facility to his South Main Street Cadillac dealership, where he fixed "all sorts of injuries to automobiles." William K. Cowan operated a "large and well-kept" garage adjoining his South Broadway Waverley and Rambler agency.[10] [11] Leon T. Shettler's REO facility at 6th Street and Grand Avenue included one of the largest service departments in the city, while the White Garage at 7th Street and Broadway boasted they could work on as many as one hundred cars at once.[12]

Nearby, on Broadway, Western Garage was among the busiest early independent repair shops, and it was run by E.R. Risen, who had established himself in the bicycle

ACCESSORIES

▲ Ralph Hamlin maintained a well-stocked accessories department.

business in 1887. He employed "a force of competent and skilled mechanics" who labored to keep gasoline, steam, and electric machines on the road.[13] South End Auto Station on Main Street, which gained fame building race cars, offered customers, "the best and most up-to-date" repair service for cars or bicycles.[14]

As Ford Motor Company assumed a dominant position in the fledgling automobile industry, its dealer operated repair shops were increasingly overwhelmed. Executives feared customers would turn to independent garages

(that did not use factory parts) unless they took action. In 1908, Ford established branches in fourteen cities to distribute cars and provide service and repairs in major cities for 215 dealers. By 1910, it operated twenty-five branches serving more than a thousand franchise dealers.

"Strike a ratio of fifty miles in almost any part of the country and there is a Ford dealer within it," the com-

▲ The Greer-Robbins auto repair shop on South Figueroa Street.

pany touted in national newspaper advertisements. "Every Ford dealer must carry a full stock of repair parts. At our 25 branch houses our stock repair parts is in every way as complete as our stock at the factory."[15]

Ford announced plans for twenty-three new service branches in 1916. However, it was becoming clear that customers who faced long waits expected more complimentary service and free replacement of parts from the factory service branches than they did from local dealers. Ford soon abandoned the branch system and handed responsibility for repairs back to dealers.[16]

To provide service to Los Angeles's growing legions of motorists, the Automobile Club of Southern California worked with the Young Men's Christian Association and the city's Polytechnic High School to establish an auto

repair center in 1905.[17] More than 160 students enrolled in the inaugural classes, which were open to both men and women.[18] The city's Manual Arts High School also established its popular Garage Automobile School.

When Auto Vehicle Company, Los Angeles-based manufacturers of Tourist automobiles, opened a night school in 1909 for owners of their popular vehicles, the firm expected "a score or more" would show up. They were "astounded" when, in fact, more than a hundred students crowded into the debut class. "A majority of the troubles with a car are generally traced to the owners not thoroughly understanding the mechanical construction of

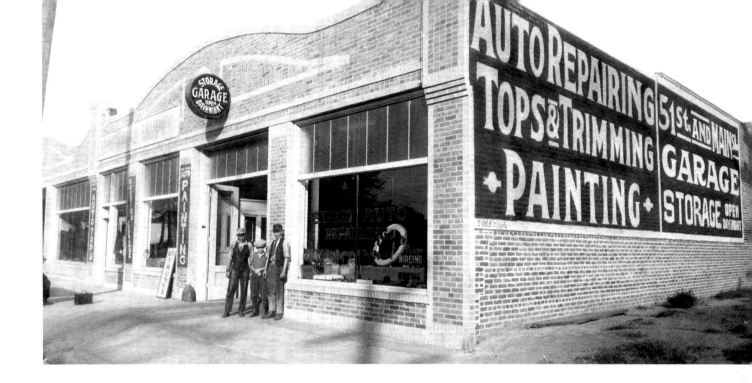

their car, so that a school of this kind should prove to be of untold benefit to all owners of the Tourist cars," the *Los Angeles Herald* observed.[19]

Franklin distributor Ralph Hamlin was among the local retailers who pressured manufacturers to provide more comprehensive training for service mechanics.[20] Franklin Automobile Company launched one of the earliest factory-run service training schools around 1910. Led by former Purdue University Professor I.O. Hoffman, the course included textbooks and covered multiple aspects of automobile repair and maintenance. Franklin car owners, including women, were encouraged to take classes to learn more about their vehicles, and the company even offered a four-year apprenticeship.[21]

Stearns-Knight Company certified fifty mechanics at a time at its Cleveland factory, and as a result, were able to offer owners of their vehicles skilled service within twenty-four hours.[22] Local representatives of Chalmers Motor Company sent seven hundred mechanics to Detroit for a two-month comprehensive training program in 1913,[23] while Reo Motor Car Company launched a 30-month service apprenticeship program in 1916.[24]

▲▼ The Morton B. Card automobile garage at 51st and Main Streets circa 1924.

Studebaker used its Los Angeles manufacturing plant on East 7th Street for a ten-day training program for mechanics. Graduates were assigned to one of the company's thirty-six service facilities in the city. The trained labor

▲ A worker from the W.I. Tupman Company delivers a serviced vehicle to its owner before returning by motorcycle to the company's Figueroa Street facility.

◄ Winslow B. Felix believed good service was key to customer retention.

allowed the company to offer a limited guarantee on service and maintenance, along with uniform charges at all of its stations.[25]

As the problem of providing adequate automotive service intensified, demands grew from dealers and motorists for a factory-backed warranty system. Local dealers did offer limited forms of "guarantees" to make repairs or adjustments within a limited amount of time (such as ten or thirty days), but no uniform policy on warranties could exist without factory involvement.

In 1916, the National Automobile Chamber of Commerce comprised of ninety-seven members announced a template for a "standard" form of service that would include free inspection and adjustments for the first month and replacement of faulty parts for 90 days.[26] Although it was only a recommendation, an estimated 90 percent of factories would follow at least a modified version.

Still, the plan had obvious limitations. If a defective

▲ A worker assists a customer with parts in the service department of a garage at 12th and Hope Streets.

part was removed and sent to the manufacturer, it was at the expense of the customer. If the factory agreed the part was defective, it would pay to ship back a replacement that the customer was forced to pay for before it would be installed. The customer would then be reimbursed for the cost of the part by the dealer. Since labor charges could be significant, dealers were often expected to absorb the costs if they wanted to retain customers.[27][28]

Despite its shortcomings, the standard warranty represented progress and several manufacturers, including Oldsmobile, Buick, Mitchell, and Studebaker, extended the 90-day limit to one full year, leaving the bulk of responsibility for repairs with the dealers.

Linking the sale of the car to the service department became a new dealer mantra and an important mar-

keting tool. "Service begins where the salesman leaves off," the *Los Angeles Times* proclaimed. "When the check is received and the new owners drive out of the shop, service should follow him and stick to him, and be at his right-hand day and night."[29]

Los Angeles Hudson and Dodge dealer Harold L. Arnold followed this advice to a T, creating what would be described as the "most elaborate system of service to patrons … in the United States." He employed twenty skilled mechanics who were "on-call" twenty-four hours a day.[30] The poorly lit garage repair pit at his South Olive facility was replaced with a new state of the art system featuring a crane and heavy-duty racks that could raise the running board of a car six feet in the air, allowing mechanics to work from below the car without climbing into a hole.[31]

Increasingly, dealers began to refer to the service and parts department as the "back end" and the sales

department as the "front end." They encouraged staff to work on customer retention, introducing the slogan, "Meet them in the front, keep them in the back."[32]

During World War I, a scarcity of skilled labor and materials forced Angelenos to pay more attention to the care and construction of their automobiles. "Home garage repairs to motor cars are just as essential at this time to all owners as the war garden movement has been to food production," Ralph Hamlin told the *Times* in August 1918. "The car owner can shift at least part of an ever-increasing burden from the harassed automobile repair man to himself. If the owner can bring himself to the realization of the needless waste of labor (under war conditions) on non-essential repairs, he will have cleared the floor of the service station for unavoidable jobs."[33]

Hamlin's views were echoed by California Cadillac distributor Don Lee. "We believe that we are safe in saying that, with well designed and correctly built automobiles, 90 percent of so-called troubles are directly traceable to a lack of lubrication, abuse, carelessness, a lack of understanding of the principals involved and proper handling generally," he explained. "Some drivers seem to think that so long as the car 'goes' that is all there is to it. It is not."[34]

In the immediate post-war years, the effort to provide efficient automobile service intensified. Los Angeles investor, Frank L. Dickinson, revealed plans in 1920 to open a chain of garages across California. Standard Motor Service Company opened its first facility on Western Avenue near Hollywood Boulevard and soon announced twenty-four more, including six locations in downtown Los Angeles.[35] Ford Motor Company, the nation's largest automaker, led the effort to standardize automobile service.[36] The company began by analyzing and establishing set costs for hundreds of repair operations on Model Ts, culminating with the creation of a "Flat-Rate" system for compensating mechanics and calculating repair costs for

◀ A mechanic at work inside the Howard Auto Company repair garage.

customers. To address concerns that repair charges were arbitrary or unfair, Ford published a price list that was the same for all owners nationwide.

"The fundamental principle … is 'equality of cost' to the consumer, for equal work well done," the *Fordowner* journal explained in April 1919. "The best repairman wins because he does the most good work, in the least time, and so his margin of profit is greater."[37]

Ford calculated the average number of hours and minutes required to complete a specific repair operation using several mechanics performing the same identical task. The flat-rate labor charges were based on a labor rate of $1 or $1.25 per hour for bigger jobs. Factored into the charge were the mechanic's time, rent, overhead, and

cost of equipment. The system offered both transparency for customers and increased control over mechanics and repair costs for dealers. Ford encouraged repair shops to keep a daily timesheet and monitor mechanics who failed to complete jobs within the flat-rate window.

The company began publishing a monthly service bulletin in 1919 detailing standardized repair practices, and in 1925, a 300-page manual, *Ford Service: Detailed Instructions for Servicing Ford Cars*, was introduced.[38] Ford urged dealers to use the manual to prevent mechanics from using their own methods of repair work and assigned

▼ A clerk takes orders for car parts at the Automotive Sales Corp. facility on South Flower Street in 1930.

field representatives to monitor these activities. The company also recommended dealers purchase more labor-saving repair tools and machine equipment. In 1919, Ford required service facilities to invest in 114 items, ranging from specialized wrenches to specialized machines. Traveling service representatives regularly inspected dealerships and reported the poorly equipped ones to the main office in Detroit.[39]

Ford also urged dealers to divide labor in the service department, separating diagnostic analysis from the repair procedures, a change that limited the ability of mechanics to use their own repair methods. In large dealerships, Ford encouraged specialization for mechanics assigned to specific areas, such as transmissions, engine, or brake repair. Less skilled mechanics removed engines from cars while experienced mechanics rebuilt them.[40]

All fifteen of the authorized Ford Motor Company dealerships in Los Angeles in 1921 had "fully equipped" shops.[41] "No matter where you buy a Ford car it is always the same list price," J. Benj. Fahy, an authorized dealer since 1916, explained in a 1923 interview. "It is the same with spare parts. The price is uniform. I fear, however, that I cannot be so positive about the complete uniformity of Ford service, due to the prairie dog growth of wayside Ford fixers… All Ford agents operate their repair

▼ The Flivver Shop located at 907 W. Pico Blvd. 1930.

Students and administrators at the Frank Wiggins Trade School of
Los Angeles pose with a Cadillac V-8 car chassis, 1931.

stations on the flat-rate labor basis. There is no haggling or arguing, no undercharging one owner and overcharging another."[42]

Despite Ford's efforts, many dealers continued to pay mechanics with regular hourly wages. The new system was resisted by small dealers who wanted to make their own decisions on how employees were paid. It was also unpopular with some mechanics who needed more time to complete a repair and rebelled by limiting their work to strictly what was required and nothing more.

Many dealers, recognizing the values as well as the limitations of Ford's flat-rate system, began to modify it in order to incentivize their own mechanics to improve their skills and produce more flat-rate hours of work. "The greatest step in servicing motor cars, from the standpoint of everyone concerned, is the adoption of what is known as the flat rate system," E.T. Strong, general manager for the Buick Motor Company, told the *Los Angeles Evening Express* in 1923.[43]

More dealers began to experiment with similar "piece-rate" payment plans that compensated mechanics for the number of flat-rate hours they accumulated versus how many actual hours they worked. The most important variation was to adjust the dollar amount paid depending upon the skill level of a mechanic. This allowed dealers to reward mechanics for increased productivity and provide

incentives for young mechanics to learn quickly.

Ford endorsed the dealer-inspired piece-rate pay plan in 1925, maintaining that it both reduced turn-over in dealership service departments and suppressed interest among mechanics in unionization. The flat-rate system would become the industry standard for the rest of the century.

"Quality sells a car, and service keeps it sold," Frank Hughes, sales manager of Greer-Robbins Company, Los Angeles Chrysler distributors, told the *Los Angeles Evening Express*. The Chrysler Institute for Service Education, a university within Chrysler's Detroit factory, was established in 1926.

"Here service managers, shop foreman and others employed by dealers in executive capacities go to school again for short intensive courses to get a better understanding of the actual meaning of service and how to render it," Hughes outlined. "Among the subjects are 'Distributor and Dealers' Service Responsibilities,' 'Supervision of Service Station Layout and Personnel,' 'Parts Department Operation,' 'Preparation of New Cars for Delivery' 'Correct Trouble Diagnosis' and 'Used Car Reconditioning.'"[44]

In 1929, more than two hundred Dodge, Chrysler, De Soto, Plymouth, and Fargo truck dealers gathered in Los Angeles to attend the Chrysler Motors Service Convention. There was so much interest, the event was staged at the Shrine Auditorium.[45] It was the first time the much anticipated event was held outside Detroit. Los Angeles proved the ideal venue with so many local facilities now providing automobile service and where a fast-growing metropolis had enabled the auto industry to rise and become a driving force in the western United States.

▶ MacFarlane's Financed Automotive Repairs, 23rd and Hill Street; Woodward Automotive Engineers, Alvarado Street; L.A. Wheel and Brake Specialists, South Olive Street.

FREE SERVICE

Among the motor dealers, both well-known and fairly famed,
Who have sold a line of autos at a price the factory named,
Though they strive in competition in most every other act,
They agree that service trouble is a well-accepted fact.
As a rule things all move smoothly, in a satisfactory way,
And the man who buys the auto gets his service any day.
He takes his car out loaded till the springs cry out in grief,
And he speeds o'er rocks and gullies, so their life is very brief.
He skids into a wagon, tears a fender from the frame,
And the way he shoves the brakes in and the gears is just a shame.
He overheats the motor, breaks a carburetor part,
And suddenly discovers that his engine will not start.
Then he quickly phones the salesroom, telling of his awful luck:
"Send me out a force of workmen and some tools, for I am stuck."
So the mechanician hurries with some parts to make repairs;
Finds the car in such condition that he very nearly swears.
But he goes to work adjusting and replacing broken parts.
And after hours of labor the motor finally starts.
The owner nods a "Thank you," which is nothing more than right,
And before the workman knows it, he has driven out of sight.
Now all the German nation and the Kaiser's sturdy will
Could not make the owner see why he should have to pay this bill.
We know that "gratis service" on each car's a staunch demand,
But wonder why no other goods must bear this same command!
If this man goes to a tailor and buys the suit that fits him best,
Does the tailor have to promise that he'll keep it cleaned and pressed?
And when he leaves the city, finds a real first-class hotel,
He knows it's going to cost him every time he rings the bell.
Now stop and think it over; maybe you will quite agree
That most car owners want to have too many bills marked "Free."

Poem by Agnes Earley, the self-proclaimed "Poetess Laureate" of
Greer Robbins Company, the Chalmers dealership located on 11th
and Flower Streets in Los Angeles.

WINSLOW B. FELIX

Winslow B. Felix used the popular cartoon character, Felix the Cat, to promote his Los Angeles Chevrolet agency, a marketing masterstroke that continues to identify the city's oldest dealership more than a century after it opened. A handsome, charismatic, and ambitious salesman, Felix rose through the ranks to become one of the city's most recognized dealers. However, his promising career would end in tragedy.

He was born Wenceslao Felix on February 12, 1891, in the town of Tucson in the Arizona Territory. His Mexican-born parents named him after his father who worked as a clerk at Zreckendorf and Company, a local merchandise store. Wenceslao would later change his name to Winslow before finding work in Los Angeles as a salesman at a local Lincoln dealership.

He was selling luxury cars for Los Angeles-based Leach-Biltwell Motor Company when he was drafted into World War I to serve as a private first class in the US Army Tank Corps.

After the war, Felix was hired as a Chevrolet salesman, and as a reward for his "keen salesmanship and aggressiveness," General Motors made him a franchise dealer on October 15, 1921. Operating as Winslow B. Felix Company, he would do business at an "ideally situated and spacious" facility at the corner of 11th and Olive Streets.[1][2]

"Mr. Felix is probably one of the most popular young automobile merchants on Los Angeles's Gasoline Promenade," the *Los Angeles Evening Express* wrote. "For years he has been associated with the Chevrolet forces in a sales capacity, and that he 'made good' is evidenced by his ability to launch into business for himself."[3]

The newspaper predicted his "experience and extremely wide circle of personal and business acquaintances" would help ensure his success. A member of Los Angeles's prestigious Jonathan Club, the Breakfast Club, and other civic organizations, Felix was also a talented polo player who learned to ride horses as a child. The sport was popular among Hollywood celebrities and the city's elite and provided excellent networking opportunities.

His society connections led to a friendship with Patrick Sullivan, the creator of the Felix the Cat comic character, and in 1923, the two made an agreement to cross-market the curious and mischievous feline with Chevrolet.[4]

First conceived by cartoonist Otto Messmer who worked for Sullivan, Felix the Cat appeared in the funny pages of many newspapers on the East Coast. He made his silver screen debut in the short *Feline Follies*, released in 1919, nine years before Mickey Mouse appeared in Disney's *Steamboat Willie,* and Felix the Cat quickly became one of the most recognizable images in popular culture. In exchange for using Felix the Cat as his dealership's mascot, Felix provided Sullivan and his friends with good deals on Chevrolets.[5][6][7]

"I have secured permission to adopt Felix as my own," he revealed. "And I am going to give the happy feline a ride through to the end. I have had brass plates made upon which is pictured the bright yellow cat carrying a banner, on which reads, 'Buy Yours from Felix.' Every car that I sell will carry this motif and bring good luck to the driver.

"One window in my showroom I have painted a large reproduction of this most famous of cats, and likewise the inscription. My idea in selecting this cat was, first, because it has the same family name as mine, although I can boast no relationship with him. I considered it a wonderful opportunity for tying up with a nationally known character of interest to young and old alike."[8]

Felix took full advantage of both the growing popularity of Felix the Cat and Chevrolet. "If there is anyone who doubts that cats like to ride in motor cars, let them take a look at the new sport roadster Chevrolet that I have dolled up for myself," he told the *Los Angeles Times* in 1924 after installing a large head of Felix the Cat in the passenger seat of his Chevrolet sport roadster.[9]

Felix made Felix the Cat integral to his business, using the cartoon image on his letterhead and in advertising material. At a time when automobiles had radiator caps on the front of their hoods, he produced custom caps in the image of Felix the Cat and sold them as a popular accessory. He also marketed tire covers that featured the Cat's smiling face.

"Drive anywhere you will, in any part of Southern California, and it's a two-to-one bet that you'll see cars sporting the Felix cat emblem," the *Times* observed. "It is said that Felix has come to mean Chevrolet and Chevrolet has come to mean Felix."[10]

Felix's impressive sales earned him respect and a central role in the formation of the Chevrolet Dealers Association of Los Angeles in 1924. Although he initially served as its secretary and treasurer, within three months he was elevated to president of the organization.

Chevrolet sales skyrocketed following World War I, and soon, General Motors boasted fourteen approved dealers in the city. It became the best-selling brand in Los Angeles in August 1925, and the following year, General Motors executives predicted Chevrolet would soon reach the one million car sales mark.[11]

"It is the policy of some makers to improve their cars only when they have to, but Chevrolet, in the middle of their biggest sales year in their history has added new colors and new improvements that make the car much more attractive than ever," Felix explained.[12]

Felix differentiated the vehicles he sold by offering unique custom features. "In developing the Felix special sport model Chevrolet, I make it possible for the owner to get all the necessary accessories at the time he buys his automobile," he noted. "Not only that but I make certain that he gets the kinds of accessories that are full value for the money involved, obviating the possibility of the motorists later purchasing some attachment or another that looks good, but lacks quality."[13]

Felix's new "special sport" Chevrolet roadsters and touring cars featured special front and back bumpers that protected against damage in traffic jams; plate-glass wind wings to add comfort for front seat passengers; balloon tires mounted on natural finish wheels and a spare tire and tube; four cast-aluminum floor plates (featuring the image of Felix the Cat); and a special oversized walnut steering wheel.[14]

Felix also offered customers a personalized service experience. If clients lived in Hollywood, Beverly Hills, or other nearby cities and didn't want to travel downtown for maintenance, Felix dispatched a porter driving a three-wheel motorcycle (embellished with a Felix the Cat insignia) to their homes. The motorcycle was attached to the back of the vehicle, then driven back to the dealership. Similarly, a salesperson would deliver the serviced vehicle back to the customer and return downtown on the motorcycle.

He also adopted the slogan, "Felix Service is as Close as your Telephone," and assigned his personal representative, Paul Parson, to call every new owner to make sure he or she was completely satisfied.[15] Felix proudly displayed an "immense" map of Los Angeles in his showroom with colored pins to show the location of every customer to whom he had sold a car.[16] This display helped him to decide where to target his advertising campaigns.

A master marketer, Felix introduced a "Trial Purchase Plan" in 1926 allowing customers to drive a new vehicle for two days and return the car for a total refund if they were not fully satisfied. He also covered the cost of gas. "The purpose of his plan is not only to further broaden the well-known liberal Felix merchandising policy, but to open new avenues through which the many possible Chevrolet buyers, previously unfamiliar with…this sturdy little car, may find out for themselves, uninfluenced by the usual selling methods," he explained.[17]

Felix sponsored parties, athletic events, auto races, shows, and dance contests where winners were awarded a new Chevrolet roadster.[18]

Passionate about polo, Felix often compared the sport to the cars he sold. "A polo pony has to be able to twist and turn like a cat…starting, stopping, and turning. Driving through modern city traffic is not a little like diving into a scrimmage in a polo game," he reflected.[19]

Felix would suffer fatal injuries playing the sport he loved. He collided with Reginald Leslie 'Snowy' Baker, considered Australia's greatest all-round athlete, when his horse stumbled in a club match at the Riviera polo field. He was transported to a hospital in Santa Monica where he died after an emergency operation to relieve the pressure on his fractured skull. *Variety* reported that many good players decided "to duck the hazardous practice of playing with the picture colony's poloists."[20]

Following Felix's demise, it was suggested General Motors had objections to allowing his dealership to be inherited by his wife, Ruth Felix, perhaps believing that a woman was not qualified to run an automobile business. However, County Superior Court Judge Arthur Keetch ruled she was entitled to her husband's estate, including his automobile enterprise.[21][22]

In his all-too-brief career, Felix proved to be a gifted innovator and master marketer whose unique approach to selling cars helped build a lasting legacy.

◀ Winslow B. Felix display in the Broadway Arcade Building, 1926.

▲ Winslow B. Felix's new dealership opened on December 17, 1933.

▼ Invitation to the new Felix Chevrolet dealership

▶ Winslow B. Felix breaks ground on a new Chevrolet facility at 12th Street and Grand Avenue in Los Angeles.

THOMAS "TOMMY" PILLOW JR.

Thomas "Tommy" Pillow Jr. was a pioneering automobile racer and one of the first African Americans to build, drive, and sell cars in Los Angeles. As a fourteen-year-old boy, his talent for rebuilding engines was discovered by the *Los Angeles Times* which boldly predicted his cultural impact could one day rival that of Booker T. Washington or Frederick Douglass.

"He is engaged in building an automobile for himself," the newspaper marveled in 1902. "He is a natural machinist, knows all about governor, flywheels, and in fact, everything that has to do with mechanics. He has his auto partially constructed. It is a small affair, about one horse-power, but when it is finished, in about two weeks, he expects to begin the construction of a larger one, a real horseless carriage."[1]

Thomas J. Pillow was born in Great Bend, Kansas, but grew up in Pasadena where he used the Hodge Bros. auto-delivery and machine shop on Union Street to advance his mechanical skills. He was behind the wheel of a Hodge Bros. electric automobile in 1902 when he was involved in one of Pasadena's most serious early car accidents.

"His attention was diverted for a moment from his machine when he startled at hearing an outcry from almost in front of the automobile, and a moment later there was shock as if it was passing over an obstruction," the *Los Angeles Express* stated.[2]

Pillow had driven over the neck and shoulder of Eaton T. Sams, secretary of the Y.M.C.A., who attributed no blame to the young driver as he had been riding his bicycle on the wrong side of the road when the collision occurred. A few months later, Pillow was fined five dollars for "riding his machine through town at a high rate of speed about midnight."[3][4]

He found himself at the center of more headline-making drama in 1904 when a "large, high-power" Co-

▲ Tommy Pillow Jr. behind the wheel of the Stevens-Duryea car that won a hill-climbing contest in Riverside, 1906.
▶ The Hodge Brothers auto-delivery and machine shop in Pasadena.

lumbia automobile he was riding in crashed through a six-foot fence on the side of the Raymond Hill bridge and went partly over the side. "John Pearson, a professional chauffeur with the West Coast Autocar company of 7th and Main Streets was in charge of the machine, and with him were W.E. Holcomb and Tom Pillow, the latter a colored chauffeur in Pasadena," cited the *Express*.[5]

With the car suspended over the edge of the bridge, the three men fell thirty feet to the railroad tracks below but none of them were seriously injured by the crash or the fall. "If it was my bad driving that caused it, I am willing to stand for it, as I ought to," Pearson told a local newspaper.[6][7]

Pillow's skill behind the wheel led to him being hired as a chauffeur for Charles Fuller Gates, an early leader of the Automobile Club of Southern California. He drove Fuller and two of his associates in a car sponsored by the *Los Angeles Examiner* in an endurance race from Los Angeles to Santa Barbara. When wealthy local automobile enthusiasts participated in endurance runs, they typically looked to chauffeurs to drive, as well as to make necessary emergency repairs and adjustments.

Fifty-three cars of all makes and models began the contest and most were able to finish by 6 p.m. Participants

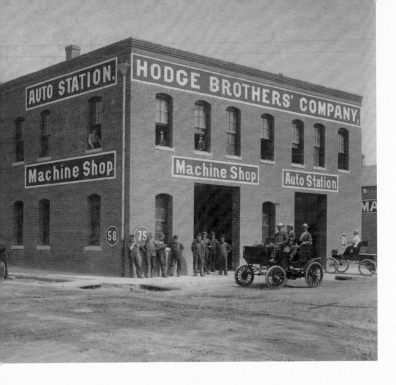

included well-known dealers such as Ralph Hamlin, William K. Cowan, and Earle C. Anthony and local luminaries including Harry Chandler of the *Los Angeles Times*.[8]

Pillow was recruited by millionaire racing enthusiast, A.B. Daniels of Coronado, to drive the six-cylinder Stevens-Duryea that won the 1906 hill climbing race in the Box Springs Mountains near Riverside in a record time. The contest was sponsored by the Los Angeles Motor Car Dealers' Association and according to the *Automobile,* Pillow guided "the big machine up the hill like a bird" although it was almost on its side at the first turn. "Pillow, instead of cutting the corner, tried to keep in the center of the road, and the wheels on one side went a foot off the ground," the journal described. "The crowd gathered at this point thought it was curtains for the big car, but Tommy steadied the monster, and it flew on to win first honors."[9]

Pillow claimed victory in five minutes and forty-one seconds, an average speed of 45 miles an hour, and would have won by an even larger margin had he not "killed a big dog" along the route. "The glory goes to Tommy Pillow," the *Los Angeles Times* declared. "He

understands the devil locked up in the high-power cars and takes no chances and makes no foolish moves. Life is too sweet, and besides there are some more races and hill climbs yet to win."[10]

He would also excel in a May 1907 race sponsored by the Seattle Automobile Association which attracted six thousand spectators. "'Tommy Pillow, despite the handicap of a suggestive slumbersome name, proved that he was very much awake by scoring the fastest time of the afternoon, on the 30th by covering the dust covered track in 1:12 ½, in his Pope-Toledo," the *Motor World* reported. He also won two hundred dollars on the second day of the event for driving the fastest mile of the meet and winning a five mile race.[11]

Pillow won again in Seattle the following week in a five-mile road race organized during the city's Auto Carnival. He drove a Pope-Toledo belonging to Pacific Coast Auto Company to the finish line with 300 yards between him and his nearest rival.[12]

His mastery of the automobile led to a position with Packard distributor Earle C. Anthony who utilized his talents to demonstrate the capability of new models. "On second speed the big car had shown her ability to reach the thirty-mile limit in less than ten seconds, and 'Tommy' was eager for a chance to see what the 'twelve' would do with a few more seconds opportunity," the *Times* wrote in 1915 after Pillow showed off the new Packard Twin-Six on Wilshire Boulevard for the newspaper's automobile editor.[13][14]

Los Angeles automobile dealer A.G. Faulkner hired Pillow to drive the Marmon cars he sold in the Economy Run from Los Angeles to Camp Curry in Yosemite beginning in 1915. He was behind the wheel of a Stephens Six owned by White Auto Company in 1923 delivering its third Economy Run victory in record time.[15]

In the 1930s, Pillow worked as a salesman before finding employment as a superintendent in a state-owned building.[16] His son, Townsend, completed four years of high school and was employed as a chauffeur. Pillow died on January 7, 1981 at age 93.

6 　　USED AUTOMOBILES

"Los Angeles has been termed the 'bottomless pit' into which hundreds and thousands of automobiles are dumped every year, to quickly disappear, and the market never seems to be exhausted."

Paul G. Hoffman, Retail Manager, Studebaker Corporation, November 12, 1916[1]

Los Angeles's passion for automobiles began with new cars, but quickly evolved to embrace used vehicles. As the market became flooded with second-hand cars, dealers began to refer to the "used-car problem" or "the used-car evil." The city would become home to the largest second-hand sales operation in the world, and it was a local enterprise that published the most celebrated, nationally recognized list of wholesale and retail prices for used vehicles.

Many early dealers who built their reputations selling automobiles to wealthy clients vehemently resisted the second-hand market, believing that displaying anything other than a new car was "below their dignity."[2] Manufacturers also refused to get involved, insisting second-hand cars were a problem for the dealers to solve.

The initial antipathy to used vehicles led the Motor Car Dealers' Association of Los Angeles to pass a June 1905 resolution prohibiting their sales.

> The members of the association agree not to trade in any second-hand cars, as part payment on any new machines. This motion was made sweeping in its intention, in order that there be no evading this rule.[3]

Yet, as sales of new cars multiplied, dealers inevitably relented and began allowing customers, who already owned cars, to trade them towards the purchase of a new vehicle.

 An advertisement for used cars at the rear of Don Lee's downtown Cadillac facility.

Ralph Hamlin's new and used-car dealerships on Flower Street

Franklin

SERVICE DEP'T.

NEW MODEL
FRANKLIN
49% MORE POWER

RALPH HAMLIN INC.

FRANKLIN

RALPH HAMLIN INC.
USED CARS
FRANKLIN DISTRIBUTORS

CARS

"Although the demand for automobiles fresh from the factory continues to increase daily there is a feature of the local trade which has developed wonderfully during the past few months, namely the selling and buying of second-hand cars," the *Los Angeles Herald* reported in August 1906. "A few years ago, second-hand machines could not be sold, owing to the undeveloped conditions of the automobile manufacturer which prevailed."[4]

Experimenting in the fledgling used-car business was complicated by the vast variety of early automobiles available, requiring dealers to have an extensive knowledge of market prices. It also put some of them at risk of violating the terms of their franchise agreements. Early manufacturers often forbade any kind of discount, in-cluding compensation for trade-ins, insisting new cars were to be sold at nationally advertised prices. The used-car market also created cash-flow problems for dealers who could only recover the funds they paid for a trade-in—often days or weeks after it had been reconditioned, repaired, and sold to another buyer.

Further adding to dealer woes was the distrust developed on the part of customers who studied news-paper prices for used cars before a potential trade-in or sale and failed to consider how dealers would make an offer only after considering the need for repairs, new tires,

▼ Greer-Robbins Company used Chrysler dealership.

and paint.[5] If they could not get a decent return on their investment, dealers were forced to offload vehicles at a wholesale price at one of the many used-car operations sprouting up on the edges of auto row.

Established dealers faced competition in the second-hand market from start-up sellers unencumbered by the cost of expensive facilities or service departments. Free from having to pay hefty deposits on new cars, these independent sellers could offer discounted rates on vehicles they found in newspaper advertisements, sometimes purchased from repair shops after a customer failed to pay his bill or from dealers who paid too much in a trade. The city's pleasant year-round climate led to many a local parking lot being transformed into an "open-air used-car emporium."[6][7]

With a consistent supply of reliable cars, many used-car sellers began converting them into trucks and other useful commercial vehicles, manufacturers took note and started developing new vehicles to exploit the emerging truck market. "There is a steadily increasing demand for second-hand touring cars from business men who remove the old bodies and replace them with those of express wagons or other vehicles for which they want to use them," the *Los Angeles Times* reported in 1908.[8] "Light delivery service, taxi companies, and liveries absorb a great number of the used cars," *The Outlook* observed.[9]

As Los Angeles's used-car market grew, the city council introduced a controversial annual license fee for all retailers of second-hand vehicles. "I have refused to pay this license, and I understand several other dealers here have taken the same attitude," Leon T. Shettler, president of the Motor Car Dealers' Association of Los Angeles, wrote to fellow members in 1909. "I personally do not object to paying the nominal sum required by this tax, but I do object to being classed with second-hand dealers and junk men."[10]

The association urged members to refuse to pay the tax and to notify the organization should they be sued. When Parley A. Lord of Lord Motor Company was arrested for selling a used car without a license, the association voted to find an attorney to defend him and contribute $500 towards his legal fees.[11] Similar action was approved two months later when a representative of the Grundy Motor Sales Company was also arrested.[12]

Eager to find a solution to the "used-car problem," in 1911, the organization explored the idea of establishing the Los Angeles Auto Dealers Rebuilt Car Company, a central, shared venue for members to sell cars at set prices, while offering customers a 90-day guarantee. Although the business model would reduce the individual burden of reconditioning vehicles and hiring staff, it was deemed "impractical" by James S. Conwell, the new president of the association, as it would be a potential violation of national and state trade laws.[13]

The Dealers' Association produced the first edition of their Second-Hand Automobile Price Value Book in 1913. It included information from retailers detailing what prices they charged for various makes and models, inspired by a similar journal published by the Chicago Automobile Trade Association.[14]

"Automobile dealers of the Pacific Coast will read with interest of the efforts now being made … to nationalize its used-car central market report," stated *Motor West*, observing the success of the Chicago publication. "So keen is the competition for new business that in many instances dealers, in their frantic desire to close a sale, have allowed from 20 to 25 percent too much for a used car taken in exchange as part of the purchase price of a new one."[15]

As sales of used cars grew, Los Angeles dealers were compelled to add additional display, storage, and repair space. The Studebaker dealership at 10th and Los Angeles Streets expanded to accommodate used vehicles and was selling fifty per month by 1912.[16]

Don Lee established a small used-car department at his Main Street Cadillac dealership the same year, and when he expanded in 1917 with a South Olive Street facility, both locations handled used vehicles. "Our expansion was due primarily to the fact of our increased business and because so much of our floor space in our present quarters is taken up with the work of renewing the cars we offer

Mechanics at work at the Kelley Kar Company.

KELLEY KAR CO
1·449·011
19 CALIFORNIA 28

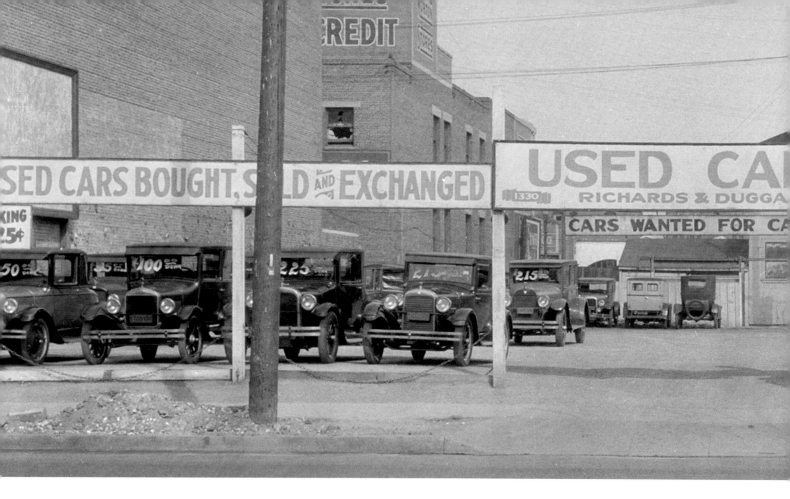

for sale," Manager Felix Guinney explained.[17] In the first five months of 1917, Lee's Los Angeles operation sold four hundred used cars.[18]

Others followed, including Troy Motor Sales Company, local Nash distributors who opened a used-car facility on Flower Street to complement their new-car operation on Figueroa, while John T. Dye, who promoted himself as being "among the largest and most prominent used-car dealers in America," converted an old church into a used-car operation on Figueroa and Pico.[19]

"Before a car is taken in ... every part of that car is gone over by the inspection department," C.J. Welch, manager of the second-hand car department at Earle C. Anthony's Packard dealership, described in 1915. "We inspect the rear axle, examine the transmission gears, and

'stethoscope' the motor, as well as trying the car on the road ... Our mechanics go over it thoroughly and put it in first-class mechanical condition ... The buyers of second-hand cars are rapidly coming to appreciate the fact that the best place to buy second-hand cars is from an established and reliable dealer in new cars."[20]

Beginning in 1915, Anthony included a coupon book, good for a certain number of hours of service and labor, with every used car he sold. He had done the same thing with new Packard and Reo automobiles that left his dealership. "Second-hand sales are yearly becoming a more and more important part of the business of every motor car dealer," he told the *Times*. "It is just as important to us to keep faith with our second-hand patrons as our new-car buyers."[21] The coupons could be redeemed

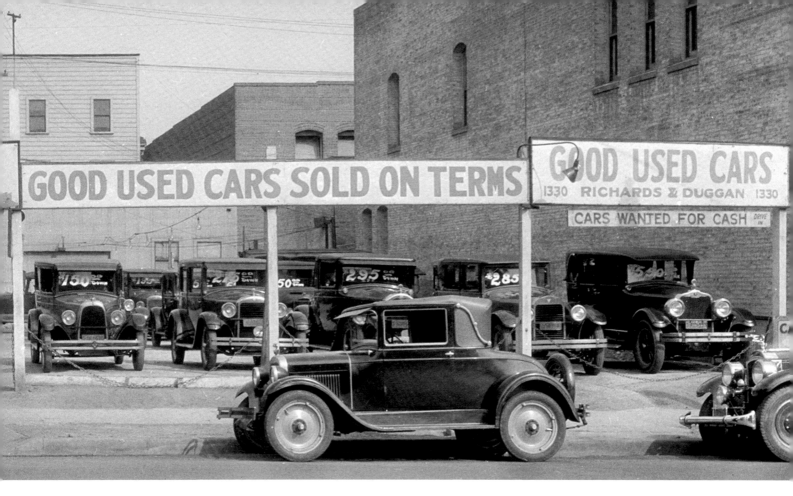

▲ Richards & Duggan used-car lot, 1330 S. Figueroa St.

at Anthony's repair shops, as well as at the 177 California service stations he operated.

"It has been estimated that fully 75 percent of the new cars purchased are bought by purchasers who already own motor cars," N.H. Williams, manager of Anthony's used-car department, revealed in 1916. "That means that in number of cars sold, the used-car business today is three-quarters as great in volume as the new car business."[22]

The same year, Studebaker's local distributor, Paul G. Hoffman, suggested the city's used automobile business had grown into three distinct sectors. "First, the 'legit,' who pays house rent, has a regular address and sells both new and used automobiles in the regular way," he explained. "Second, 'the wrecker,' who knocks 'em to pieces

in their old age and sells the parts to the army of repair and garage men who make a living rejuvenating run-down rolling stock, from the one-lung chugger, to the salon star with a cylinder for every month of the year. Third and last, but no means least, is the eminent psychologist, and festive proprietor of 'the gyp field,' whose roof is the star sprinkled floor of heaven by night and empyrean dome of blue by day. His stock of decrepits need not the protection of roof or wall—in fact, his business flourishes in the open, like the seller of superheated hot tamales."[23]

The value of used cars rose dramatically during World War I. While the economy boomed during the first two years of the war, and automobile production more than doubled from 569,000 cars in 1914 to 1,617,000 in 1916, all that would change when the United States formally entered the war in April 1917.[24]

A shortage of steel and other materials led Bernard Baruch, head of the War Industries Board, to threaten to shut down automobile production to free-up resources for the war effort. Congress classified automobiles as non-essential "pleasure cars" and slapped a 5 percent excise tax on them. Manufacturers and dealers henceforth referred to them as "passenger" cars.

"If the telephone is a necessity; if electric lights are not a needless extravagance; if sewing machines are not merely a recreation for the tired mother—then certainly automobiles are absolutely indispensable in this work-a-day world," R.C. Rueschaw, sales manager of Reo Motor Car Company, argued.[25]

While production remained relatively steady in 1917, by the following year, it declined by 700,000 units. Carmakers survived because prices continued to rise. The average wholesale price of an automobile rose from $670 in 1916 to $1,000 in 1918.[26]

"The continual advance in the price of new motor cars, made necessary because of the war taxes and the scarcity of material and labor, has made the low-priced car of today as expensive as the moderate-priced car of yesterday," Martin A. Leach, of Leach-Biltwell Company dealership on Grand Avenue, told *Motor West*.[27]

The end of the war did not curb high inflation which continued through 1919 and into the early months of 1920. Automobile manufacturers greatly expanded production capacity with modern factories. However, the cost of cars remained high and used cars were sometimes selling at a higher price than when they were brand new.[28] "The day of the used car may be said to have come," *Motor West* declared.[29]

While many Los Angeles dealers traveled to the eastern states in search of used-car inventory, dealers from the East were doing the same thing arriving in California. "Few people realize how many used cars from other States are shipped and driven into Southern California," George Kussman, manager of Earle C. Anthony's used-car department, revealed. "Not one in ten of these cars is as good a buy as a California used car. If it is a car from the far East and has been used through the mud and slush and snow of an eastern winter and spring it has had far more severe usage than the California used car will ever get."[30]

However, the *Times* maintained, "Good used cars are about as difficult to obtain as new cars" and gave the example of Paul G. Hoffman who recently returned from an East Coast search for used Studebakers with just one in his possession.[31]

In 1919, more than 75,000 used cars were sold in Southern California, representing a total expenditure of $45,000,000. The used-car business was now the fourth-largest industry in the region.[32] In March of the same year, the *Times* claimed to have published a record twenty-two columns of classified automobile advertisements.[33]

To exploit the popular interest in used vehicles, the newspaper formed a commercial partnership with the newly formed Used Car Dealers Association of Southern California, established by twenty-three of the region's largest second-hand automobile retailers.

"To date, the association's efforts have worked an almost marvelous change in the used-car market conditions in Los Angeles by eliminating to a large extent the 'fly-by-night' curbstone auto broker," the group's president, M.A. Leach, explained. Every member of the association was issued an emblem to be displayed prominently at their business. "That emblem stands for square dealing and is the buyer's assurance that what the dealer sells is just as he represents it."[34]

By 1920, the group had more than sixty members and organized its own used-auto show in April, held at Praeger Park with more than $500,000 worth of vehicles. Organizers promised, "The most wonderful display of renewed autos ever exhibited in the United States."[35]

"Next to the sale of new automobiles, perhaps the most important branch of the entire motor car industry is the marketing and conditioning of used automobiles," the

Times declared in January 1922. "Early in the history of the motor industry the used car presented a very minor problem. New cars were scarce enough and few people, either owners or manufacturers, gave any thought to the time when the driver would turn in his machine for a new one. But during the past two decades automobile manufacturing has jumped into third place in the nation's industries and the used-car problem has kept pace." [36]

American auto dealers sold 2.2 million new cars in 1922, but to do so, they had to take in 1.3 million in trades. Thus, only 950,000 customers were first-time buyers. Dealers needed to sell their new and used inventory, which amounted to 4.5 million cars. By year's end, they were left with about 400,000 unsold used cars.

Due to increased capacity and technological advances, new-car production soared. In 1923, dealers sold 3.6 million new cars. But to sell those 3.6 million, dealers had to accept 2.8 million trade-ins, putting the overall total of cars for sale at a stunning 6.4 million. But that same year would see a dramatic decline in the pool of first-time buyers, which dropped to 800,000.

The National Automobile Dealers Association reported the average allowance for a trade was $322 while the average resale price for the trade-in was $308, meaning every used car sold cost the dealer an average $14, contributing to an overall forty million dollars loss among the nation's dealers. [37]

White Auto Company, Southern California Stephens distributors, reported in the summer of 1923 the demand for good, used automobiles remained strong. "You don't hear so much weeping and wailing about the used-car situation as you did a few months ago," President O.R. Fuller explained. "We have introduced the one price policy in selling our used cars. We tag each car and mark on that tag the definite price at which that car will be sold … There is no dickering to be done." [38]

George Nelson, head of the used-car department at Albertson Motor company, local Dodge Brothers dealers, added, "Used cars have stepped up in the world, you might say. They are no longer a 'Main Street' bargain. They are Figueroa Street value." [39]

For many years, however, a handful of dealers and automakers had voiced concern that a "saturation point" of auto sales might soon be reached as manufacturers continued to produce cars that dealers were unable to sell. And early in 1924, Los Angeles dealers began to complain. Jack Benell, Southern California Haynes distributor, was one of them:

> When 95 percent of the automobile prospects that come in the door had a car to trade in, that is getting pretty close to saturation point, isn't it? … When a salesman brings in a clean deal, cash and no trade-in, these days, the sales manager usually faints on the office rug … The plain fact of the matter is that nine dealers out of ten are carrying too heavy a load of used cars. This condition has been largely forced on them by the factories who have compelled them to take large allotments of new cars … If new-car production were held within proper limits, there would of course, be no used-car problem. That was demonstrated plainly during the war, when new car production was curtailed. [40]

Adding to the problem, automobile manufacturers were now producing more durable, reliable cars that lasted longer. A new emphasis on updated styling for new cars after 1920 also meant that many car owners were trading relatively new cars for brand-new, restyled cars, creating a large group of much newer used cars flowing into the market. As Earle C. Anthony admitted:

> It has been allowed to grow and has even been fostered by the automobile manufacturers themselves until it has reached the point where it is now rightfully referred to as the used-car evil … Problem, evil or what not, the question of the used car is the most important facing the automobile industry today, and one of vital importance to

the whole country. It is the next object of attack by the industry. No business can be permanently successful unless it serves the public and with economy. Until the used car is disposed of, proper economy is impossible. The greatest cost of operating an automobile today lies in depreciation, and the used-car evil is responsible for a far greater depreciation loss to the original owner than all the driving in the life of an automobile … Central appraisal bureaus and all the other cure-alls which have been suggested will serve little purpose in solving the present great problem of the automobile business. It will be eradicated only by going right at the source. There will be no 'used car evil' when the original purchasers of automobiles keep their cars and drive them until all the useful and desirable miles have been exhausted. Every car is worth far more in the hands of the original owner than on the floor of a used-car showroom."[41]

Auto finance companies which came into their own in the 1920s played a large role in the used-car problem, as they introduced a broader range of buyers and removed some financial barriers that checked overproduction tendencies on the part of the manufacturers.[42]

The automakers generally dismissed the used-car dilemma as something for the dealers to resolve, but alarmed by "a high dealer mortality rate," several manufacturers began to experiment with various ways to aid and strengthen their dealers.[43]

The National Automobile Dealers Association recognized dealers often took in used cars on trade for less than they were able to sell them, and in 1923, began compiling detailed information on the number of used cars sold on a quarterly basis, the average trade-in allowance and eventual sale price, and the total number of losses to dealers across the nation. This information was provided to dealers to help them determine the allowance for trades

and pricing for used-car sales.[44]

The most meaningful effort to create a used-car price guide would come from used-car dealer, Ransom Leslie "Les" Kelley, who kept track of data on the vehicles he sold through the Los Angeles-based Kelley Kar Company. In 1926, he published the first *Kelley Blue Book* of Motor Values.[45] The book proved so popular, it became instrumental in establishing "standard values on all makes of used cars." When Kelley's business moved to South

Figueroa Street, it would become the largest used-car facility in the world.

Paul Hoffman's Los Angeles-area Studebaker dealerships sold more than a thousand used cars in the first four months of 1927.[46] Hoffman understood the used-car problem was an unavoidable reality for the automobile business and required cooperation between manufacturers and dealers.

"We constantly hear discussions of the so-called "used-car problem" as something annoyingly foreign to automobile distribution," he wrote in the 1929 book, *Marketing Used Cars*. "It is part and parcel of the new car business, the phase which calls for the exercise of the maximum of judgment, skill, and shrewdness."[47]

▲ The Apperson Motor Company used-car showroom on South Flower Street, 1922.

USED AUTOMOBILES

PAUL G. HOFFMAN

Paul G. Hoffman began his career in Los Angeles selling Studebaker automobiles, but he is best remembered as a car company executive, statesman, and global development aid administrator. His confident, decisive management style and innovative training programs earned him the respect of President Harry Truman who recruited him to help Europe rebuild after World War II. When touted as a possible presidential candidate himself, he rejected the idea suggesting being a businessman was not a qualification to run a country.

Born in Chicago in 1891, young Hoffman, like many teenage boys, was fascinated by the automobile. In 1907, his father invested in a Pope-Toledo, billed as the world's first mile-a-minute automobile. "Roads were wretched. Cars were inferior. Servicing facilities were poor," he recalled.[1]

Hoffman attended the University of Chicago, with the intention of pursuing a legal career, but dropped out following disappointing exam results and a general lack of interest in classes.[2] He instead went to work for the Chicago distributor for Halladay automobiles. He was em-

ployed as a foreman in the repair shop until the business was bought out by a new owner who recognized he was wasting his talents and recommended he try selling cars.

Hoffman's family headed to Southern California in 1911 where he was hired as a Studebaker dealer in Los Angeles. In 1912, he won a contest for Studebaker sales staff with an essay entitled, "How to Sell Studebaker Automobiles," and was invited to South Bend, Indiana, where he met with J.M. Studebaker, one of the original Studebaker brothers who co-founded the company.

"We are successful because we always give our customers more than we promise," Studebaker told Hoffman. "This way you hold customers and get more customers. But don't give them too much more, or you'll go broke."[3]

Within three years, Hoffman won a national sales contest and was offered a position running the Studebaker Corporation's New York distribution center and a $50,000 annual salary. But he turned it down insisting he still wanted to continue to sell cars. In 1917, he was put in charge of Studebaker's Southern California operation.[4]

Hoffman's career was interrupted by World War I, in which he served as a first lieutenant of the artillery division of the army, but resumed when his military service ended. In March 1919, he acquired the Southern California Studebaker distributorship and during the first three months of 1920, sales increased by 300 percent. He was soon selling four thousand cars a year.[5][6]

In 1921, he invested $35,000 to help debut the KNX radio station, primarily to advertise his automobile operation. In 1936, CBS bought the station for one million dollars.[7]

As his business grew, the company relocated to a new purpose-built facility at Pico and Figueroa Street and erected a separate 40,000 square-foot, two-story building downtown to act as a receiving station for Studebakers where they could be tuned, tested, and serviced before being sent to local dealers.[8]

Paul G. Hoffman Company had sixty thousand dollars in capital in 1919 and by 1925, it had $1.5 million in assets.[9] Studebaker Corporation took note of Hoffman's

▲ Paul G. Hoffman Co. moved into a new building on South Figueroa Street in 1920.

success and elected him to vice president in charge of sales and also appointed him to its board of directors in 1925.

Hoffman worked to improve the corporation's relationship with dealers and introduced the "Friendliest Factory" plan which encouraged retailers with complaints to visit his office.[4] He also established a retail course for the eight thousand Studebaker staff and a factory school for traveling representatives of the corporation's twenty-two branches.[10]

In 1929, he co-wrote a very useful book *Marketing Used Cars,* which explained how new car dealers should organize their used-car departments; how to buy, recondition, merchandise, and sell used cars; and how to control inventory.[11]

Studebaker Corporation, like many other automakers during the Great Depression, went into receivership in 1933. However, unlike other businesses that had been forced to liquidate their assets to pay debts, Hoffman,

now president of sales and vice-president of the corporation, used his salesmanship to convince Federal Judge Thomas W. Slick to allow Studebaker to reorganize and continue doing business.

It was the first time an automobile company had weathered receivership and the first time any major manufacturing enterprise had been recapitalized with private investment under section 77-(b) of the Corporate Reorganization Act.[12]

Hoffman's sense of civic responsibility led him to serve as the head of the executive board of the Traffic Commission of the City and County of Los Angeles and chairman of the roads committee of the Los Angeles Chamber of Commerce. He was also the director of the National Planning Foundation which worked to improve

traffic systems and was central to founding a traffic research center at Harvard University that developed programs for Chicago, San Francisco, Los Angeles, and other major cities.[13]

In the aftermath of World War II, President Harry Truman named Hoffman to lead the European Economic Cooperation Administration, generally known as the Marshall Plan, to utilize American assistance to rebuild war-torn Europe.

A founder and the first chairman of the President's Committee for Economic Development, Hoffman's name was floated in 1953 as a potential candidate himself for president. According to Herbert Stein, chairman of the Committee for Economic Development under Presidents Nixon and Ford, Hoffman made it clear he was not interested in the job.

"Hoffman not only disclaimed any interest for himself but also said that he did not think that a businessman should be the candidate," Stein remembered. "I am still not sure that he was right about himself, but he was probably right about businessmen in general."[14]

Hoffman's friendship with Dwight D. Eisenhower led to a position on the team that helped him win the 1952 Republican presidential nomination. Hoffman later became the first president of the Ford Foundation before returning to Studebaker where he oversaw its merger with Packard Motor Company in 1954.

"Studebaker-Packard will have $249 million in assets and $92 million in capital," he explained. "We will be a very big company."[15]

He was appointed as the head of the United Nations Special Fund in 1959, which became the United Nations Development Fund in 1966, and he maintained an interest in the agency's work.

His many different jobs would earn him the sobriquet "the Everything Man." In 1973, he was awarded the United States Medal of Freedom. He died the following year at age 83.[16]

◀ Paul G. Hoffman Co. took over the Arnold Building at Figueroa and 7th Streets.

R. LESLIE KELLEY

Ransom Leslie "Les" Kelley transformed the used-car business by offering a comprehensive guide to prices still widely used today nearly a century later. His *Kelley Blue Book* would become the automotive industry standard for establishing the value of cars. He also operated what was billed as the world's largest used-car business and later would build the world's largest Ford dealership.

Born in Ash Flat, Arkansas, in 1897, the son of a Methodist minister, he first arrived in Los Angeles at the age of 17 and attended the University of Southern California in 1914. To pay for college, he used his mechanical skills to recondition inexpensive used automobiles on a lot south of the university.

Kelley applied the accounting skills he learned at USC to track his purchases and sales and analyzed the data to get a better sense of the true market value of each vehicle.

He started his used-car company with three Model T Fords and employed his "energetic" 13-year-old brother, Sidney H. "Buster" Kelley, as a lot boy to wash cars, change tires, and make sure the vehicles looked attractive.[1]

▲ The Kelley Kar Company at Figueroa and Pico Boulevard was the largest used-car operation in the world.

In the early years, he moved the business from Central Avenue to Main Street, then to 10th and Broadway, and later to Olive Street.[2]

To acquire new inventory, Kelley created a list of makes and models, indicated what he would pay for them, and then circulated the list to new car dealers on Auto Row. At the time, most new car dealers had little interest in used cars.

Kelley's list appealed to the dealers because they knew he was paying all dealers the same price for their cars. They also took advantage of the list to show customers what their trade-in was really worth and diffuse the inherent tension between customers and dealers in agreeing on the value of a used vehicle.

As his business grew, Kelley sent his list to banks that were beginning to consider loans to customers for auto sales. Most financial institutions had little or no idea of the true market value of a used car.

In newspaper advertisements, Kelley Kars challenged buyers to visit the business and "Ask Us How We Do It."[3] Promotions typically included the message, "The following used cars represent fair values on the present market. We can't give you something for nothing— Nor can anyone else. But every car we sell is good, or we will make it good."[4] Kelley attributed the company's success to the "Blue Seal Guarantee" which accompanied the majority of cars sold.

When Leslie and Buster overstocked the business with Model T Fords, they remembered Henry Ford's famous comment that cars can be "any color as long as it was black" but decided to paint one of them pink. When the pink Model T sold immediately, they did the same to the others.[5]

If a manufacturer went out of business and left the dealers with an inventory of phased-out cars, Kelley would buy the entire inventory and sell it on their used-car lot.[6] They also provided insurance to customers and offered no-money-down auto loans to soldiers returning from wartime service.

Kelley transformed his price list into the *Kelley Blue Book* of Car Values in 1926. He cleverly incorporated "Blue Book," a term normally used to refer to the socially prominent people whose names were listed in a Blue Book. It quickly became regarded as "the bible of the used-car business in terms of establishing automobile market values."[7]

When California became one of the first states in the union to adopt uniform appraisals on motor vehicles for tax purposes, the California Tax Assessors Association made Kelley their official appraiser. They were impressed by the "scientific accuracy" and itemized list of appraisals that "covered practically every type of car and motor vehicle in use."[8]

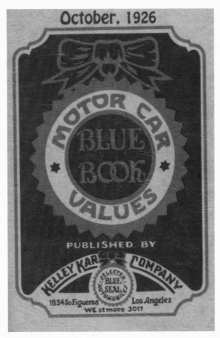

▲ The *Kelley Blue Book* of Motor Car Values was launched in 1926.

The Kelley Kar Company eventually relocated to South Figueroa Street on a site that covered nearly an entire block and became the largest used-car operation in the world.

When it was announced in 1930 the company would become the De Soto distributor for Los Angeles and Orange County, they constructed a new showroom, service station, and parts stockroom nearby. "In their experience as used car dealers, officials of the Kelley Kar Company have had an opportunity to test the value, popularity, and work of many makes of cars, and so well has the De Soto met all the tests of public preference that when the opportunity came to take this franchise Mr. Kelley was not long in deciding," reported the *Los Angeles Evening Express*.[9] By 1934, they had 80,000 square feet of floor space.[10]

During World War II, Kelley acquired a small local Ford dealership and later publicized it through television ads. It would become the largest Ford dealership in the world, employing 625 people.

In 1962, Kelley sold his automotive businesses and devoted his attention to his eponymous Blue Book, which later expanded to include valuations for motorcycles and recreational vehicles.

He died at the age of 92 in 1990.

"The notable fact which has been brought out in the auto show and in the salerooms of many of Los Angeles's motor car dealers is that women are becoming more and more of an important factor to be reckoned with in the business of selling automobiles."

Los Angeles Evening Express, January 26, 1919[1]

For Los Angeles to become the car capital of the West, both men and women had to get behind the wheel. While historians have emphasized the new age of the automobile as a man's world, the critical role women played in introducing the public to its revolutionary new means of mobility has been largely ignored.[2] Also overlooked are the many ways women influenced manufacturers in the design of automobiles and the way in which cars were sold.

When women moved from the passenger seat to the driver's seat, they challenged Victorian expectations about their place in society. Not only would they demonstrate they could handle, repair, race, and sell cars, they would also lobby for laws to govern them.

Forgotten from history is the transformative role Sybil C. Geary, the first female secretary of the Automobile Club of Southern California, played in championing standardized road signs and state automobile regulations, all while boosting the organization's membership. Also lacking recognition are the Los Angeles women who used automobiles to shepherd men to the ballot box to support the historic fight for women's rights in 1911 or those who took to the streets in 1920 to overturn the city's controversial parking ban.

"Does anyone realize how many of the 1,500 automobiles in town are owned or operated by women?" the *Los Angeles Times* asked readers in July 1905. "At almost

◀ La Fiesta Parade first prize for automobile decoration, 1908.

A MOTOR-VEHICLE WORTHY *of the* STUDEBAKER NAME

WE have not been indifferent to the introduction of the horseless carriage. Rather than push upon the market an imperfect and immature product, however, we have expended time and money in order to secure a type of automobile which would not discredit our standing in the vehicle world.

THE STUDEBAKER ELECTRIC VEHICLE

is admirably simple in construction, safe, easy to operate and remarkably free from vibration and noise. It is not a racing machine, but a strongly built practical motor-vehicle for everyday service on country roads and city streets. Extensive experiments and tests have convinced us that the electric motor, with the great improvements recently made in storage batteries, provides the most desirable equipment in every way. It is simplicity itself, clean, odorless, durable and sufficiently speedy for all practical purposes.
Now on exhibition at the following repositories. Descriptive booklet free.

STUDEBAKER BROS. MFG. CO.

NEW YORK CITY: Broadway and Prince St.
CHICAGO, Ill.: 378-388 Wabash Avenue.
KANSAS CITY, Mo.: 810-814 Walnut St.
SAN FRANCISCO, Cal.: cor. Market and 10th Sts.
Local Agencies Everywhere.

DENVER, Colo.: Corner 15th and Blake Sts.
SALT LAKE CITY, Utah: 157-159 State St.
PORTLAND, Ore.: 328-334 E. Morrison St.
DALLAS, Tex.: 194-196 Commerce St.
FACTORY AND EXECUTIVE OFFICE: South Bend, Ind

◀ A 1902 ad assures women that the car is "not a racing machine, but a strongly built, practical motor-vehicle for everyday service."

Other pioneering women in the driver's seats included Ida Dotter, who was both an accomplished chauffeur and a mechanic. "I had my automobile all to pieces last week, and I put it all together again by myself," she boasted in a 1905 interview. "Grease? I should say so, from my hands to my elbows, but that's better than paying from fifty to a hundred dollars per month for repairs."[6]

When Chicago chauffeuse Katherine Lockwood moved to Los Angeles in 1907, she hoped to escape tired expectations about her position. "Why is it that I am discriminated against, simply because I am a woman?," she wrote to the automobile editor of a local newspaper. "If I can do the same work and give more satisfaction than a man; why not give me a trial?"[7]

That same year, the *Times* noted, "It is found that not only do many women drive machines, but that in many cases own them themselves, and it not infrequently happens that the lady of the household is the real motorist, the husband not being as good a mechanic as his wife."[8] Even before California began paving highways, Los Angeles women drivers made headlines driving up the coast, into the mountains, north to Yosemite and San Francisco or south to Mexico.[9] In 1906, women competed against men in an endurance run from Los Angeles to Riverside and also in the Southern California Reliability Contest.[10][11]

Plans were made in 1908 for an all-female race between Los Angeles and Riverside. "For the first time in the history of automobile road racing, women will enter a contest arranged exclusively for them," the *Times* reported. "… it remains for Los Angeles to have the first women's road race ever held in the United States."[12]

Los Angeles dealers exploited the publicity their wives, daughters, and sisters generated, participating in long distance drives, endurance runs, or races, to boost sales. Nadi Burt, whose husband W.J. Burt headed the Burt Motor Car Company and was an Auburn dealer; Larooka Conwell, daughter of James S. Conwell, a dealer

any moment of the day half a dozen machines buzz down Broadway, guided by the fair sex who skim past streetcars, wind in and out among trucks and drays and glide around corners as skillfully as does husband, father or brother when at the helm."[4]

The first woman to operate a large car in Los Angeles was Christina Reedal, who the *Times* claimed could "rip a tire off or repair a puncture without so much as looking at a chauffeur or a mechanic." Her father, retired capitalist John Reedal, supported her passion and gifted her with a Rambler in which she drove four female friends to Santa Barbara in 1905, the first woman to make the journey without a "man or a chauffeur."[5]

▲ Two women explore Los Angeles in an Ohio Steamer, circa 1911.
▲▶ A Los Angeles woman poses with an electric car, 1914.

representing several brands; and Minnie Beardsley, wife of Volney Beardsley, who represented Firestone, Columbus, and Warren-Detroit automobiles, regularly competed in automobile contests.

Ruth Bekins—whose brother Milo established the Bekins-Corey Motor Company in 1909, the local agents for American Simplex and Atlas—was tipped for success after competing in a 1911 Santa Monica road race in her Lozier Briarcliff. "This motor maid is the likeliest woman driver in the West and is in line for amateur world championship honors," the *Times* raved.[13]

Just two years prior, Bekins drove with her mother from Riverside to Los Angeles in a record time of two hours and twenty-nine minutes, and was no stranger to press attention.[14] As a seventeen-year-old student at Los Angeles High School, she made headlines flouting two city speeding laws in one wild night. "The young lady was out for a spin with her friend Linford Lull, son of the general manager of the Auto Vehicle Company, in his car," the *Times* reported.

"On West Seventh street, near Alvarado, he offered Miss Bekins the wheel; and then the street lamps began to look like a blur as they flew by." When police finally caught up with her, she urged them to go easy as it was the night before Valentine's Day. Bekins, however, was arrested and later paid a fifteen-dollar fine to avoid spending fifteen days in the city jail.[15]

Bekins would play a central role in the formation of the Southern California Women's Automobile Club in 1910, serving as the organization's secretary. The group included more than a hundred motorists who shared her passion for the handling and racing of automobiles, as well as associated pleasure trips, exhibitions, and tours.

"There are more women owners of automobiles in Los Angeles than in any other city on the Pacific Coast," read the *Times*. "This is the reason, say the women, that Los Angeles should lead the world in an effort to make the women's club better than anything ever formed."[16]

The enthusiasm surrounding the automobile at the dawn of the twentieth century led to the formation of numerous local auto groups, many of which would later be absorbed into the Automobile Club of Southern California. The club enticed them by sharing details of member activities in its own magazine and assigning representatives to show up at their meetings.[17]

When the Political Equality League, the most influential suffrage group in Los Angeles, succeeded in placing a constitutional amendment on the ballot for the October 1911 election, women with access to automobiles used them

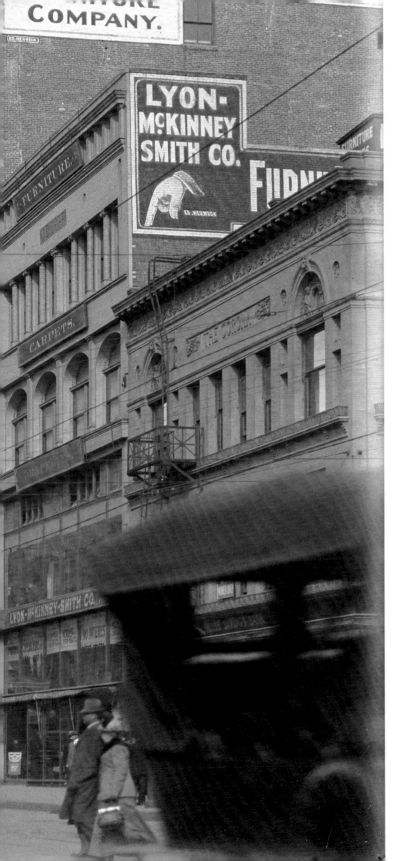

to mobilize male voters to help pass the amendment.[18] The path-breaking referendum, while heavily defeated in the San Francisco Bay Area, carried in the Los Angeles region and in most rural areas.[19]

Banners with the slogan "Votes for Women" were affixed to automobiles, as an estimated eight hundred women gathered at the polling places urging men to support their cause. "More than fifty automobiles were in service of the suffrage cause the entire day," stated the *Los Angeles Herald*. "These machines were volunteered and they hauled voters to the polls by hundreds."[20]

On election day, hundreds of women visited factories, businesses, and residences, searching for men to support their vote and then "used the telephone to call for automobiles to take them to the polls."[21]

In an historic victory, women won the right to vote in California, but the state required all voters to be legally registered to vote twenty-five days prior to voting in any election. In Los Angeles, this meant that women would not be able to vote in upcoming primary elections for mayor and city council members, but if they acted quickly to register women voters, those new female voters could cast ballots in the general election. Supporters immediately began using cars to bring women to voter-registration centers.

Women also mobilized using automobiles to campaign for candidates in the mayoral primary elections on October 31, 1911 and the December 5 municipal ballot. "The Women's Progressive League, which is ardently supporting Mayor Alexander … today is in the thickest of the battle," the *Los Angeles Evening Herald* detailed. "Twenty automobiles loaded with registration deputies, all of them young women, left the headquarters … this morning for a systematic canvass of voters in a number of important precincts."[22]

While incumbent George Alexander was backed by progressives and anti-Socialists and running on the

◀ A female driver navigates through traffic along Broadway.

◀ A Baker R&L Company advertisement, 1915.

view. "In exactly 92 percent of the accidents recorded in Los Angeles during the past six weeks, men were to blame. Perhaps the period of time chosen did not represent the average, but it shows the fair pilots have been maligned."

Morrison claimed women had grown more confident behind the wheel due, in part, to the development of electric vehicles. "The cars are light and their easy control permits those driving them to traverse the downtown streets at the busiest hours of the day without fear," he explained. "Many women graduate from the electric to the big gasoline car, and they prove the electric apprenticeship was well spent." [25]

Electric cars offered women distinct advantages. Starting a gasoline engine by hand-cranking was hard work and dangerous because failure to turn the engine could cause the crank to snap back and seriously injure, or even break an arm. By contrast, electric cars started instantly with the flick of a switch. Soon, a gendered distinction between gasoline cars and electrics began to emerge. While advertisers viewed men as interested in power and economy, automobiles were marketed to women for their comfort and convenience. [26]

"These vehicles have always been looked upon as women's cars because they require no cranking, are silent, easily controlled, and possess ample speed for city use," *Vogue* magazine wrote in 1913. [27] "The electric … is a women's car … a woman is more interested in the cushions, lights, and upholstery and finish than she is in the motor," *Automobile Salesmanship*, a 1915 training manual, noted. "Practically all electric cars are enclosed cars and these points should be played up well." [28]

Cadillac distributor Don Lee celebrated the new electric starter on the manufacturer's gas-powered 1912 car by linking it in advertising with the enactment of women's suffrage. [29] Electric car manufacturers like Baker, Milburn, Woods, Borland, and Anderson regularly featured women in their national advertising, emphasizing

"Good Government" ticket, his opponent, Job Harriman, was backed by a coalition led by Socialists. Harriman's campaign also drew support from women who formed an "Autos Committee" for mobilization at polling stations on election day. [23]

By 1913, it was claimed there were more women automobile owners in Los Angeles than any other city in the United States, with the "possible exception of New York City." [24]

"Ninety percent of the women handling automobiles in Los Angeles are as capable of driving their cars as men who have had similar experience," A.E. Morrison, of the R.C.H. Corporation, argued in a syndicated inter-

▲ The automobile gave women the freedom to explore rural areas outside of the city.

safety, comfort, and convenience. They also recognized the purchasing power of women by enclosing cars with a metal roof to provide protection from the elements. "For social functions, the closed electric car represents the types most in use among women … Thorough protection from rain, wind, and the cold is afforded by the glass sides and windows and the permanent roof," *Vogue* observed.[30]

Volney S. Beardsley, Los Angeles dealer for Columbus Electric, won praise for cross-marketing the company's new coupe with "stunning garments" at a 1912 fashion show at Bullock's department store on Broadway and 7th. As an electric car glided down the central aisle, it was surrounded by models sporting elaborate gowns, wraps, and hats. "The success of the novel living display was attested by the enormous crowds which blocked traffic for an hour or so in front of the big store," the *Times* read. "It was necessary to send several traffic officers to the spot to keep the throng moving."[31]

Manufacturers of electric cars offered women extra comfort with cushioned seating and higher-grade upholstery.[32] "Handsome body lines, together with a finish which is made up of twenty-three coats of paint and varnish, give a snappy appearance to the car upon first sight,"

the *Times* wrote, describing the new Detroit Electric in 1916. "Inside the deep-tufted upholstery and the little refinements, which are most appreciated by women, serve to make the Detroit Electric the most comfortable car to ride in."[33]

The early success of the electric car with women buyers was not enough to overcome the obvious limitations. Electric vehicles cost more to manufacture than their gas-powered competitors, especially as the assembly-line factories produced more cars at lower cost. They also had limited range as one battery charge might only provide a 20- to 50-mile run, and being heavy, they had difficulty mounting steep roads or navigating rough, unpaved roadways.

Eventually, manufacturers of gasoline-powered automobiles began to include features made popular in the electric vehicles that were designed primarily to appeal to women: non-cranking ignition systems, covered roofs, interior lighting, and comfortable seating.

Along with selling cars designed for female drivers, automobile dealers were also increasingly aware of the role women played in the selection of vehicles. "The man in the household narrows down the choice to two or three automobiles, which he believes to be mechanically right," S.G. Chapman, Bay Area distributor for Hudson automobiles, described in 1912. "Almost invariably at this point

the woman of the household is brought into the prospective purchase, by reason of her good judgment relative to automobile beauty, comfort, and convenience."[34]

The following year, Margaret R. Burlingame, a writer for *Motor: The National Magazine of Motoring*, noted, "It is beginning to be a recognized fact in the marketing of automobiles that women must be taken into consideration in almost every sale."[35] Two years later, *Harper's Bazaar* placed advertisements in *Motor* magazine that suggested seventy-five percent of automobile sales were influenced by women.[36]

"In the opinion of the officers of the J.V. Baldwin Motor Company, local agents for the Saxon Six, fully 60 percent of passenger car sales are either made directly to women or are the result of the feminine influence," the *Los Angeles Evening Express* stated in January 1919. "Motor car manufacturers, recognizing this condition, are leaving nothing undone in their efforts to include features of direct interest to prospective women purchasers."[37]

Edward Jordan, an advertising and publicity manager who created Jordan Motor Car Company, insisted,

▲ Actress Anita King arrives in Chicago on her transcontinental tour in a Kisselkar.
▶ Two Los Angeles women pose with a pristine automobile. When women moved from the passenger seat to the driver's seat, they challenged Victorian notions about their role in society.

"Men buy automobiles, but it is the women who choose them." Jordan's 1923 full-page magazine advertisement entitled "Somewhere West of Laramie," featured an attractive woman in her car racing against a cowboy riding a pony. It would become an iconic image and have a profound influence on automobile advertising.[38]

Packard distributor Earle C. Anthony, was fascinated with the role of women in choosing Packard as a family vehicle and reached out to University of Southern California psychology professor, Ernest A. Rayner, for answers.

Prof. Rayner explained that a man buys a car from purely practical considerations, thinking of price in relation to his business and family demands," George R. Bury, vice president of Earle C. Anthony, Inc., relayed.

> He has more or less of an idea of the mechanical features and purchases the car from the common sense standpoint of economy... A woman looks at the purchase of a car from a standpoint of appearance and class, since these are the values which more especially appeal to her. To be sure she is not unmindful of the practical considerations, but she is inclined to give full regard to lines, appointments and general effect. Then when she finds a car that meets all of these requirements, she buys that car, and we might add that their husbands seem willing enough to sign the checks when the choice is Packard.[39]

The drive to sell automobiles to women led local dealers, manufacturers, and enthusiasts to customize cars based on female motorists' demands, incorporating some of the posh features seen earlier in electric luxury cars, such as fine upholstery, custom coachwork, and interior lighting.

Los Angeles auto shows already appealed to women with floral displays and fashion shows, but began to display

◀ Women in Los Angeles were employed as auto mechanics during World War I.

cars with female-focused accessories, such as adjustable windshields that protected drivers and passengers with hats, as well as custom interior and exterior paint jobs in audacious colors.[40]

White Motor Company marketed its new 1910 covered gasoline car as offering doors, "wide enough to accommodate cumbersome skirts and a driver's seat that folded up 'to make entrance easy from either side.'"[41] Meanwhile, executives at Cartercar insisted the transmission in their vehicles made them ideal for women. "The gearless transmission of the Cartercar eliminates the clutch and gears and, for that reason, we feel perfectly safe in saying that the Cartercar is essentially a woman's car," Harry R. Radford, vice-president and general manager, told the *Los Angeles Evening Express*. "It is operated as easily as an electric vehicle, yet it has the range of any gasoline car."[42]

Los Angeles dealers also used women to market to other women. William E. Bush, Inc., Los Angeles representatives for DeSoto Six, hired two local motorists, Gay Barton and Mary Bowden, to drive its cars around the city as a publicity stunt. "A month ago this company employed the two girls to drive the roadsters about merely to impress the public of the car's beauty, its smart appearance and ease with which a woman can handle it, even in heavy traffic," P. Parks Harris, vice-president of the dealership, revealed.[43]

As the motion picture industry came of age, female movie stars were recruited to exploit their cross-marketing potential. Paramount Pictures promoted Anita King's movie career in 1915 by arranging for the actress to drive a new Kisselkar from Los Angeles to New York, a solo trip covered by a crew of Paramount's publicists anxious to gain publicity for the car and its star behind the wheel.[44] *Motor Age* described King as "the first woman driver to attempt a transcontinental trip without a companion, male or female."[45]

Apperson marketed their 1917 Roadaplane as "The Proven Car For Women" after vaudeville star, Claire Rochester, drove one "without a stop due to mechanical trouble" from New York to San Francisco in 11 days and 22 hours, a record for women drivers.[46]

While women were making an impact on the design of automobiles, they were underrepresented on the sales floor. The first female automobile dealer in the United States was Mary D. Allen, whose husband, Ives Marshall Allen, established Allen Automobile Agency after securing Brooklyn's first franchise for the Stevens-Duryea car in 1903. When he died in 1905, Mary took over the business and ran it for ten years, exhibiting cars at auto shows at Madison Square Garden in New York City, as well as Newark and Atlantic City.[47]

Patricia K. Webster, the Alameda and Contra Costa Counties dealer for Jordan cars, was reported to be the only female dealer on the Pacific Coast in 1923. "It is a field where men have had absolute sway, and where they probably felt that women could not compete, although in this they showed their usual aptitude to underrate the feminine capacity for adaptability," the *Oakland Tribune* expressed.[48] Webster had sold various makes of cars before going into business for herself. "Her repair and service department is among the most complete and largest on the entire coast, and is entirely under her management," the newspaper noted.[49]

The increasing number of women drivers led various Southern California organizations to set up classes to educate women about automobiles. The Young Men's Christian Association automobile school in Pasadena opened its doors to women in 1914. According to the *Times*, the six attendees of the inaugural women-only class found the science of spark plugs and "the manner of driving cars" particularly interesting.[50] In 1919, Santa Monica High School offered a series of popular classes for women in mastering the automobile, while the Los Angeles Chamber of Commerce organized lectures for women in 1921 on the "fine points of their cars and how to drive them safely and tend them."[51][52] The lessons were used and prepared by the National Safety Council.

In 1917, Lillian Spannagel, Southern California representative for the United States Department of Labor, actively encouraged more local women to train as automobile mechanics to fill in for their male counterparts who were serving in World War I.[53] Bristol Taxi Company was among the first to recruit female drivers during the war. "If I can secure more drivers … I shall certainly employ them as vacancies occur, for I believe it is the duty of this and every other company to release men for war work where it is possible to satisfactorily replace them with women workers," proprietor H.J. Bristol told the *Times*.[54]

"We find that women are much more conscien-

▲ ◄ A female service station attendant adds water to a customer's car.
▲ Women work together to detail a 1929 automobile.

tious in their work than the men were," Harry H. Knoll, route manager for a local dairy which hired women to work as truck drivers in 1918, told the *Los Angeles Evening Express*.[55] Other local female motorists supported the war effort by volunteering to transport US Army or Navy officers on official business or loan them their automobiles.[56]

By 1920, there were an estimated 300,000 women driving automobiles in the United States. The *Los Angeles Times* suggested 20 percent of the drivers in Los Angeles were women.[57] Many of the city's female motorists would join forces to overturn a new city parking ordinance intended to reduce traffic congestion by limiting street parking downtown in an area within Main, Spring, Broadway, and Hill Streets, from 1st to 9th Streets.

The ordinance, adopted by the city council on April 10, 1920, banned private vehicles from street parking between 11:00 a.m. and 6:15 p.m. "The 30,000 autos, which daily park in the forbidden area represent 82,500 people, who will be forced to do one of three things: Stay at home, leave their cars outside the no-parking area (thereby creating as much congestion on its edges as now exists downtown) and walk in or take the street cars, or use the streetcars all the way from home," the *Times* concluded.[58]

It drew immediate outrage from women who were accustomed to driving downtown to do their shopping and banking or to attend a matinee movie, as well as a coalition of local merchants who braced for a dramatic decline in sales.

Although no women or members of women's organizations spoke out at public hearings, they demonstrated their displeasure in other ways, boycotting stores and staging protests. Actress Clara Kimball Young, angry that women could not find parking spaces, organized a petition of merchants and a parade of protest for which she served as grand marshal.

Young entered eighteen automobiles and nine

▶ A woman adds Pennzoil to car as part of a 1926 publicity campaign.

trucks used at Garson Studios in a procession of hundreds of vehicles that stretched several miles. The *Los Angeles Evening Express* called the protest, "one of the most urgent demands ever made by the business interests of the city for immediate action on the part of the city council to relieve a condition threatening to the convenience of the automobilists and disastrous to business."[59][60] Facing growing opposition, the city council buckled under the

◀ Actress Betty Boyd poses with a Chevrolet in 1926. Los Angeles
dealers regularly used movie stars to help market cars.

▶ A 1927 Ford advertisement promises to save women time and money.

pressure and voted to amend the ordinance to allow passenger car parking for forty-five minutes between 10:00
a.m. and 4:00 p.m.

In the coming years, the automobile would help
facilitate and accelerate the decentralization of commercial activities from the historic downtown center to outly-
ing areas including Wilshire Boulevard, Hollywood, and
Pasadena, where parking was easier and more space was
available to build stores and other attractions.

"There was a time when many people laughed at
women drivers, but that day is gone," Cadillac distributor
Don Lee proclaimed in 1920. "There are as many good
women drivers in proportion to the total number as there
are men, and no matter where you tour, you will always
find women at the wheel of cars."[61] He claimed there were
at least three thousand women driving Cadillacs in California.

Innovations driven by the demands of women were
becoming commonplace with most new cars. "Women
have revolutionized the design of steering gears in automobiles," Don P. Smith, Los Angeles-based Moon Six
distributor, told the Los Angeles Evening Express in 1926.
"With so many of the fair sex driving, the demand for easy
steering apparatus has grown universal and engineers have
gone to great lengths in eliminating arm strain.

"… The Moon car is an example of what was accomplished in advanced steering design. A frail girl can
turn the balloon-tired wheels with one hand while the
car stands still on the street. She can park and circle the
car with ease."[62]

When the Model A Ford was unveiled in 1929, it
was promoted for the ease with which it could be handled. "The average woman likes an automobile that will
give her speed when she wants it, that will show agility
in traffic and that will be reliable," local Ford dealer, Ray
F. Chelsey, explained. "The Ford coupe is a type that has

Her habit of measuring time in terms
of dollars gives the woman in business
keen insight into the true value of a
Ford closed car for her personal use.

This car enables her to conserve minutes, to expedite her affairs, to widen
the scope of her activities. Its low

first cost, long life and inexpensive
operation and upkeep convince her
that it is a sound investment value.

And it is such a pleasant car to drive
that it transforms the business call
which might be an interruption into
an enjoyable episode of her busy day.

TUDOR SEDAN, $590   FORDOR SEDAN, $685   COUPE, $525   (All prices f. o. b. Detroit)

Ford
CLOSED CARS

appealed strongly to women drivers. Like the other Model
A bodies it is offered in various colors. It has simple but
distinguished lines and the richness of its appearance is ac-
centuated by the bright, black, artificial leather covering
the rear quarter."[63]

"It was a few years ago that the number of women
drivers were almost negligible and little or no consideration paid them in connection with the design and construction of automobiles," according to the Los Angeles
Evening Express. "But those times have changed in recent
years, with the number of women drivers increasing by
tens of thousands each year."[64]

SYBIL C. GEARY

▲ An Automobile Club of Southern California sign on Topanga Canyon Boulevard, Topanga, California, circa 1915.

Sybil C. Geary transformed the Automobile Club of Southern California into the largest motor club in the world. She championed legislation to support automobile owners and was the driving force behind a campaign to improve signposting. She also lobbied for dedicated courts to deal with automobile offenses and is credited with inventing the term "jaywalker."

Born in Edina, Minnesota, in 1881, Geary first found work with the Automobile Club of Southern California as a stenographer in 1909. She quickly became editor of *Touring Topics*, the club's monthly journal and in May 1910 was elevated to acting secretary and then secretary (aka executive director) of the organization. "She has only women assistants, and these are able to do the work far better than the same number of men could, she says," read the *Los Angeles Times*.[1]

"Very few people realize what good work the Automobile Club of Southern California is doing and has done for Southern California," Geary wrote in the *Los Angeles Herald* in October 1910.[2] She estimated the club had 2,300 members. Under her stewardship, it would surpass the Automobile Club of Buffalo as the largest motor club in the nation in May 1913.[3][4][5]

"The club was organized in 1900 and jogged along like similar organizations, content to let well-enough alone," *Motor Age* reported in April 1914. "No effort was made to boost membership until 1909 when Miss S.C. Geary was installed as assistant secretary and instructed by the directors to make it a real club. The present policy was outlined in the rough, and Miss Geary followed instructions with such vigor that the Automobile Club rapidly developed into a do-something organization."[6]

The club, which began as a social organization to hold automobile races and lobby for legislation on behalf of motorists, now offered discounts on automobile insurance, free legal advice, and would even act as a mediator in disputes between dealers and customers.

Geary spoke for the organization on public issues and regularly orchestrated boycotts or recall campaigns when local government officials lowered speed limits in order to generate new speeding ticket revenue. She campaigned for better street lighting, uniform speed laws, and made it a personal mission to repeal legislation that failed to grasp how essential motoring would become.[7]

"As is the case when ignorance and power go hand in hand, a lot of useless laws were made, many ridiculous," she argued. "The cry for automobile legislation reached such a point of intensity—through enemies whose business it menaced and through the fanatics who always look upon progress with fear—that the United States enacted so many laws in her various legislatures as to almost kill the industry."[8] Among the high-profile targets of Geary's focus was Secretary of the Interior Walker L. Fisher whom she lobbied to allow automobiles to pass through the scenic valley roads of Yosemite National Park.[9]

Since its inception, the Auto Club had made signing the roads of Southern California a high priority, but Geary took it to a whole new level. In November 1912, she announced the club was launching a new signpost program for the most desolate, as well as the most traveled, routes of the desert areas extending as far away as Albuquerque, New Mexico.[10] [11]

She teamed up with the club's engineers to install road signage throughout the San Joaquin Valley and added more than a hundred new signs between Los Angeles and San Diego. By March 1913, the auto club had placed 4,510 signs covering 3,495 miles and soon announced plans to add even more along the Pacific Coast from Los Angeles to San Francisco.[12]

"More than $80,000 has been expended in this work, but it's worth in rendering the roads safer for all classes of travelers is impossible to estimate," the *Los Angeles Express* noted. "What the block signals mean to the

▲ A 1926 advertisement celebrates the work done by the Automobile Club of Southern California to post road signs.

engineer, the automobile signs mean to the auto driver."[13]

Geary, described by the *Times* as "an expert driver," was often tasked with navigating her Franklin touring car along a new route or racetrack before it could be declared safe. She accompanied Ralph Hamlin on a trip to the summit of Mount Wilson in 1912, and the following year, was called upon to inspect part of the route of a celebrated road race that began in Corona and featured some of the "world's greatest motor pilots."[14]

"The plucky young woman was surprised when she found that it was possible to keep the car with the throttle wide open for the entire circuit of the fast three miles of road," the *Times* wrote.[15]

Geary made national headlines when it was revealed she was working with Charles Sebastian, Los Angeles chief of police, to regulate the speed of automobiles in the city.

"Speed Cop is a Woman" was the headline repeated above a widely syndicated 1912 newspaper story. "Miss Geary is also a deputy sheriff. She has had considerable experience in curbing violators of the law," the report noted.[16]

"There are 21,000 automobiles in this city, and the number is increasing rapidly," Geary told the *Times* the following year. "The police force is not adequate to properly handle the situation, and every member of the Automobile Club of Southern California will be asked to co-operate with Chief Sebastian's men and the county officers to bring an end to the driving of machines with utter disrespect for human life, which has become such a scandal in this city recently."[17]

Geary also gained attention when she announced

a national effort to urge pedestrians to use caution when crossing busy streets. "'Jaywalker' is the new name for people who pay no attention to where they are going while crossing the congested traffic districts," the *Express* reported. "The term originated with Miss S.C. Geary, secretary of the Automobile Club of Southern California."[18]

In September 1912 when Geary was forced to take time off from work to recover from appendicitis, the *Times* declared, "The work already mapped out by the secretary would keep about ten men busy. But then, nevermind, with the right determination it is possible to accomplish anything."[19]

Geary worked with local authorities in 1913 to establish the first auto court in the city. The dramatic rise in vehicles had become a burden on the legal system.

"The plan is to obtain a special judge to try all automobile cases in the courts and to have all such cases segregated for separate trial," she explained. "Many complaints have been made to the club by members and non-members regarding the objectionable conditions under which motorists have been forced to appear in court in company with all the disreputable law-breakers in the community."[20]

Geary also worked with leaders of the automobile club to address the need for new statewide automobile regulations. She established a legislative committee and began an intensive study of existing laws in states with the most automobiles. After nearly two years, she unveiled a carefully drafted measure to present to the Los Angeles delegation of state lawmakers.

"The new vehicle act … has been pronounced by experts as the most comprehensive and just measure for the regulation of all traffic using the public roads, that has ever been prepared in any state or country in the world," *Touring Topics* proclaimed in February 1913.[21]

Geary spent several weeks in Sacramento helping to push the vehicle act through the legislature. In March 1913, it was reported she had ignored her physician's demands to rest and was "completely exhausted by months of work."[22][23]

Just weeks later, it was revealed she was on an indefinite leave of absence. "Miss Geary's illness was largely due to the strain of the additional work of preparing the proposed new law governing automobile traffic and registrations," informed the *Times*.[24]

The Vehicle Act of 1913, which passed the California State Assembly and the Senate on May 9, 1913, was a comprehensive act of forty-three sections that repealed the old act of 1905.[25] The bill had been altered from the original club-backed version to now require annual registration of vehicles with the state treasurer with fees based on horsepower, a feature that was highly unpopular with motorists.

Geary was in the difficult position of publicly opposing legislation she had worked tirelessly to promote. Making matters worse, she had broken her ankle and remained confined to her home. Nearly a year later, in the last days of 1914, the state legislature approved a new bill that reconciled some of the more controversial issues that had caused public outcry.

Sybil Geary was not present when the 1915 Vehicle Act was passed. She had resigned her position with the Automobile Club of Southern California in March 1914. In an ironic turn of fate, her mother, Catherine, was killed in 1919 after being struck by an automobile at the intersection of Jefferson Boulevard and Vermont Street. Geary moved to San Francisco and then San Diego, where she died in 1935 at the age of 54. Her achievements, largely unknown and unrecognized until recently, contribute to our understanding of the history of the automobile in Los Angeles.

Some content in this essay originally appeared in "Sybil Geary, Women, and the Automobile in Los Angeles, 1900–1920," Southern California Quarterly, v.103 n.2, Summer 2021.

▶ The Automobile Club of Southern California took responsibility for posting road signs before the local government took over.

HOLLYWOOD ➤
SANTA MONICA BAY DIST. ➤
◄ GLENDALE 4
◄ U. S. HIGHWAY #99
AUTOMOBILE CLUB ⬤ SOUTHERN CALIF.

WARNING
KEEP TO RIGHT
OF
CENTER LINE
AUTO CLUB ⬤ OF SO. CAL.

SCHOOL
ZONE
AUTOMOBILE CLUB ⬤ SOUTHERN CALIF.

CALIFORNIA
US
101

CAUTION
SPEED LIMIT
15
MILES
ON CURVES
AUTO CLUB ⬤ OF SO. CAL.

WILSONA VALLEY 2 ➤
EL MIRAGE VALLEY 15 ➤
ADELANTO 26 ➤
VICTORVILLE 35 ➤
AUTOMOBILE CLUB ⬤ SOUTHERN CALIF.

CALIFORNIA
US
99

CALIFORNIA
STATE LINE
AUTO CLUB ⬤ SO. CAL.

LOS ANGELES
COUNTY LINE
AUTOMOBILE CLUB ⬤ SOUTHERN CALIF.

CALIFORNIA
US
6.6

STOP
AUTO CLUB ⬤ OF SO. CAL.

A crowd of men gather in 1912 outside the Automobile Club of Southern California headquarters at 8th and Olive Streets where Sybil C. Geary worked. According to the *Los Angeles Times*, Geary and her female assistants performed tasks "far better than the same number of men could."

8

LOS ANGELES AUTOMOBILE SHOWS

"For one week the automobile is to reign as king in Los Angeles and chug wagons from the great roaring touring cars to natty little runabouts and silent electric machines will puff proudly about."

Los Angeles Herald, January 21, 1907[1]

Los Angeles car dealers recognized there was no more tantalizing place to sell and celebrate cars than an auto show. What would become an annual tradition in the city actually began as an act of defiance against the nation's leading automobile manufacturers association. The local auto show was a first of its kind forum to display new models and accessories to Southern California motorists and one of the most anticipated dates on the city's social calendar. It was also an opportunity for Los Angeles to compete directly with more established cities. As the city's ambition and population grew, so too did the scale and complexity of its auto shows. However, the spectacle would be devastated by a disaster in 1929 that sent shockwaves through the nation's automobile industry.

The world's first auto show was held in Paris in 1898 and was sponsored by the Automobile Club of France. Interest soon spread to America and in 1900, small shows took place in five US cities.[2] Organized by local automobile clubs, bicycle clubs, or sporting clubs, their popularity and obvious lack of regulation proved problematic for carmakers that struggled to produce enough display models to keep pace with exhibitor demands.[3]

New York City's Madison Square Garden hosted the national auto show on November 3, 1900. Sponsored by the Automobile Club of America, it showcased 160 different vehicles from thirty-four carmakers, mostly steam and electric powered, as

◄ The 1919 Los Angeles Auto Show featured more than sixty makes of cars and was decorated with three thousand lanterns.

well as newer machines with internal combustible engines. After the show, twenty-three manufacturers concerned by the "coercive methods" being used to "induce" them to exhibit at other auto shows came together to form the National Association of Automobile Manufacturers.

"The objects as stated now are to regulate shows so that manufacturers will not be muleted by showmen pure and simple; to prevent price cutting; to prevent injurious legislation, and to cooperate with clubs to obtain good roads," read the *Brooklyn Daily Eagle*.[4]

The association quickly asserted itself, insisting members only exhibit at shows or enter endurance or speed contests it sanctioned.[5] Initially only two shows, one in New York City and one in Chicago, were approved. *The Automobile Review* said the action prevented manufacturers and auto clubs from being, "milked for the personal gain of the promiscuous show promoter."[6] But by 1906, cities including Boston, Cleveland, Detroit, and Washington, DC, all defied the National Association to plan unsanctioned shows, and Los Angeles would soon follow with an event organized by the Motor Car Dealers' Association of Los Angeles.

The premiere Los Angeles Auto Show was held in January 1907 at Morley's Grand Avenue skating rink, giving organizers just enough of a window to narrowly claim bragging rights to being the first auto show in the West. A similar event would be staged in San Francisco the following month. The Los Angeles show was trumpeted as "the social event of the season" with "one million dollars worth of autos."[7] Morley's rink offered 17,000 square feet of display space, which sold out more than a month in advance.[8] To select who got the prime spots, the twenty-two participating dealers drew numbers, although at least five of them were forced to relinquish their space when their factories could not deliver cars in time.[9]

Los Angeles Mayor Arthur C. Harper opened the show on January 21 by pressing a switch, illuminating ten thousand bulbs of "dazzling brilliancy" suspended overhead on long festoons. "We are not surprised when this city does large things, for it is destined in time to be the greatest place west of Chicago," he told the enthusiastic crowd.[10]

The four thousand visitors who paid the one dollar entrance fee (later reduced to fifty cents) marveled at the nearly a hundred automobiles on display accompanied by two hundred eager salesmen. Individual booths were decorated in colors chosen by dealers and embellished with floral displays that local newspapers described as "far too costly for cold country exhibitors to attain."[11]

The sounds of the Ladies Mandolin Orchestra and the Royal Hawaiian Sextet filled the venue as spectators competed for a glimpse of Barney Oldfield and his famous Peerless Green Dragon; stood in awe of the long red body of the Stoddard-Dayton roadster; and crowded around the Cadillac Model H coupe in Don Lee's display.[12]

"Necessarily an automobile must be pampered and petted like a thoroughbred equine, and as a result everything in connection with the buzz wagon life is being thoroughly inspected at the show," the *Herald* informed.[13]

The *Los Angeles Times* reported Henry Ford, who attended Friday night, was "delighted with the beauty of the show" and proclaimed it to be "one of the most attractive he has ever seen in any part of the country."[14] By popular demand, it was extended an extra day. "Every dealer and every other exhibitor had something to show that was a little bit out of the usual," read the *San Francisco Chronicle*.[15]

Local automobile enthusiasts would have to wait another two years for the next show, which was held in the basement of the Hamburger department store on Broadway. "By comparison of the show held last year in San Francisco, with the coming automobile display to be held Jan. 23 to 30, Los Angeles motorists will realize that the Angel City is far superior in an automobile way to her northern sister," the *Los Angeles Evening Express* hailed.[16]

The festivities began with a parade kicking off at the intersection of Pico and Main Streets and celebrating advances in transportation with horseback riders, old stagecoaches, early automobiles, and modern 1909 models. More than 30,000 advance tickets were sold and Hamburger's interior was transformed into a "fairyland of polished cars" illuminated by 12,000 incandescent frosted globes and two hundred auto searchlights with an electric fountain as the centerpiece.[17] "The big pillars, which support the largest department store west of Chicago, have been made to lend themselves to the general decorative scheme," reported the *Times*. "Greenery, studded with lights has been festooned around the columns."[18][19]

Of the pristine automobiles on display, ninety were gasoline-powered, seven electric, and two with steam engines.[20] The popular exhibits included Don Lee's Cadillac Model 30, which held the record for local sales; a touring car displayed by the Auto Vehicle Company with accommodation for eating and sleeping; and the new six-cylinder Franklin.

It was a glorious success until tempers flared during preparations for what was called Society Night. For one evening, organizers allowed dealers extra freedom to embellish their booths with ribbons, flowers, and other elements as long as they complemented the show's green-and-white color scheme. But when Don Lee was told his decorations were excessive and needed to come down, he angrily threatened to quit the Dealers' Association.

Harry O. Harrison, secretary of the association, demanded staff at the Rambler display remove their newly installed pink drapery. An argument erupted, descending into a fist fight when Harrison aimed a blow to the head of L.B. Harvey, a guest at the company's booth. Rambler dealer William K. Cowan stepped between the two men, breaking the force of the blow and taking a mild hit to the mouth. It took a half-dozen dealers to restrain Harrison, who was escorted away only to return moments later to be held back once more.

"The affair created a tremendous sensation on the floor of the show, and dealers on all sides were quick to condemn Harrison for allowing his temper to run away with him, especially as he is the secretary of the association under whose auspices the show is being given," the *Herald* detailed.[21] There were immediate calls for Harrison to resign.

The following year, Los Angeles would stage two back-to-back competing auto shows in February and then again in December, as a result of a 1909 ruling by United States Circuit Judge Charles M. Hough. Hough ruled that all American manufacturers and importers of motor vehicles should pay a royalty to George B. Selden, inventor of a one-cylinder internal combustion engine attached to a four-wheeled vehicle.

Selden, a Rochester, New York, attorney and frustrated engineer, first filed a patent for his creation in 1879. In subsequent years, he filed a series of amendments until a US patent was granted in 1895. Although he had not yet produced a working model of an automobile, he sold his patent rights in 1899 to William C. Whitney, owner of the Electric Vehicle Company. Together, the two men sought to capitalize on the so-called "Selden patent" and collect royalties from dozens of auto companies.

Supporters of the Seldon patent, who agreed to pay a royalty on cars they sold, came together to form the Association of Licensed Automobile Manufacturers. Other carmakers formed the American Motor Car Manufacturers Association to fight the patent.

In Los Angeles, dealers representing licensed brands formed a new organization, the Licensed Motor Car Dealers of Los Angeles. When the group's board of directors discovered that independent dealers, led by event organizer Walter Hempel, were planning a February auto show in 1910, they responded with a rival event of their own.

Hempel's event on February 7 at the Grand Avenue skating rink featured 103 cars, fifty-three exhibitors, and a two hundred-automobile parade along Grand Avenue.[22] It promised Angelenos a close-up look at the first torpedo-body cars on the West Coast, including a Columbus roadster. More than two hundred vehicles were sold at the show. "The machines at $1000 and less have had a wonderful run," observed the *Los Angeles Times*. "The public at the auto show lingered long around the booths where the low-priced product was on display."[23]

The Licensed Car Dealers show, held a week later in Fiesta Park at Pico Street and Grand Avenue, was staged

▲ Los Angeles Auto Show, 1910.

beneath what was reported to be "the largest canvas ever thrown over a place of amusement in the United States or the World."[24] The 90,000 square foot area it covered was embellished with four truck loads of redwood bark and branches from the Santa Cruz Mountains, thousands of flowers, and a giant 1,008 foot-long California-themed backdrop painted by the Thompson Scenic Company.[25] The opening day of the event drew a crowd of more than five thousand and by week's end, it was estimated at least 50,000 people had seen the show.[26]

Some ten months later in December, the Motor Car Dealers' Association held a show at the Shrine Auditorium, showcasing two hundred automobiles, including the Kissel racer that won the Phoenix race; the Fiat racer that recorded the fastest laps in the Santa Monica road race; and Barney Oldfield's Blitzen Benz, billed as the fastest motorcar in the world.[27] Not to be left behind, the

rival Licensed Car Dealers group hosted its second auto show, also with two hundred cars, just a week later over the Christmas holidays and featured a 52-foot-tall Christmas tree.[28]

Ford and other carmakers in 1910 had appealed the decision upholding the Selden patent and the next year, an appeals court in New York City reversed the decision, concluding it only applied to a specific type of engine and not all internal combustion engines in general. Nevertheless, conflicting views over auto shows—how they were

organized, who bore the financial burden, what types of vehicles were displayed, and what these events were intended to accomplish—meant Los Angeles would not have another auto show until 1914. Proposals to stage an electric car show at the Bullock's department store or possibly a two-day open house on Auto Row were considered but failed to materialize.[29]

To much fanfare, the Los Angeles Auto Show returned in January 1914 with the Grand Avenue pavilion reinvented as a Japanese tea garden, replete with green

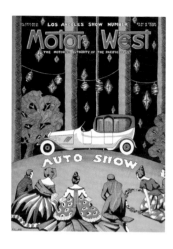

◀◀ Motor West celebrates the 1916 Los Angeles Auto Show.
◀ Advertisement for the 1917 Los Angeles Auto Show.

carpet, pagodas, dwarf trees, and other plants.[30] More than twice the crowd anticipated by manager Walter Hempel bought tickets and the *Times* noted brisk sales meant "there was not a booth where one to three cars" were not "rolled out to a prospective buyer instead of being sent back to the salesroom."[31] A second show later in October exhibited both cars and trucks and transformed

the Shrine Auditorium into a garden oasis filled with a hundred palm trees.[32][33]

The Shrine also hosted the first of two shows in 1915. A September event produced by Walter Hempel attracted a strong audience but was overshadowed just weeks later by the Broadway Automobile and Flower Show. The event, endorsed by the Motor Car Dealers' Association, made use of all four floors of the old Boston Department Store on Broadway, opposite Los Angeles City Hall. The first two levels displayed cars and accessories, the third floor featured floral exhibits, and the fourth was reserved for dancing and entertainment. Among the highlights were the new 1916 Hupmobile and Chalmers models that arrived days earlier from Detroit.[35] Barney Oldfield's wife Bessie was so impressed by the new Maxwell Model 25, she wrote a check for a convertible model within two minutes of the show opening.[36]

By 1916, Los Angeles had the largest number of automobiles per capita of any metropolitan city in the world, and the Motor Car Dealers' Association wanted a show that reflected the city's growing importance to the automobile industry.[37] Just five weeks before the event, organizers finally secured a venue, settling on a half-finished three-story structure being built by the Earl Automobile Works at Pico and Los Angeles Street. The event was called the "Los Angeles Auto and Truck Show" in recognition of the rising number of truck retailers, and promoted as the "Million Dollar Show" despite the value of the 244 vehicles (204 cars and 40 trucks) easily exceeding the moniker.

While early Los Angeles auto shows had been dominated by basic touring cars and roadsters, the 1916 exhibit featured more luxury cars that rode closer to the ground, including coupes, limousines, landaulets, and town cars. The new Owen magnetic car, which ran without gears, was highlighted, as was a giant Mack tractor and car decorated by celebrated British designer, Lady Lucy Duff-Gordon.[38] There was also a proliferation of Los Angeles-crafted add-on styling features, such as the Victoria Top and disc coverings for wheels and other distinctive custom items.[39] The inclusion of trucks reflected the reality that "commercial cars" had evolved into "trucks" just as "pleasure cars" were now described as "passenger cars," no longer a luxury but a necessity of modern life.

"As an education in the automobile industry, the show is really a wonder," critic Warde Fowler wrote in the *Los Angeles Times*. "Technical experts explain every working part of the car … Cut-away chassis are an education in themselves. Many of the exhibits have demonstrating engines which give a wonderful idea of the heart of the car."[40] Fowler further added, "The painting of bodies, once entirely black, has given way to colors that were once unknown, tints unheard of before, and daring schemes of decoration that, yesterday, would have been

turned down as too bizarre."[41]

The *Los Angeles Evening Express* described the show as, "the most comprehensive display of motor vehicles ever held in the West."[42] While Los Angeles was now an established force in the automobile industry, the United States entry into World War I in 1917 meant future auto shows were put on hold indefinitely.

Following the war, the Motor Car Dealers' Association organized the first auto show anywhere in the nation in Los Angeles, but planning efforts were hindered by the death of James S. Conwell who had helped coordinate many previous events. Perry Greer, a Chalmers and Hupmobile dealer, reluctantly assumed Conwell's role but expressed reservations the public might not be ready to spend money after cutting back on unnecessary expenses during the war.

Greer initially had difficulty finding a venue but eventually secured Praeger Park, a large open space located at Washington Street and Grand Avenue. He wrangled two large tents from the National Orange Show of San Bernardino and a third from the Downie Brothers Company in Los Angeles before convincing his colleagues to

▶ Perry H. Greer (center), chairman of the organizing committee for the 1919 Los Angeles Auto Show.

▲ The new Essex model was displayed for the first time at the 1919 Los Angeles Auto Show.

push the start date back to January 11, 1919.[43,44]

"Since the close of the war the motor car business in Southern California has never known such a boom," Earle C. Anthony, who helped plan the show, explained. "For several years the people have been making their old cars do. They are ready for the new models, and this buying spirit will be a big factor in making the coming motor car exhibit the biggest thing of the kind Los Angeles has ever known."[45]

Greer teased journalists by keeping the theme of the show secret, telling them only that a small army of scenic artists were planning elaborate decorations. But behind the scenes, he was struggling to find the embellishments needed to fulfill the committee's desire for an entirely "oriental" show. He eventually turned to F. Suie

▲ Harley J. Earl won rave reviews when he added a custom body to a Chandler town car and painted it brilliant blue for the 1919 Los Angeles Auto Show.

One, a "well-known Chinese importer and dealer in Chinese goods" to acquire the more than three thousand Chinese lanterns that lit up the venue.[46]

"Somebody conceived the brilliant idea of trying oriental decorations for a change, and those who crowd into the big tents will see the light streaming through creamy canvas on gaily-colored Chinese lanterns, tapestries and artwork valued at more than $150,000," the *Los Angeles Times* reported.[47]

The show highlighted the many innovations in California automobile customization, including the special bodies and permanent tops designed and built by George Bentel, an Oakland and Studebaker dealer, which drew large crowds, as did the work of Harley J. Earl, who adapted his father's coachbuilding techniques to create unique automobiles. A custom body he attached to a four-passenger Marmon Sport sold to a New York banker for seven thousand dollars. The *Los Angeles Times* described a custom body he added to a Chandler town car, painted brilliant blue, as "the classiest thing of its kind ever shown on the Coast or anyplace else."[48]

Greer noted in his post-event report that the newspapers had been particularly supportive, as a lack of automobile-related advertising revenue meant they "were doubly anxious to boost the business back to pre-war conditions."[49]

In the 1920s, carmakers produced more reliable, powerful, and comfortable automobiles. The Los Angeles Auto Show also solidified its position as one of the most significant events of its kind in the country. While the Motor Car Dealers' Association originally began staging auto shows as a way for dues paying members to exhibit and sell cars, the show itself had become more complex and its purpose was changing.

At the group's ninth-annual automobile show in December 1920, manufacturers recognized that most of the thousands of spectators who crammed into the Arnold building at the corner of 7th and Figueroa were not coming simply to purchase a car, but also to see the new models and learn what new features and innovations were available. General Motors had led the way by updating its automobiles annually to stimulate demand, and now the show was deliberately timed to coincide with the imminent release of new vehicles, ahead of national shows in New York and Chicago.[50 51]

For the latest show, Los Angeles organizers promised "more special built and 'dolled-up'" cars than any previous event.[52] "The national shows are for the purpose of selling strictly stock cars to the distributor, while the Los Angeles show has as its purpose the display of the very best in motor cars to a very discriminating buying public, the object being fully as much artistic as commercial," read the *Santa Ana Register*.[53]

Taking a detour from the traditional auto show in 1921, local dealers experimented with what was billed as "Call of the Open Road" week. In April, showrooms from Main Street to Figueroa Street were decked out with displays celebrating the theme of "the infinite variety of scenery and touring advantages enjoyed by the Californian."[54] The concept was so popular that when it was repeated the following year, brisk sales comparable to the regular auto show were reported.

"This sales volume was almost exclusively for standard models and was an additional indication that business has staged a complete recovery from its temporary slump of last year and that buyers are seeking more than ever for dollar-for-dollar value in their purchase," stated the *Los Angeles Evening Express*.[55]

In November 1922, more than 100,000 people attended the Dealers' Association's tenth Auto Show held beneath four giant tents in Praeger Park. It returned to the same venue in 1923 for what Manager Burt Roberts boasted would be the "first time in the history of the motor car industry that the premier announcement of the latest automotive creations will be made west of New York."[56]

The following year, Exposition Park was the site for the largest and most expensive auto show the Dealers' Association had ever attempted. Roberts took full advantage of the extra space for a flower-filled, Chinese-themed affair that showed off nearly four hundred immaculate new vehicles to an eager public.

As interest accelerated over the years, dealers began to look at a more intimate, luxurious way of complementing the auto show. Manager Burt Roberts floated the idea of a specialized event highlighting top of the line enclosed cars (as opposed to the open-top models) as a "high-class and dignified" way of selling expensive cars to wealthy Angelenos.

The First Annual Enclosed Car Salon took place in March 1924 at the newly opened Biltmore Hotel at 5th and Olive Streets. It was trumpeted as the first event on the Pacific Coast to offer a "tribute to the meteoric rise in popularity of the enclosed car," which now rivaled open cars.[57] Held in the hotel's lavish ballroom, the event showcased thirty-five different automobile brands exhibited by twenty-nine distributors. In a memo entitled "Let

Los Angeles car dealer Harold L. Arnold's Hudson
display at the 1919 Los Angeles Auto Show

◄ The Auto Show held in Exposition Park in 1924 was the most expensive ever staged.

Courtesy Be Our Watchword," Roberts told dealers only three representatives were allowed for each dealership and they should wear business attire during the day and tuxedos for evening wear.

The Howard Automobile Company proudly displayed a new Buick Brougham, custom-painted in sagebrush green for California clients. Earle C. Anthony featured a chauffeur-driven Packard sedan, and Paul G. Hoffman included Studebaker's highest-priced Big Six. More than 17,000 people attended the event, which produced such good sales; it was repeated the following October and again in 1926 with a show focused largely on female motorists.

"In no other single thing are as many interested as in automobiles," the *Los Angeles Evening Express* told readers in a passionate editorial explaining why they should attend the thirteenth Los Angeles Automobile Show. It was set to take place beneath four massive tents in Washington Park at Washington and Hills Streets in February 1926.[58][59] "The motor car has become a dominant factor in the social, recreational and industrial life of America. It has become a member of far the larger number of American families. The show gives the opportunity to become better-acquainted with the new member."[59]

By February 1927, the excitement surrounding an exclusive custom-built body salon at the Biltmore Hotel

was enough for the *Los Angeles Examiner* to exclaim the city was now "the third motor metropolis of the United States!"

"Up to this time, the coach and body builders of America have felt that New York and Chicago were the only cities of sufficient importance to warrant an exclusive custom-built salon," the newspaper argued. "It shows that Los Angeles has become universally known not only as an important market as regards quantity, but as a quality market as well," George R. Bury, vice president of Earle C. Anthony Inc., maintained. "Los Angeles not only has more cars per capita than any other city in the United States, but an observer of cars on our boulevards cannot fail to be impressed by the high-quality and fine type of cars our people drive."[60]

The Los Angeles Auto Show would return to Washington Park in 1927, 1928, and again in 1929. In anticipation of the March 1929 event, Manager Burt Roberts sent out a series of bulletins to exhibitors, including an order from the Los Angeles Fire Department: "ALL GASOLINE MUST BE REMOVED FROM MOTOR VEHICLES BEFORE THEY ARE ALLOWED TO ENTER THE TENTS" and "INSPECTORS WILL BE ON HAND TO SEE THAT THE ABOVE IS COMPLIED WITH." Another stated that matches, cigarettes, and cigars should not be thrown anywhere in the facility.[61]

Opening day on Saturday, March 2, drew an estimated 5,135 visitors. The next day, 10,460 enjoyed the show, and the following day, 7,150 spectators attended. On Day 4 in the afternoon around 4:10 pm, as nearly 2,500 visitors were perusing automobiles, a small fire broke out in the northeast corner of Tent No. 2, near the show offices and restrooms. "When the fire was first discovered it was a small, red spurt, leaping up the hangings to the top of the tent," *The New York Times* reported. "The flames soon burned a hole in the canvas and the wind whipped the blaze to a fury. Then it jumped from tent top to tent top with the speed of an express train."[62]

Fortunately, the fire erupted in the afternoon and

▲ Tents erected in anticipation of the Los Angeles Auto Show, 1929;
Los Angeles Auto Show souvenir program, 1929.

not in the evening when attendance would likely have doubled. Exhibitors hurriedly pulled up the sides of the tents to allow panicked spectators to flee. In what was described as a miracle, no one was seriously injured in the blaze, although an electrician suffered serious burns cutting the light and power wires that ran through the venue, and two firefighters were also injured.[63]

The raging inferno made headlines across the nation. The next morning, throngs of curious motorists flocked to view the destruction first-hand. The devastation caused losses of well over a million dollars and left behind an urban wasteland of red-hot embers, charred wood, twisted steel, and smoking rubber tires. As many as 320 cars were lost in what was described as "the worst single automotive disaster in history."[64]

Among the cars lost was a 1907 Model 30 Packard roadster which had been driven more than 510,000 miles. It had traveled "more than twice the distance to the moon without a mishap" the *Times* pointed out, "only to be destroyed by the fire that razed the Los Angeles Auto Show."[65] The fire also decimated an airplane exhibition and motor boats.

Before the ashes had cooled, members of the Motor Car Dealers' Association met at the Los Angeles Athletic Club and made plans to reopen the auto show at the Shrine Auditorium. It took less than eighteen hours before insurance companies began issuing checks to automobile distributors.[66] The Shrine donated its facility and worked with the show's planning committee and twenty-five volunteers from the Automobile Club of Southern California to get the event up and running again.

Remarkably, the Los Angeles Automobile Show resumed just twenty-seven hours after the fire. The Shrine was hastily decorated with tin foil flowers and five thousand yards of fireproof cloth. Capt. Fred W. Walker, theater inspector at the fire department, declared the exhibition had been made as fireproof as was humanly possible.[67] The number of cars on display was reduced to 173, and most of the original exhibits were lost, but enthusiasm was at an all time high as congratulatory messages flooded in from major manufacturers and automobile organizations.[68]

"There may be bigger and better shows in the future, but to a lot of the participants here there will never be a show quite equal in all respects to the Shrine Automobile Show now in progress, conceived and consummated in twenty-four hours out of the wreck and ruin of the blackest disaster Los Angeles motor car dealers ever experienced," Jack Howe, the *Examiner's* automobile editor, reflected.[69]

Spectators gather to witness the wreckage of the 1929 Los Angeles Auto Show fire. According to the *New York Times* the flames spread with "the speed of an express train."

Don Lee took the chassis of a Cadillac destroyed in the fire, rehabilitated it, and put it back on display. "It does not show effects of having been through fire," the *Times* marveled.[70] The Ford exhibit included a continuous motion-picture projector showing fifteen minutes of amateur footage of the fire's devastation that proved compelling with firefighters, police officers, and others who were on the scene.[71]

Speculation swirled as to what caused the blaze and early reports laid the blame on an errant cigarette thrown by a woman near the Monocoupe Aircraft display. However, an investigation by the fire department concluded a short circuit in wiring carrying electric current to a light above an airplane exhibit was the source.

The city's fire department refused any blame for being unable to quell the blaze as they had not issued a permit for the show, citing concerns about the event being held underneath a tent. Instead, the permit had been issued by the Los Angeles City Council. Fire Commissioner E.R. Werdin urged city officials to provide a fireproof building for events such as the auto show. But it would be several decades before the Los Angeles Auto Show found a home at the Los Angeles Convention Center.[72]

"The 'boys' of the local automobile world have exhibited a fine spirit of sportsmanship under trying conditions and heavy losses," columnist A.Y. Tully wrote in the *Los Angeles Evening Express*. "They are of that which has made Los Angeles the greatest city on the western coast."[73]

The city had shown its resilience and the automobile community too had proven it could unite to overcome the worst of circumstances. Los Angeles was now a driving force in the national automobile industry and its importance would only grow in the coming decades.

▶ As many as 320 cars were destroyed in the 1929 Auto Show fire. It was described as "the single worst automotive disaster in history."

The 1929 Los Angeles Auto Show fire made headlines across the nation and caused well over a million dollars of damage.

COMPLETE
OTIVE SERVICE

FENDER AND BODY
REPAIRING

AUTO TOPS
AND
UPHOLSTERING

BRAKES
RELINED

Let Us Repair Your Car
24 HOUR S

TIRES,
TUBES,
ACCESSORIES

WHI
REPA

The A-1 Auto Works yard filled with burned cars after the auto show fire.

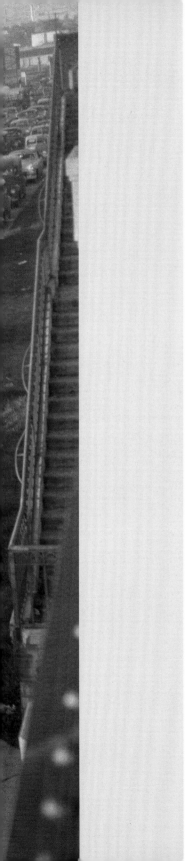

9

AFTERWORD

Los Angeles's infatuation with automobiles has only intensified in the years since 1930. The popular embrace of cars, advances in their design, and improvements in roads meant automobiles were quickly integrated into every aspect of daily life. The city, which for decades had experienced the most "phenomenal and sustained" growth in American history, grew dependent on automobiles to facilitate development in areas that the rail lines didn't reach.[1]

When Fred S. Ferguson, president of the Newspaper Enterprise Association, arrived in Los Angeles in 1942 to write a syndicated story about the local workers and work plants, he noted:

> Surveys of aircraft and industrial plants in the area (Los Angeles) reveal that 90 percent of the employees go to and from their work in their own cars. Bus, street car, and train facilities are entirely inadequate for the transportation of this vast army of workers.[2]

For many years, Los Angeles had led the United States in the building of homes. However, now architects such as Richard Neutra, John Lautner, Edward H. Fickett, and others embraced the youthful enthusiasm of cars in their residential designs. Traditional detached garages were replaced or complimented by carports that led to the kitchen, as porches and grand entrances gave way to a more informal, car-centric way of life.

The 1940 opening of the Arroyo Seco Parkway (also known as the Pasadena Freeway) reaffirmed the region's commitment to an automobile based future. The six-lane, six-mile freeway was the third superhighway in the nation and the first on the Pacific Coast. It was designed to accommodate as many as 27,000 cars daily.

"These freeways (such as the Arroyo Seco Parkway) form the only solution to our traffic problem," California Highway Commissioner Amerigo Bozzani predicted.[3]

Los Angeles County ranked second in comparison to other US counties in industrial activity in 1940 (in 1920 it was 27th). It produced almost as many tires as Akron, Ohio, and was second only to Detroit in the assembly of cars. When the first Dodge rolled off the production line at the Chrysler Motors of California plant in 1946, Los Angeles was producing the same number of car makes as Motor City.[4]

◀ Traffic jam at Venice and La Cienega Boulevards, 1953.

"Progress of any city or state usually is measured in generations—or at least in decades—but not Los Angeles or California," the *Los Angeles Mirror* marveled in 1949 while reporting the population of Los Angeles County had increased by 151,230 in the twelve months from July 1948 to July 1949. "They brought their cars and then some," the newspaper wrote. "The number of automobiles registered in Los Angeles County increased from 1,016,932 to 1,421,249 in a single year."[5]

After driving on the newly expanded Hollywood Freeway in 1951, a reporter for the *Chicago Tribune* wrote, "The new automobile freeways are a delight for motorists weary of struggling thru dense traffic."[6] The same year, approximately one of every 120 cars registered in Los Angeles County would be stolen, according to the California Highway Patrol.[7] As far back as the 1920s, car theft had become California's most lucrative crime.

When the Los Angeles Auto Show returned to the Pan-Pacific Auditorium in 1952, after a twelve-year hiatus caused by World War II, record crowds thronged to get a glimpse of more than five million dollars worth of vehicles. "Los Angeles has beaten San Francisco to the punch in presenting the first big West Coast show since the start of the war," the *Los Angeles Times* boasted as the city's passion for the event was reignited.[8]

The following year, the Pacific Electric Railway Company, which had done so much to fuel the city's expansion, sold its passenger business to Western Transit System, Inc., for eight million dollars. A steady decline in ridership and the popularity of the automobile were blamed for the demise of the business. The new owners would convert the existing routes to bus transportation.

A survey conducted by Fortune surveyors in 1957 found commuting motorists in Los Angeles would use public transportation if it could compete in cost and convenience with that of their cars. "The crowding problem is real enough, as every Los Angeles driver knows," the

Los Angeles Times opined. "If the city stopped growing now the highway system could not catch up with the automobile demand for years."[9]

The growing number of cars in Los Angeles in 1959 led city leaders to forecast the metropolis would soon be choked by traffic. "We are now approaching a crisis which cannot be put off," City Administrative Officer Samuel Leask argued. "By 1970 we will have an estimated 1,400,000 to 1,600,000 automobiles registered in Los Angeles city. Placed bumper to bumper that would stretch 3200 to 3600 miles in length or from here to New York City with an extra link connecting to Washington D.C."[10]

In 1970, there were 3,670,496 motor vehicles registered in Los Angeles County. That number would grow to 4,048,996 by 1980. The region had long since become synonymous with gridlocked freeways, smog, high insurance rates, and permit parking, and yet the bond between people and their cars remained as unbreakable as it had ever been.

In 1993, the Los Angeles Auto Show moved to the Los Angeles Convention Center. There was so much interest in the 1998 show that more than a million visitors were expected to attend. "The Los Angeles show isn't just a showcase for new production models and designers' dreams," the *Los Angeles Times* reported. "It has become a critical player in the drive to promote alternatives to the internal-combustion engine."[11]

As the automobile industry transitions towards an electric future, Los Angeles continues to be a leading hub of automobile innovation, design, and sales. There were an estimated 62,851 electric vehicles on the city's streets in 2021 and more electric vehicles in California than any other state in the nation. Sales of hybrid and EVs continue to increase dramatically.

Early fears of a potential saturation in local car sales have never been realized. In 2021, there were 6,386,830 motor vehicles registered in Los Angeles County. While the early pioneers of auto retailing may be long forgotten, their legacy has come to define the city and continues to impact everyday life in Los Angeles.

Used cars fill a 1930s Los Angeles storage lot.

ACKNOWLEDGMENTS

I would like to thank many colleagues and friends for offering valuable assistance in writing and producing this book. The project started for me when staff members of the California New Car Dealers Association (CNCDA) came across several old boxes containing archival materials from the Motor Car Dealers Association of Los Angeles (MCDALA) and the Los Angeles Auto Show from 1905 into the 1950s.

Discovering that valuable trove of primary documents led me to the Transportation collections of the Natural History Museum of Los Angeles County. The museum's President and Director Lori Bettison-Varga opened the door to collaboration with William Estrada, Beth Werling, Brent Riggs, and the collection managers of the Seaver Center for Western History Research including John Cahoon and, especially, Betty Uyeda. Generous funding from the Greater Los Angeles Dealers Association allowed the Center's Kim Walters to organize and process the Motor Car Dealers Association's archival materials so future historians will be able to access these documents. Publishers Paddy Calistro and Scott McAuley of Angel City Press recognized the importance of the project from the very beginning.

Auto enthusiast Bruce Meyer introduced me to Jay Leno and our discussions of an early draft of the book resulted in Jay's generous offer to write the foreword. I also benefited from comments on an early draft by Morgan Yates, archivist at the Automobile Club of Southern California, and Leslie Kendall, research director of the Petersen Automobile Museum. Peter Welch, former president of the National Automobile Dealers Association; Brian Maas, president of CNCDA; and Bob Smith, executive director of Greater LA New Car Dealers Association, all enthusiastically supported my research. Andrea Gronwald helped me keep track of documents, photos, and working drafts of the manuscript.

The more deeply I delved into this story, the longer the manuscript became. This was complicated by my desire to feature nearly a hundred images. After a discussion with Stephen

▶ A patrolman from the Highway Patrol Service of the Automobile Club of Southern California provides directions, 1925.

Gee regarding the architecture of early Los Angeles dealerships, he and I decided to collaborate by editing the manuscript for space and clarity. Stephen's valuable input helps the book appeal to a broader group of readers.

Driving Force is dedicated to the most distinguished historian in our family, my wife Carole Shammas, who at age thirteen, began working during summers in the business office of Felix Chevrolet, which was owned by her parents. Carole is acknowledged for listening to me talk about this subject for the last five years and for offering invaluable historical advice.

—Darryl Holter

I am grateful to Darryl Holter for the invitation to work on *Driving Force* with him. Writing and researching about the pioneers of the Los Angeles automobile business was a fascinating experience. I would like to say a personal thank you to Jo for her detailed, skillful work reviewing the text. I also would like to thank the staff of the Los Angeles Public Library, including Christina Rice. I am grateful to Erin Chase, assistant curator of Architecture and Photography at the Huntington Library, Art Museum, and Botanical Gardens, for access to the archive of architects John and Donald B. Parkinson, and to Pamela Kellogg for sharing information and images from the Parkinson Family Archive. I also very much appreciate the material from Ralph Hamlin Archive provided by Mr. Hamlin's relative Kerry Galton. The team at Custom Auto Service in Santa Ana including Toby DeLeon, Robert Escalante, and Cathy Hull very graciously allowed access to the Earle C. Anthony publicity and advertising scrapbooks. I also thank Paul R. Spitzzeri, museum director at the Workman and Temple Family Homestead Museum; Maria Christopher at Rancho Camulos Museum; the staff at the California State Library and the Detroit Public Library; David Haberstich, archives center coordinator at the National Museum of American History; Richard Gilreath, archivist at the Smithsonian Institution Archives; Dave Smeds; Dydia DeLyser; the staff at the Chris and Kathleen Koch AACA Library and Research Center; Robert Signom III, curator at America's Packard Museum; and historian and writer Leon Dixon.

—Stephen Gee

ENDNOTES

The following abbreviations are used throughout the endnotes to designate sources whose names repeat often. Publications are shown in italics.

ECASB	Earle C. Anthony Advertising and Publicity Scrapbook, Custom Auto Service (Santa Ana)	LAT	*Los Angeles Times*
		MCD	Motor Car Dealers' Association of Los Angeles
HA	*The Horseless Age*	MW	*Motor West*
LAE	*Los Angeles Examiner*	SCWHR	Seaver Center for Western History Research, Natural History Museum of Los Angeles
LAEE	*Los Angeles Evening Express*		
LAEH	*Los Angeles Evening Herald*	SFC	*San Francisco Call*
LAEX	*Los Angeles Express*	SFE	*San Francisco Examiner*
LAH	*Los Angeles Herald*		

Preface

1. Automotive history rarely finds its way into the business classroom. For example, a review of twenty-five years of *Business History Review*, 380 articles turned up only three articles about the auto industry, along with two others on the tire industry. Jace Baker, Pat McInturff, C.E. Tapie Pohm, Jr., "The Business School Curriculum and the Study of Automotive History." *International Journal of Management in Education*, v.2 v.1, 2008: 31. Going back to the beginning of the journal in 1980, I found twelve articles about the automobile industry: five on foreign industries, three on tires, and four on the industry in the US, one of which is a research note that deals with the automotive franchise system. None are concerned with auto retailing. Two books deserve mention, although neither are academic. Martin H. Bury's *The Automobile Dealer*, was written by a dealer to describe what dealers were doing in the mid-twentieth century. *America's Auto Dealer: The Master Merchandisers*, is an attractive image-filled, coffee-table book by Art Spinella, Beverly Edwards, Mo Mehlsak, and Larry Tuck that includes a useful section on early retailing.

2. Steven M. Gelber. Horse *Trading in the Age of Cars: Men in the Marketplace*: 42

3. Walter A. Friedman. *Birth of a Salesman: The Transformation of Selling in America*, in Gelber: 42

4. James Rubenstein. *Making and Selling Cars: Innovation and Change in the U.S. Automotive Industry*: 251-254, 267-270, 273-276

5. Charles Coolidge Parlin, and Henry Sherwood Youker. *Automobiles*, v.13, *Gasoline Pleasure Cars: Report Investigation*, Curtis Publishing Company, 1914, Chapter 111

Introduction

1. "Three Thousand Autos In Motion." *LAH*, Jul 29, 1906

2. "Automobile Exception to One Old Rule." *LAT*, May 15, 1927 [ECASB]

3. Art Spinella, Beverly Edwards *et al.*, *America's Auto Dealer*: 11

4. "College Boy Auto Pioneer" *LAT*, Feb 20, 1916 [ECASB]

5. "Superior Auto Company." *Greater Los Angeles Illustrated*, 1907: 123

6. "The Motor Industry Through Western Eyes." *Out West*, Feb 1913

7. "Publicity Men Begin New Year." *LAT*, Jan 7, 1914

8. "California is Playground of Motor-Car Men." *LAE*, Mar 14, 1915 [ECASB]

9. "This Year to be Greatest for Auto, Belief." *LAT*, Jan 10, 1926 [ECASB]

10. "$4,000,000 Spent Annually for Los Angeles Garages." *LAEE*, May 17, 1930

11. "Automobile Exception to One Old Rule." *LAT,* May 15, 1927 [ECASB]

12. Bert Smith, "Gasoline Row." *LAT,* Mar 10, 1912

13. "Avoid Problem of Used Cars by Using Them." *LAT,* Feb 6, 1927 [ECASB]

1: City of Cars

1. Frederick Wagner, "Southland Has 580,000 Autos." *LAEE,* Feb 29, 1924

2. "Three Thousand Autos In Motion." *LAH,* Jul 29, 1906

3. Geo. L. Thompson, "Auto Leaves Toy Class." *LAH,* Dec 15, 1907

4. James J. Flink, *The Automobile Age*: 140, 143

5. Ashleigh Brilliant, *The Great Car Craze: How Southern California Collided with the Automobile in the 1920s*: 69

6. "Auto Show to Open in Blaze of Splendor." *LAH,* Jan 21, 1907

7. Christopher Finch, *Highways to Heaven: The Auto Biography of America*: 27

8. "Good Roads is Autodom's Cry." *LAH,* Apr 1, 1906

9. Los Angeles Chamber of Commerce, *The Members' Annual,* Mar 1908

10. Los Angeles Chamber of Commerce, *The Members' Annual,* 1922 and 1923: 156-157

11. "How the Auto Will Dash in Los Angeles." *LAT,* Nov 1, 1903

12. "Efficacy of Racing As Seller of Autos." *LAH,* Dec 18, 1909

13. "Will Surpass Expectations." *LAT,* Jan 13, 1907

14. "See Big Success for Auto Show." *San Francisco Chronicle,* Jan 30, 1907

15. "Auto Trade in San Francisco Never Better Than It Is Now." *San Francisco Chronicle,* Apr 21, 1910

16. "Honks from the Autos." *Baltimore Sun,* Jan 24, 1910

17. "Honks from the Autos." *Baltimore Sun,* Jan 24, 1910

18. Virginia Scharff, *Taking the Wheel: Women and the Coming of the Motor Age*: 117

DEL VALLE, BRUSH AGENT, PLANS TO ENLARGE PRESENT QUARTERS

Plans are being prepared by Y. R. Del Valle, Southern California agent for the popular Brush car and the new Detroiter automobile for the enlarging of his present quarters in Grand av., near W. Pico st., this step being taken principally to provide room for the big stock of Detroiters which he has ordered, and which are now on their way to Los Angeles.

Y. R. DEL VALLE DRIVING THE NEW 25-HORSEPOWER DETROITER TOURING CAR.

The Detroiter is the latest motor creation of the Michigan city, which has been made famous by the automobile industry. The new car has already won its place as a leader among low-priced cars, and will undoubtedly prove a good running mate for the popular little Brush, of which Mr. Del Valle has disposed of hundreds in this territory. Recently he put the new Detroiter through a series of gruelling tests over local roads, and has informed the factory that the new car stands up to the road and hill conditions in this part of the country in royal style.

19. "Home of the Motor is Prediction of Del Valle." *LAT,* Jan 25, 1914

20. "Eleven Types of Tourists Built By Auto Vehicle Co." *Los Angeles Evening Post Record,* Oct 2, 1909

21. "Local Car is Now on Roads." *LAT,* Sep 29, 1907

22. "Massive Ford Factory Nears Completion." *LAT,* Nov 2, 1913

23. "Leach Biltwell Motor Co. Acquires Big Factory." *LAEE,* Dec 13, 1919

24. "Will Employ at Capacity 800 Workers." *LAEE,* Feb 6, 1929

25. "Inventions of Los Angeles Citizens Play Important Part In Automobile Industry." *LAT,* Nov 12, 1916

26. Kevin Nelson, *Wheels of Change: From Zero to 600M.P.H The Amazing Story of California and the Automobile*: 82-83

27. "Automobile is Essential to 'Movie' Directors." *Los Angeles Tribune,* Feb 6, 1916 [ECASB]

28. "This Packard Camera Car was Used by M-G-M in Filming of 'The Wind.'" *Woodland Mail,* Jul 3, 1927 [ECASB]

29. Christopher Finch, *Highways to Heaven*: 120-121

30. Carl Breer with Anthony Yanik, *The Birth of Chrysler Corporation…* Society of Automotive Engineers, 1995: 11, 13-15, 17

31. Albert Drake, *Hot Rodder! from Lakes to Street*: 17, 29

32. Kathleen Franz, *Tinkering: Consumers Reinvent the Early Automobile*: 8-12, 19-20

33. "Southland Has 580,000 Autos." *LAEE,* Feb 29, 1924

34. "State Seen as Motor Leader." *SFE*, Jan 10, 1926 [ECASB]

35. "Lots of Cars in California." *LAT*, Oct 2, 1927

36. Mark S. Foster, "The Model T, the Hard Sell, and Los Angeles's Urban Growth: The Decentralization of Los Angeles during the 1920s." *Pacific Historical Review*, 4, Nov 1975: 459-484

2: Dealers and Manufacturers

1. "Among The Auto Agencies." *LAT*, Aug 28, 1904

2. *Automobile Manufacturers Association, A Chronicle of the Automotive Industry in America, Detroit*, no date: 5

3. "Here Autos Flourish." *LAEX*, Apr 25, 1903

4. "Among The Auto Agencies." *LAT*, Aug 28, 1904

5. "The Automobile Industry and the Men at the Head of It." *LAT*, Jan 1, 1912

6. "The Deposit System." *HA*, v.18 n.15, Oct 10, 1906

7. "Dealers' Commission." *HA*, v.17 n.4, Jun 13, 1906

8. James Zordich interview of Ralph Hamlin, GC-1342-Box 190v, 1880-1974 Collection, SCWHR: 19

9. "Auto Dealers Form Combine." *LAH,* May 19, 1905

10. "Auto Dealers World Beaters." *LAT,* Oct 24, 1909

11. Charles M. Hewitt, *The Development of Automobile Franchises*: 259-260

12. Henry Ford, *My Life and Work: Autobiography of Henry Ford*: 59

13. James M. Rubenstein, *Making and Selling Cars: Innovation and Change in the US Automotive Industry*: 265

14. Lawrence H. Seltzer, *A Financial History of the American Automobile Industry*: 96, 98

15. James M. Rubenstein: 266

16. "Anthony, Earle C., Auto Industry Ranks Among Largest of the Country." LAE, Jan 31, 1915 [ECASB]

17. "Sees Demands on Factories." *LAT,* Aug 8, 1915

18. "Head of Chandler Factory Here For Visit." *LAEE,* Oct 30, 1915

19. "Successful Auto Firm Moves into New Home." *LAT,* Dec 2, 1917

20. Charles M. Hewitt: 17-18

21. Charles M. Hewitt: 55-56

22. Lawrence H. Seltzer, *A Financial History of the American Automobile Industry*: 25-26 and Charles M. Hewitt, *The Development of Automobile Franchises*: 58

23. "Head of Chandler Factory Here for Visit." *LAEE,* Oct 30, 1915

24. The Deposit System." *HA*, v.18 n.15, Oct 10, 1906

25. "Many Autoists are Arriving in this City." *LAE,* Jan 17, 1915 [ECASB]

26. Frederick Wagner, "1918 Turbulent Year for Los Angeles Motor Trade." *LAEE,* Jan 12, 1919

27. "'Cleveland Six' Secures a Los Angeles Headquarters." *Long Beach Telegram,* Sep 13, 1919

28. "Great Future for Motor Sales." *LAEE,* Mar 71, 1920

29. "L.A. Smashes Record for Auto Sales In Quarter." *LAEE,* May 6, 1921

30. "Expects Sales to Show Improvement." *LAT,* Jun 19, 1921

31. "A Report on Conditions." *LAEE,* Nov 20, 1921

32. Paul G. Hoffman, *Trends in Motor Car Distribution, Consumer Marketing Series #1.* New York: American Management Association, 1930: 19

33. Charles M. Hewitt: 11-13.

34. Federal Trade Commission, *Report on the Motor Vehicle Industry*, Washington DC, US Printing Office, 1939: 361

35. Frederick Wagner, "Sales Sweep Upward at High Speed." *LAEE,* Aug 15, 1928

36. Frederick Wagner, "New Car Sales for Year 1928 Show Increase." *LAEE*, Feb 6, 1929

William K. Cowan

1. "City Board Holds Its Initial Meeting." *Eagle Rock Sentinel* Mar 8, 1911

2. Robert J. Burdette, *Greater Los Angeles and Southern California*: 134

3. "Los Angeles to San Diego: All Ready for the Great Relay Bicycle Race." *LAH,* May 23, 1892; "The Bicycling World." *LAH,* Jul 27, 1892

4. Rambler Bicycles Advertisement, *LAH,* Aug 19, 1894

5. Rambler Bicycles Advertisement, *LAH,* Dec 21, 1899

6. "Going Back to Early Days of Industry," *MW,* v.28 no.2, Nov 1, 1917

7. "'Traffic Trouble? Here's Man Who Started It,'" *LAT,* Jun 10, 1946

8. "Many Ramblers Used." *LAT,* Feb 26, 1905

9. "W.K. Cowan, Automobiles, Etc." *LAH,* Sep 3, 1905

10. "Going Back to Early Days of Industry," *MW,* v.28 no.2, Nov 1, 1917

11. Auto Dealers Form Combine, *LAH,* May 19, 1905

12. "Traffic Trouble? Here's Man Who Started It," *LAT,* June 10, 1946

13. Mrs. W.K. Cowan, "The Ramblings of Two Ramblers in California." *The Rambler Magazine,* Mar 1906

$1200 TO $5500
Choose Your
Automobile or Truck
ALL 1913 MODELS, HIGH-GRADE, STANDARD-MAKE AUTOMOBILES OR TRUCKS
Full Factory Guarantees
$300 Cash and $125 Per Month for Six Months or
$600 Cash and $50 Per Month for Eleven Months
Why allow your business to suffer for want of a Truck to increase the business?
Why not purchase an automobile the same way you would a home?
Automobile Funding Company of America
CHAS. A. BRADLEY, President
Telephones—Home A3873—Broadway 2493
Suite 502 L. A. Investment Building
Infringements on Copyrights of the Automobile Funding Company of America Will Be Vigorously Prosecuted.

14. "'Traffic Trouble? Here's Man Who Started It,'" *LAT*, Jun 10, 1946
15. "Rambler Moves into New Home." *LAH*, Nov 15, 1908
16. "Rules Adopted for Altadena Road Race," *LAH*, Feb 11, 1909
17. J. Allen Davis, *The Friend to All Motorists: The Story of the Automobile Club of Southern California Through 65 Years,* ACSC
18. "City Board Holds Initial Meeting." *Eagle Rock Sentinel*, Mar 8, 1911
19. "W.K. Cowan Makes Announcement of Entrance in Race." *Eagle Rock Sentinel*, Feb 27, 1931
20. "Mr. Cowan Takes Agency," *Eagle Rock Sentinel*, Mar 4, 1915
21. "The American Car since 1775." *Automobile Quarterly*: n.p.
22. "Back on Automobile Row." *Eagle Rock Sentinel*, Jul 19, 1917
23. "'Traffic Trouble? Here's Man Who Started It,'" *LAT*, Jun 10, 1946

Ralph Hamlin

1. James Zordich interview of Ralph Hamlin, GC-1342-Box 190v, 1880-1974 Collection, SCWHR
2. "Ralph Hamlin, Pioneer Auto Dealerships in Los Angeles." *Valley News*, Oct 27, 1967
3. James Zordich, Ralph C. Hamlin, untitled publication, Kerry Cunningham Galton Archive
4. James Zordich interview, *op. cit.*
5. Zordich and Hamlin, *op. cit.*
6. Jacque Wright, "Jonathan Number One." *The Jonathan*, Mar 1972
7. Zordich and Hamlin, *op. cit.*
8. "Ralph Hamlin Made The First Cycle Car." *LAT*, Apr 5, 1914
9. "Pro-Delivery Service on the New Car." *Motor Age*, v.27 n.25, Jun 17, 1920
10. James Zordich interview, *op. cit.*
11. David Traver Adolphus, "Sand Special." *Classic Car*, n.75, Dec 2010
12. James Zordich interview, *op. cit.*
13. Ralph Hamlin, "The Great Desert Race." *Desert Magazine*, Oct 1962
14. James Zordich, *op. cit.*
15. Kevin Nelson, *Wheels of Change: From Zero to 600 MPH...*: 35-36
16. "Hamlin's Biplane to be Assembled." *LAEE*, Jan 19, 1911
17. "Hamlin Smashed Last Year's Phoenix Record." *LAT*, Oct 29, 1912
18. Bert C. Smith, "Ralph Hamlin in Franklin Leads Race." *LAT*, Oct 28, 1912

▼ The Ajax Division of Troy Motor Sales Co. at 11th and Flower Streets adjoined the Nash showroom at 11th and Figueroa Streets.

19. "Pro-Delivery Service on the New Car." *Motor Age*, v.27 n.25, Jun 17, 1920

20. *The Franklin Automobile Company*, Society of Automotive Engineers

21. "Hamlin Made De Vaux Distributor." *LAT*, May 29, 1932

3: Auto Rows and Retail Facilities

1. "Coming of the Auto." *LAT*, Jun 16, 1899

2. "A Horseless Carriage." *LAH*, May 30, 1897

3. "W.F. Pipher Moves to New Main St. Quarters." *LAH*, Aug 31, 1912

4. "Leavitt Talks of Bicycle Days." *MW*, v.46 n.11, Mar 15, 1927

5. "Three Thousand Autos In Motion, *LAH*, Jul 29, 1906

6. James J. Flink, *America Adopts the Automobile*, 1895-1910: 52

7. "Three Thousand Autos In Motion." *LAH*, Jul 29, 1906

8. "The Garage Business in Los Angeles." *HA*, v.23 n.16, Apr 21, 1909

9. "Many New Garages on Olive Street." *LAH*, v.35 n.305, Aug 2

10. "Franklin Garage to Move to South Olive." *LAEE*, Oct 03, 1908

11. "The Hamlin Garage, Los Angeles." *HA*, v.23 n.16, Apr 21, 1909

12. "Dealers' Directory." *Touring Topics*, Aug 1910

13. "The Garage Business in Los Angeles." *HA*, v.23 n.16, Apr 21, 1909

14. "The Garage Business in Los Angeles." *HA*, v.23 n.16, Apr 21, 1909

15. "The Garage Business in Los Angeles." *HA*, v.23 n.16, Apr 21, 1909

16. "The White Garage," Los Angeles, *HA*, v.23 n.16, Apr 21, 1909

17. "The White Garage." *Greater Los Angeles Illustrated*, 1907: 119.

18. "Leon T. Shettler" *Greater Los Angeles Illustrated*, 1907: 135.

19. "Apperson Cars in New Home." *LAT*, Jan 21, 1912

20. "The Automobile Industry and the Men at the Head of It." *LAT*, Jan 1, 1912

21. Betty Uyeda, "The Hotel Figueroa and Figueroa Street Name Origins." *Los Angeles Revisited*, Jan 22, 2011

22. "Ornate Packard Home is Planned." *LAT*, Jun 25, 1911

23. "Ornate Packard Home is Planned." *LAT*, Jun 25, 1911

24. "Salesroom on Auto Row Described by Los Angeles Motorists as a 'Dream.'" *LAT*, Jan 14, 1917

25. "Salesroom on Auto Row Described by Los Angeles Motorists as a 'Dream.'" *LAT*, Jan 14, 1917

26. "Many Buildings Go Up Along L.A. Auto Row." *LAH*, Jan 13, 1917

27. "Salesroom on Auto Row Described by Los Angeles Motorists as a 'Dream.'" *LAT*, Jan 14, 1917

28. "Bekins-Speers Builds New Quarters." *MW*, v.27 n.4, Jun 1, 1917

29. "Rich Man Deeds $800,000 of Estate to Heirs." *LAH*, Mar 12, 1913

30. "Auto Block Started." *LAT*, May 20, 1917

31. "Troy Motor Sales Co. In New Quarters." *LAH*, Nov 9, 1918

32. "Chandler to Have Fine New Home." *LAH*, Jun 23, 1917

33. "Auto Row Has A New Name." *LAT*, Sep 2, 1917

34. "Two Celebrations in One, is Plan: New Cars To Be Shown in New Quarters." *LAT*, Oct 7, 1917

35. "Lincolns are Treated in an Exclusive Way." *LAT*, Sep 16, 1923

36. The property and building was purchased by Nickolas Shammas in 1957 to relocate Felix Chevrolet from 12th Street and Grand Avenue.

37. "Takes Place with the Best on Any Row." *LAT*, Oct 17, 1920

38. The building still stands but has been substantially reconfigured to house an electrical manufacturing firm.

39. "Elaborate Plant Planned by Maddux in New Building." *LAT*, Dec 5, 1926

40. "Maddux Plans New Building on Auto Row", *LAT*, May 9, 1926

41. Meredith Drake Reitan. "Lost Parkinson Auto Showroom Discovered on Figueroa." *LAvenues Project*, SAVENUEPROJECT, Jul 9, 2017

42. Mark Wilson, *Bernard Maybeck*, 12

43. Carl Haverlin, Carl Grant, Earle C. Anthony, *Romance of Transportation and the Story of the Packard Building: 4*

44. *Los Angeles City Directory*, 1927

45. Charles Coolidge Parlin and Henry Sherwood Youker, "Automobiles Volume 1B. Gasoline and Pleasure Cars. Report of Investigation." Curtis Publishing Company, 1914: 111-112, quoted in James M. Rubenstein, *Making and Selling Cars: Innovation and Change in the U.S. Automotive Industry*: 253.

Don Lee

1. "Cadillac Tradition is Maintained." *LAEE*, Jan 22, 1930

2. "Donald Musgrave Lee." Press Reference Library, Notables of the Southwest, 1912: 414

3. "Royal Changes Hands." *LAT*, Oct 20, 1907

4. "Movie Studio had 22 Cadillacs." *MW*, May 1, v.29 n.2, 1918

5. "Big Automobile Body and Top Factory Now Property of Cadillac Distributor Here." *LAEE*, Jul 12, 1919

6. "Big Automobile Body and Top Factory Now Property of Cadillac Distributor Here." *LAEE*, Jul 12, 1919

7. "East Seeks Motor Car Body Styles in California." *LAEE*, Aug 9, 1919

8. "East Seeks Motor Car Body Styles in California." *LAEE*, Aug 9, 1919

9. Nick Georgeano, *The American Automobile A Centenary 1893-1993*

10. "Cadillac Tradition is Maintained." LAEE, Jan 22, 1930

Two People with a Rambler Gasoline

On Sunday, June 14th, went to Riverside and back, starting at 9 a.m., returning 7:30 p.m., stopping 2½ hours on the road, covering the round trip of 140 miles in 8 hours, making an average of 17½ miles per hour. The whole trip was made on high speed gear, not once putting in the hill-climbing clutch. No other vehicle in California can duplicate the performance. The Rambler is looked upon as a modest little touring car, but it will do the work that cannot be done by many $2500 machines. Call and see this machine, as well as our other models.

W. K. COWAN
207 West Fifth St.
Our New Home is 830-32-34 S. BROADWAY.

11. "L.A. Cadillac Firm Outsells N.Y. and Chicago During '23." *Monrovia Daily News*, Mar 19, 1924
12. "Radio KHJ is in New Hands." *LAT*, Nov 12, 1927
13. Greg Fischer, "Don Lee and the Transformation of Los Angeles." *Southern California Quarterly*, v.96 n.1, Spring 2014
14. "Mrs. Don Lee Wins Divorce." *SFE*, Jan 28, 1925
15. "Young Beauty Sues Don Lee, Auto Magnate." *Los Angeles Record*, Sep 14, 1933
16. "Widow Says Don Lee's Love Affairs Were Costly." *Sacramento Bee*, Apr 13, 1935
17. "Lethal Drug Given Lee, Kin Charges." *Pasadena Independent*, Dec 16, 1951

Earle C. Anthony

1. Lynn Rogers, "Automotive: Highlights." *LAT*, Sep 11, 1949
2. Lynn Rogers, "Automotive: Highlights." *LAT*, Sep 11, 1949
3. "Earle C. Anthony." Biographical File, Los Angeles Central Library, History Department
4. "Will Edit the Blue and Gold." *SFC*, Mar 14, 1901
5. "Burlesque Will Follow Football." *SFE*, Nov 7, 1902
6. "College Boy Auto Pioneer." *LAT*, Feb 20, 1916 [ECASB]
7. "College Boy Auto Pioneer." *LAT*, Feb 20, 1916 [ECASB]
8. "Automotive: Highlights." *LAT*, Sep 11, 1949
9. "Packard Plum Hanging High." *LAT*, Jun 13, 1909
10. "Packard Not in Auto Show." *LAT*, Nov 18, 1956
11. Kevin Nelson, *Wheels of Change: From Zero to 600 M.P.H.: The Amazing Story of California and the Automobile*: 56, 59
12. "Builds Auto Gas Station on Coast." *National Petroleum News*, v.5 n.10, Dec 1913
13. "New Owners for Supply Stations." *LAT*, Apr 19, 1914
14. "College Boy Auto Pioneer." *LAT*, Feb 20, 1916 [ECASB]
15. "Tracing Absence: Enduring Methods, Empirical Research and a Quest for the First Neon Sign in the USA." *Area*, Royal Geographical Society, v.46 n.1, Mar 2014
16. "Lindbergh Rides in Packard Car." *Glendale News* (Glendale CA), Oct 13, 1927 [ECASB]
17. Packard Motor Car Company advertisement, *LAT*, Feb 22, 1929
18. "Romance of Transportation Depicted at Beautiful New Anthony-Packard-Bldg." *LAEE*, Feb 21, 1929
19. "Anthony Has Colorful Career." *Oakland Tribune*, Nov 24, 1940
20. "Dreams of Great Bay Bridge." *Appeal-Democrat* (Marysville CA), Nov 28, 1936
21. "Celebration! 35th Year for Anthony." *SFE*, Feb 26, 1939
22. "See the Premiere of KFI Television." *Los Angeles Evening Citizen News*, Oct 6, 1948
23. "Automotive: Highlights and Fact." *LAT*, Jul 2, 1939
24. "Automotive: Highlights and Fact." *LAT*, Jul 2, 1939

4: Selling Cars on Credit

1. "Time Sales of Automobiles Have Reached Enormous Proportions." *Automotive Industries*, v.49, Jul 26, 1923
2. Art Spinella, Beverly Edwards *et al.*, *America's Auto Dealer: The Master Merchandisers*: 31
3. Ralph C. Epstein, *The Automobile Industry: Its Economic and Commercial Development*: 63
4. Martha L. Olney, *Buy Now, Pay Later: Advertising, Credit, and Consumer Durables in the 1920s*: 119-120.
5. James Zordich interview of Ralph Hamlin, GC-1342-Box 190v, 1880-1974 Collection, SCWHR: 90-91
6. William A. Grimes, *Financing Automobile Sales by the Time-Payment Plan*: 11
7. James Zordich, "Tourist Automobiles-Made in Los Angeles, Cal." *Horseless Carriage Gazette*, v.35, n.6, Nov-Dec 1973
8. "Studebaker Adopts Credit Plan." *Motor World*, v.29 n.11, Dec 7, 1911
9. "Studebaker Adopts Credit Plan." *Motor World*, v.29 n.11, Dec 7, 1911
10. "Big Concern Novel Project." *LAT*, Feb 9, 1913
11. "Charles A. Bradley, Pres. and Gen'l Mgr. of the Automobile Funding Co. of America." *Out West*, v.6 n.3, Sep 1913

▲ Walter M. Brown sold Stutz Motor Car Company vehicles at Figueroa Street and Washington Boulevard.

12. "Supt. French Reviews New Automobile Law." *SFE*, May 23, 1915

13. "Los Angeles Autos Transport U.S. Army." *LAT*, Aug 15, 1915

14. James J. Flink, *The Automobile Age*: 191

15. "Guaranty Plan." Advertisement, *LAT*, Jul 12, 1916

16. "Buying Automobiles on 'Time on Payments.'" *MW*, v.25 n.1, Apr 15, 1916

17. James J. Flink: 190

18. Against Deferred-Payment Plan." *MW*, v.25 n.2, May 1, 1916

19. Martha L. Olney, *Buy Now, Pay Later: Advertising, Credit, and Consumer Durables in the 1920s*: 120

20. Martha L. Olney: 120

21. "Financing Automobile Sales." *MW*, v.32 n.8, Feb 1, 1920

22. James J. Flink: 191

23. "Time Sales of Automobiles Have Reached Enormous Proportions." *Automotive Industries*. v.49 n.4, Jul 26, 1923

24. "Time Sales of Automobiles Have Reached Enormous Proportions." *Automotive Industries*. v.49 n.4, Jul 26, 1923

25. "Millions Cars Are Bought on Time and Bad Debts Are Almost Nil." *LAT*, Aug 3, 1924

26. "Star and Durant Motor Interests Show Marked Increase in Los Angeles." *LAEE*, Apr 29, 1925

27. Martha L. Olney: 125

28. Ralph C. Epstein: 119

29. "Felix Favors Short Term Payments." *LAEE*, Nov 4, 1925

James S. Conwell

1. "Councilman Conwell is Called by Death." *LAT*, Dec 16, 1917

2. Indiana Bicycle Advertisement. *SFC*, Jan 12, 1896

3. "Cycle Dealers United." *SFC*, Apr 10, 1896

4. "Cyclers Out for Smooth Streets." *SFC*, Jul 24, 1896

5. "Cycle Board of Trade in Line." *SFC*, Jan 8, 1897

6. "Cycle Trade Loses an Earnest Worker." *SFE*, Sep 24, 1897

7. "Waverley Electric Vehicle." *Electrical World and Engineer*, v.33 n.20, May 20, 1899

8. "Automobile Races and Expositions." *Electrical World and Engineer*, v.36 n.13, Sep 29, 1900

9. *Who's Who in the Pacific Southwest, A Compilation of Authentic Biographical Sketches of Citizens of Southern California and Arizona*, 1913: 98

10. "Tourist Automobile: Made in Los Angeles, California." *Horseless Carriage Gazette*, Nov-Dec 1973

11. "Auto Man to Change Base." *LAT*, Nov 8, 1908

12. "Big Crowd to Greet Tourists." *LAH*, Aug 23, 1908

13. "Auto Man to Change Base." *LAT*, Nov 8, 1908

14. "Auto Man to Change Base." *LAT*, Nov 8, 1908

15. "Conwell is a Dean of Ideas." *LAH*, Mar 14, 1909

16. "Conwell is a Dean of Ideas." *LAH*, Mar 14, 1909

17. MCDA minutes, May 2, 1910

18. MCDA minutes, Nov 17, 1911 and Dec 8, 1911

19. MCDA minutes, Dec 29, 1911 and Mar 8, 1912

20. "Deaths." *Northwestern University Bulletin Alumni Journal*, v.18 n.19, Dec 15, 1917

21. Bert C. Smith, "Twenty-Five Million for Ocean to Ocean Highway." *LAT*, Sep 15, 1912

22. "Motorists Should Retain Conwell in Council." *The Tribune* (San Luis Obispo CA), v.7, n.4, May 1915

23. "J.S. Conwell Returns to Auto Row." *LAE*, Aug 9, 1913

24. "Politics." *LAT*, Jul 1, 1917

25. "To Force Stand of Council on Billboards." *LAEH*, May 29, 1917

26. "Auto Man to Change Base." *LAT*, Nov 8, 1908

27. "Council Head J.S. Conwell Expires." *LAEE*, Dec 15, 1917

Ygnacio R. del Valle

1. Liberty-Brush advertisement. *Norfolk Daily News*, Jul 21, 1911

2. Ygnacio's brother, Reginaldo, was a California state senator and a founder of Los Angeles Normal School (later UCLA).

3. "Tammany's Topical Talk." *LAH*, Apr 8, 1894

4. Brush advertisement. *LAT*, May 23, 1909

5. "Brush Runabout Demonstration." *Pomona Daily Review*, Apr 15, 1909

6. "Going to Factory to Study Machine." *LAEX* Dec 23, 1911

7. "Going to Factory to Study Machine." *LAEX* Dec 23, 1911

8. "Along Auto Row." *LAEH*, Jun 29, 1912

9. "Auto Man Says to Make Up for Shortcomings He Needs Motor That'll Sell Itself." *LAEE*, Jul 13, 1912

10. "Detroiter is Touring West." *LAEX*, Aug 2, 1913

11. "Going to Factory to Study Machine." *LAEX*, Dec 23, 1911

12. "Koehler Car Result of 14 Years of Work." *LAEH*, Sep 14, 1912

13. "Koehler Truck One of New Arrivals." *LAT*, Jun 1, 1913

14. "Koehler Truck One of New Arrivals." *LAT*, Jun 1, 1913

15. "Touraine Six New Model on Market." *LAT*, Apr 6, 1913

16. "New Product, Little Truck." *LAT*, May 10, 1914

17. "Motor Car Shipped Via Panama Canal." *LAEH*, Dec 5, 1914

18. "Light Truck Aid to Industrialism." *LAEE*, Aug 29, 1914

19. "Will Make Convertible Body for Vim Truck." *LAEH*, Sep 19, 1914

5: Service and Repairs

1. "Garage Bill, Bitter Pill." *LAT*, Oct 3, 1906

2. "Repairs Are Difficult." *HA*, v.8 n.21, Aug 21, 1901

3. Stephen L. McIntyre, "The Failure of Fordism." *Technology and Culture*, v.41 n.2, Apr 2000

4. "Garages and their Repair Shops." *MW, v.*27 n.9, May 25, 1911

5. "Barney's Advice." *LAT*, Aug 28, 1904

6. "Auto Leaves Toy Class." *LAH*, Dec 15, 1907

7. "Delivery Auto in Local Use." *LAT*, Sep 1, 1907

8. "Interesting Statistics." *LAH*, Apr 15, 1906

9. "Among the Auto Agencies." *LAT*, Aug 28, 1904

10. "Lee Automobile Company." *LAH*, Sep 03, 1905

11. "Lee Automobile Company." *LAH*, Sep 03, 1905

12. "Garages and their Repair Shops." *MW, v.*27 n.9, May 25, 1911

13. "Among the Auto Agencies." *LAT,* Aug 28, 1904

14. "South End Auto Station." *LAH*, Sep 3, 1905

15. "When Ford Speaks the World Listens." Advertisement. *Long Beach Press*, Nov 4, 1910

16. "Repairs Are Difficult." *HA*, v.8 n.21, Aug 21, 1901

17. "Schoolboys Run Garage." *LAT*, Apr 2, 1916

18. "Automobile School." *LAT*, Oct 20, 1907

19. "Tourist 'Automobile Night School' Proves Instant Success and Attracts Throng." *LAH*, Mar 14, 1909

20. *The Franklin Automobile Company*, Society of Automotive Engineers, Inc.: 180-181

21. "Training Men for Dealers' Service." *Motor World*, v.32 n.11, Sep 5, 1912

22. "Service Men for Stearns." *LAT*, Jan 19, 1913

23. "Chalmers Repair School Will Open." *Detroit Free Press*, Aug 17, 1913

24. "Training Given to Apprentices." *LAT*, Mar 26, 1916 [ECASB]

25. "Many Service Stations Open." *LAT*, May 31, 1914

26. "Effort Made to Standardize 'Service' to Customers." *New York Tribune*, Jun 25, 1916

27. "Garages and their Repair Shops." *Motor World*, v.27 n.9, May 25, 1911

28. Stephen L. McIntyre: *op. cit.*

29. Stephen L. McIntyre: *op cit.* On car jokes, see B.A. Botkin, "Automobile Humor: From the Horseless Carriage to the Compact Car." *Journal of Popular Culture*, v.I, iss.4, Spr, 1968, in McIntyre: 276

30. Stephen L. McIntyre: *op. cit.*

31. "Training Men for Dealers' Service." *Motor World*, v.32 n.11, Sep 5, 1912

32. "Discontinuance of Retail Sales." Aug 1916, acc. 78, box 1, FA/EI, in McIntyre: 277

33. "War Teaching Owners of Autos to be Handy Men." *LAT* Aug 11, 1918

34. "Owners Give More Attention to Cars Now." *LAEE*, Jul 28, 1918

35. "Standard Motor Service Company of California." *LAT*, Jan 1, 1920

36. "Service Men for Stearns." *LAT*, Jan 19, 1913

37. "Chalmers Repair School Will Open." *Detroit Free Press*, Aug 17, 1913

38. "Many Service Stations Open." *LAT*, May 31, 1914

39. "Effort Made to Standardize 'Service' to Customers." *New York Tribune*, Jun 25, 1916

40. Ralph C. Epstein, *The Automobile Industry*: 85-86

41. "Ford Parts Hold To Old Price List." *LAEE*, Jan 8, 1921

42. "Planning Ford Structure Here." *LAEE*, Mar 28, 1923

43. "Service System Established by Buick Factory." *LAEE*, Mar 28, 1923

44. "Chrysler Institute for Service Influence Wide." *LAEE*, Feb 22, 1930

45. "Chrysler Service Men Gather." *Los Angeles Record*, Sep 18, 1929

Winslow B. Felix

1. "Felix Now Directs Chevrolet Agency of his Own in L.A." *LAEE*, Oct 22, 1921

2. "W.B. Felix Named Chevrolet Dealer." *LAEH*, Oct 15, 1921

3. "Felix Now Directs Chevrolet Agency of his Own in L.A." *LAEE,* Oct 22, 1918

4. John Canemaker, *Felix: The Twisted Tale of the World's Most Famous Cat*: 88; Jon G. Robinson, *Classic Chevrolet Dealerships*, Motorbooks: 95

5. "Cats Like Rain*." LAT,* Mar 9, 1924

6. "You Ought to Hear it Purr..." *LAT,* Jan 11, 1925

7. "Cats Will Follow These Chevrolets." *LAT,* Feb 8, 1925

8. "Felix Selects Cat for Mark." *LAEE,* Aug 22, 1923

9. "Dolled-Up Car Speaks Loudly." *LAT,* Jan 6, 1924

10. "Felix the Cat Makes Business Up to Scratch." *LAT,* Mar 29, 1925

11. "Chevrolet Dealers in Los Angeles Who Stepped on it During August." *LAEE,* Sep 16, 1925

12. "Dealer Creates a New Special Touring Model." *LAT,* Apr 19, 1925

13. "Chevrolet to Reach Million Mark Soon." *LAEE,* Aug 25, 19261

14. "Dealer Creates a New Special Touring Model." *LAT,* Apr 19, 1925

15. "Telephone Slogan Adopted by Felix." *LAT,* Mar 22, 1925

16. "Pins in Map Tell of Sales in City." *LAT,* Jun 21, 1925

17. "Trial Purchase Plan is Latest Felix Feature." *LAT,* Jun 6, 1926

18. "The Last Word." *LAT,* Aug 6, 1926: 24; "Café Notes: Plantation Dance Prize." *LAT,* Nov 12, 1926

19. "Autoist Is Also Horseman." *LAT,* Aug 15, 1926

20. "H'Wood Poloists Rank Novices, But Risk Necks to Hop Up Sport." *Variety,* v.123, iss. 2, Jun 24, 1936

21. "Felix Widow Given Reins." *LAT,* Jun 2, 1936

22. Nickolas Shammas, the author's father-in-law, now deceased, purchased the dealership from Ruth Felix in 1955. He relocated the business to the corner of Jefferson and Figueroa in 1958 and built the giant Felix the Cat-Chevrolet sign in 1959.

Thomas "Tommy" Pillow Jr.

1. "Bright Colored Boy." *LAT,* Apr 6, 1902

2. "Run Over by a Mobe." LAEX, Nov 27, 1902

3. "Auto Leaps off Bridge." *LAT,* Jan 11, 1904

4. "Big Automobile Crashes Through Bridge, Hurling Occupants Down Steep Bank." *LAH,* Jan 11, 1904

5. "Dropped From a Bridge." *LAEX,* Jan 11, 1904

6. "Auto Leaps off Bridge." *LAT,* Jan 11, 1904

7. "Big Automobile Crashes Through Bridge, Hurling Occupants Down Steep Bank." *LAH,* Jan 11, 1904

8. "Successful Termination of the Run to Test Automobile." *Santa Barbara Morning Press,* Aug 6, 1905

9. "Climbing from Orange Blossoms to Snow." *The Automobile,* v.15 n.24, Dec 13, 1906

10. "Stevens-Duryea Wins Riverside Hill Climb." *LAT,* Nov 30, 1906

11. "Seattle Sees Track Racing." *Motor World,* v.16 n.11, Jun 13, 1907

12. "Seattle's Auto Carnival." *The Automobile,* v.16 n.24, Jun 13, 1907

13. "'Twin-Six' In 'Pick-Up' Test." *LAT,* Nov 7, 1915

14. "'Twin-Six' Designers Follow Pioneer Lead." *LAT,* Sep 5, 1915

15. "High Mileage Made By Cars." *LAEE,* May 23, 1923

16. *Los Angeles City Directory, 1930*: 1810

6: Used Cars

1. "What Becomes of Old Cars?" *LAT,* Nov 12, 1916

2. Theodore H. Smith, *The Marketing of Used Automobiles*: 1

3. MCDA minutes, Jun 1, 1905

4. "Second-Hand Machines Sell." *LAH,* Aug 10, 19065

5. Paul G. Hoffman, "What Becomes of Old Cars?" *LAT,* Nov 12, 1916

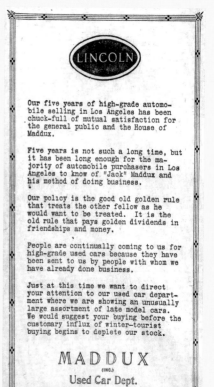

LINCOLN

Our five years of high-grade automobile selling in Los Angeles has been chuck-full of mutual satisfaction for the general public and the House of Maddux.

Five years is not such a long time, but it has been long enough for the majority of automobile purchasers in Los Angeles to know of "Jack" Maddux and his method of doing business.

Our policy is the good old golden rule that treats the other fellow as he would want to be treated. It is the old rule that pays golden dividends in friendships and money.

People are continually coming to us for high-grade used cars because they have been sent to us by people with whom we have already done business.

Just at this time we want to direct your attention to our used car department where we are showing an unusually large assortment of late model cars. We would suggest your buying before the customary influx of winter-tourist buying begins to deplete our stock.

MADDUX (INC.)
Used Car Dept.
1059 So. Figueroa   WE. 4114

Daily 8 A. M. to 9:30 P. M.   Sundays 9 A. M. to 5 P. M.
6. "Beware of the Automobile 'Gyp'!" *MW,* v.23 n.4, Jun 1, 1915

7. "Beware of the Automobile 'Gyp'!" *MW,* v.23 n.4, Jun 1, 1915

8. "Use Second-Hand Cars." *LAT,* Jan 5, 1908

9. Henry Farrand Griffin, "The Problem of the Used Motor Car." *The Outlook,* v.105 n.12, Dec 27, 1913

10. MCDA Minutes, Dec 28, 1909

11. MCDA Minutes, Jul 15, 1912

12. MCDA Minutes, Aug 20, 1913

13. MCDA Minutes, Sep 12, 1912

14. MCDA Minutes, Oct 10, 1913

15. "The Used Car Problem." *MW,* v.22 n.8, Feb 1, 1915

16. "Second-Hand Car Business Booming." *LAT,* Jul 28, 1912

17. "Business Demands Larger Quarters." *LAT*, Dec 30, 1917

18. "Hundreds Buying Used Automobiles." *LAT*, Jul 15, 1917

19. Advertisement. *LAT*, May 2, 1920

20. "Second-Hand Sales a Big Part of Business." *LAT*, Apr 4, 1915

21. "Anthony's Used Car Service Innovation." *LAT*, Jul 25, 1915

22. "Good Used Cars Always on Market." *LAH*, Apr 29, 1916 [ECASB]

23. "Old-Time 'Hoss' Trader Now Makes Living Swapping Cars." *LAT*, Nov 26, 1916

24. E.D. Kennedy. *The Automobile Industry*: 88

25. "Autos, Once a Luxury Now a Necessity." *LAT*, Jun 10, 1917 [ECASB]

26. E.D. Kennedy: 102-103

27. "Making New Cars from Old Ones." *MW*, v.30 n.1, Oct 15, 1918

28. E.D Kennedy: 104

29. "Little Possibility of Local Automobile Shows." *MW,* v.30 n.1, Oct 15, 1918

30. "Best Used Car if Home-Grown." *LAT*, Jan 22, 1922

31. "Through East for Used Motor Cars." *LAT*, Nov 16, 1919

32. "A Stronger Organization." *LAT*, Aug 22, 1920

33. "The Times and Used Autos." Advertisement, *LAT*, Mar 9, 1919

34. "Used-Car Dealers are Incorporated." *LAT*, Oct 5, 1919

35. "Automobile Show." Advertisement. *LAEE*, Apr 15, 1920

36. "Used Car Business is on Solid Basis Now." *LAT*, Jan 22, 1922

37. E.D. Kennedy: 140

38. "Steady Demand for Used Cars." *LAT*, Aug 19, 1923

39. "Used Car Now Welcome Here." *LAEE*, Jul 23, 1924

40. "Sticks by His Guns to Limit." *LAT*, Feb 24, 1924

41. "Avoid Problem of Used Cars by Using Them." *LAT*, Feb 6, 1927 [ECASB]

42. Charles Mason Hewitt, Jr., *Automobile Franchise Agreements*: 63-64

43. Charles Mason Hewitt, Jr.: 63

44. "Cut Down the Used Car Losses." *LAT*, Oct 28, 1923

45. "R. Leslie Kelley, Car-Pricing Pioneer, 93." *New York Times*, Feb 11, 1990

46. "April Business a Bit Below March." *MW*, v.47 n.3, May 15, 1927

47. Paul G. Hoffman and James H. Greene. *Marketing Used Cars*: 1

Paul G. Hoffman

1. Paul G Hoffman, *Seven Roads to Safety*: 30-33

2. Alan R. Raucher, Paul G. Hoffman, *Architect of Foreign Aid*: 4

3. Stephen A. Longstreet, *Century on Wheels: The Story of Studebaker: A History, 1852-1952*: 81-83

4. C.B. Glasscock, *The Gasoline Age: The Story of the Men who Made It*: 261

5. "Shows Rapid Expansion." *LAT*, Apr 4, 1920

6. "Beware The Super-Salesman!" *Lubbock Avalanche Journal*, Oct 27, 1929: 24

7. Alan Raucher, Paul G. Hoffman: 8

8. "Storage Plant Will be Built." *LAT*, Jan 13, 1924

9. "Studebaker Elects a New Vice-President." *Press-Democrat* (Santa Rosa, CA), Apr 12, 1925

10. "Beware The Super-Salesman!" *Lubbock Avalanche Journal,* Oct 27, 1929

11. Paul G. Hoffman and James E. Greene, *Marketing Used Cars*: 11

12. "Reorganized Firm is Ready to Go Forward." *South Bend Tribune*, Mar 9, 1935

13. "Beware The Super-Salesman!" *Lubbock Avalanche Journal,* Oct 27, 1929

14. "Risky Business—A Non-Politician as President." *Wall Street Journal*, Jul 9, 1992

15. "Hoffman Reports Studebaker-Packard Merger Will Make 'Very Big Company.'" *Palladium Item (Richmond, Indiana)*, Sep 27, 1954

16. "Paul Hoffman Dies, Headed Europe Aid." *Intelligencer Journal,* Oct 9, 1974

R. Leslie Kelley

1. "Sidney H. Kelley, 92: Sold Cars, Blue Book." *LAT*, Dec 7, 2001

2. "Kelley Kar Co. Old-Timer Here." *LAT*, Jul 26, 1934

3. Kelley Kar Co. Advertisement, *LAEH*, Nov 24, 1920

4. Kelley Kar Co. Advertisement, *LAEH*, Nov 29, 1921

5. "Kelley Blue Book Company, Inc." *International Directory of Company Histories*, v.84, n.d.: 219

6. "Kelley Blue Book Company, Inc." *International Directory of Company Histories*, v.84, n.d.: 219

7. "R.L. Kelley, 93; First Published Blue Book on Used-Car Values." *LAT*, Feb 9, 1990

8. "State Tax on Car Equalized." *LAT*, Oct 14, 1928

9. "New Dealer if Named to Handle Line." LAEE, Dec 17, 1930

10. "Kelley Kar Co. Old-Timer Here." *LAT*, Jul 26, 1934

7: Women in Cars

1. "Designers Aim to Please Women Motorists." *LAEE*, Jan 26, 1919

2. Darryl Holter, "Sybil Geary, Women, and the Automobile in Los Angeles, 1900-1920." *Southern California Quarterly*, v.103 n.2, Summer 2021: 220-255

3. Darryl Holter, *op. cit.*

4. "Women Chauffeurs Now after Automobile Honors." *LAT*, Jul 26, 1905

5. Women Chauffeurs Now after Automobile Honors." *LAT*, Jul 26, 1905

6. Women Chauffeurs Now after Automobile Honors." *LAT*, Jul 26, 1905

7. "Wanted — Job For a Woman." *LAT,* Oct 13, 1907

8. "Many Women Drivers." *LAT,* Dec 22, 1907

9. "Women Chauffeurs Now After Automobile Honors." *LAT,* Jul 26, 1905

10. "Most Successful Endurance Run in the History of Automobiling in America." *LAT,* Jun 30, 1906. Ralph C. Hamlin Collection, Box 19ov, SCWHR

11. "Notes from the Archive." SCWHR, Jun 2020

12. "Woman's Challenge Leads to New Race." *LAT,* Oct 4, 1908

13. "Lozier's Motor Maiden Likely World Champion." *LAT,* Mar 12, 1911

14. "Pretty Girl Makes Record Auto Drive from Riverside." *LAT,* Sep 26, 1909

15. "Beauty's Fast Drive An Invitation Affair." *LAT,* Feb 15, 1908

16. "Up San Jacinto In Oldsmobile." *LAT,* Jan 09, 1910

17. Morgan Yates and Matthew Roth, "Mergers and the Growth of the Automobile Club of Southern California." Automobile Club of Southern California, unpublished research, Mar 2010: 1

18. "Electrifying the Corpse." *LAH,* Dec 30, 1909

19. Rebecca J. Mead, *How the Vote was Won: Woman Suffrage in the Western U.S., 1868-1914:* 146

20. "Thousand Women at Polls Work for Right to Vote." *LAH,* Oct 11, 1911

21. "Thousand Women at Polls Work for the Right to Vote." *LAH,* Oct 11, 1911

22. "Big Building to House Army of Workers for Alexander." *LAEH,* Nov 6, 1911

23. "Socialists Speak Throughout City." *LAEH,* Nov 7, 1911

24. "Los Angeles Claims Honor." *The Tribune* (San Luis Obispo CA), Dec 27, 1913

25. "Praises Women's Handling of Autos in Cities." *Buffalo Times,* Jun 29, 1913

26. Virginia Scharff, *Taking the Wheel: Women and the Coming of the Motor Age,* New York: The Free Press, 1991: 37

27. "Woman's Influence on the Motor Car." *Vogue,* v.41 n.1, Jan 1, 1913

28. Jacob H. Newmark, *Automobile Salesmanship:* 103-104

29. Greg Fischer, "Don Lee and the Transformation of Los Angeles." *Southern California Quarterly,* v.96, n.1, Spr. 2014

30. "Woman's Influence on the Motor Car." *Vogue,* v.41 n.1, Jan 1, 1913

31. "Living Fashion Bullock's Idea." *LAT,* Mar 15, 1912

32. Space Ad, *Vogue* v.37 n.3, Feb 1, 1911

33. "Agents Proud to Sell Pretty Cars." *LAT,* Dec 17, 1916

34. Woman is 'Boss' in Auto Buying." *SFC,* Nov 3, 1912

35. "Needs Must, When—Woman Asks." *Motor: The National Magazine of Motoring,* 1913

36. Virginia Scharff: 199

37. "Designers Aim to Please Women Motorists." *LAEE,* Jan 26, 1919

38. Jacob H. Newmark: *op. cit.*

39. "Femininity's Views Bared by Packard." *San Diego Union-Tribune,* Jul 17, 1927 [ECASB]

40. Jacob H. Newmark: *op. cit.*

41. Virginia Scharff: 48

42. "Shifting of Gears Bugbear of Women." *LAEE,* May 30, 1914

43. "William Bush Inc., Finds Fair Drivers Take No Risk in City Traffic." *LAEE,* Apr 10, 1929

44. M.M. Musselman, *Get a Horse: The Story of the Automobile in America:* 246-249

45. "Movie Star Reaches Chicago." *Motor Age,* v.28, n.14, Sep 30, 1915

46. "The Proven Car For Women." Advertisement, *LAT,* Aug 13, 1916

47. "Mrs. Allen, First Woman Auto Dealer In US, Dead at 89." *Transcript-Telegram* (Holyoke MA), Sep 5, 1961

48. Howard Simpson, "Woman Wins Success in Auto Trade." *Oakland Tribune,* Mar 18, 1923

49. Howard Simpson, "Woman Wins Success in Auto Trade." *Oakland Tribune,* Mar 18, 1923

50. "Hundreds at Charity Ball." *LAT,* Feb 6, 1914

51. "Women Wanted To Work As Elevator Boys." *Monrovia Daily News,* Jul 14, 1917

52. "Lecture Courses Given For Women Motorists." *Hilo Daily Tribune* (Hilo HI), Apr 14, 1921

53. "Women Drivers Needed To Help Win the War." *LAT,* May 19, 1918

54. "Girls Take Men's Places at Wheels of Taxicabs." *LAT,* Jun 9, 1918

55. "Women Drivers of Dairy Trucks Make Hit in City." *LAEE*, Sep 14, 1918

56. "Whole Family Scholars Now." *LAT*, Sep 21, 1919

57. Virginia Scharff: 117

58. "The Perils of a Parkless Town." *LAT*, Feb 29, 1920

59. "Parade To Point Protest." *LAT*, Apr 22, 1920

60. "Expect Action on Parking Law Today." *LAEE*, Apr 23, 1920

61. "Women Drivers On Jump." *LAT*, Oct 24, 1920

62. "Women Cause Auto Changes." *LAEE*, Jan 13, 1926

63. "Features of New Ford are Attractive." *South Gate Daily Press-Tribune* (South Gate CA), Jul 2, 1929

64. "Unusual Driving Ease Appreciated by Women." *LAEE*, Mar 2, 1929

Sybil C. Geary

1. "Auto Club Sets High Mark in Membership Enrollment." *LAT*, May 22, 1910

2. S.C. Geary, "Automobile Club of So. California." *LAH*, Oct 16, 1910

3. J. Allen Davis, *The Friend to All Motorists: The Story of the Automobile Club of Southern California through 65 Years, 1900-1965*: 36

4. C.G Sinsabaugh, Motoring's Good Samaritan, *Motor Age*, v.25, n.18, Apr 30, 1914

5. "Auto Club Members All Special Speed Officers." *LAT*, Nov 10, 1913

6. "C.G Sinsabaugh, Motoring's Good Samaritan, *Motor Age*, v.25, n.18, Apr 30, 1914

7. "Present Low Speed Unnecessary." *Long Beach Press*, Oct 19, 1912

8. S.C. Geary, "Automobile Club of So. California." *LAH*, Oct 16, 1910

9. "Open Gates to Yosemite Park." *LAT*, Oct 14, 1912

10. "Desert Reaches Are to Be Marked By Signs." *LAEH*, Nov 16, 1912

11. "Desert Charting Much Appreciated." *Los Angeles Evening Post Record*, Dec 14, 1912

12. J. Allen Davis: 43

13. "Silence Policy Forced on Club." *LAEX*, May 18, 1912

14. "Mt. Wilson Trail Safe for Autos." *Santa Ana Register* (Santa Ana CA), Jul 1, 1912

15. "Corona Calls Motorists, Auto Club to Sign Roads." *LAT*, Aug 29, 1913

16. "Speed Cop is a Woman." *SFE*, Jul 6, 1912

17. "Auto Club Members All Special Speed Officers." *LAT*, Nov 10, 1913

18. "'Educate Jaywalker' Auto Club's Slogan." *LAEX*, Jul 26, 1913

19. Bert Smith, "Gossip Along Gasoline Row." *LAT*, Sep 8, 1912

20. "Auto Club Sets High Mark in Membership Enrollment." *LAT*, May 22, 1910

21. "Synopsis of Club's Vehicle Bill." *Touring Topics*, v.5 n.1, Feb 19135

22. "Miss Geary Suffers Collapse; Overwork." *LAEH*, Mar 28, 1913

23. "Auto Club Plans Better Motor Laws." *LAT,* Apr 6, 1913

24. "Auto Club Plans Better Motor Laws." *LAT,* Apr 6, 1913

25. J. Allen Davis and Harry V. Cheshire Jr., "California Motor Vehicle Legislation" *66 West's Annotated California Codes 12-57,* 1960: 6-7

8: Los Angeles Automobile Shows

1. "Auto Show to Open in Blaze of Splendor." *LAH*, Jan 21, 1907

2. James J. Flink, *The Automobile Age*: 18

3. The Detroit auto show began in 1899 and was sponsored by the sporting goods department of the Fletcher Hardware Company and the Tri-State Automobile and Sporting Goods Association. The show consisted of automobiles, bicycles, firearms, and fishing tackle. Robert Szudarek, *The First Century of the Detroit Auto Show*: 3

4. "Auto Manufacturers Organize." *Brooklyn Daily Eagle*, Dec 4, 1900

5. "The National Association of Automobile Manufacturers." *Automobile Review*, v.4 n.1, Jan 1901. A similar development took place in Great Britain when twelve manufacturers formed the Society of Motor Manufacturers and Traders largely to allow only one show in 1903 and to prevent "a multiplicity of shows." "Crystal Palace and Motor Traders' Show." *Automobile Topics*, v.4 n.20, Aug 30, 1902

6. "The Chicago Show and its Management." *Automobile Review*, v.4 n.4, Apr 1901

7. "Automobile Show." Advertisement, *Los Angeles Evening Post-Record*, Jan 21, 1907

8. "Floor Space is All Sold." *LAT*, Dec 12, 1906

9. James J. Flink: 18

10. "Amid Brilliant Display of Flowers and Lights Automobile Show Opens." *LAH*, Jan 22, 1907

11. "Auto Show to Open in Blaze of Splendor." *LAH*, Jan 21, 1907

12. "Amid Brilliant Display of Flowers and Lights Automobile Show Opens." *LAH*, Jan 22, 1907

13. "Auto Show Will Close Tonight." *LAH*, Jan 26, 1907

14. "Auto Show For Sunday." *LAT*, Jan 26, 1907

15. "See Big Success for Auto Show." *San Francisco Chronicle*, Jan 30, 1907

16. "Los Angeles Auto Show Excites Much Interest." *LAEE*, Jan 16, 1909

17. "Notes of Show." *LAT*, Jan 24, 1909

18. "Notes of Show." *LAT,* Jan 24, 1909

19. "Big Preparations for Los Angeles Auto Show." *Los Angeles Evening Post-Record*, Jan 23, 1909

20. "The Los Angeles Show." *HA*, v.23 n.5, Feb 3, 1909

21. "Starts Fight at Auto Show." *LAH*, Jan 30, 1909

22. "Everything in Readiness for 1910 Auto Show." *LAH*, Feb 6, 1910

23. "Auto Show Lights Soon to Be Dimmed." *LAT*, Feb 13, 1910

24. "Record Canvas to Cover Auto Show." *LAH*, Feb 12, 1910

25. "Big Tree Bark to Be Used At Licensed Show." *LAH*, Feb 6, 1910

26. "Daylight Peep at Licensed Gems Thrills Fiesta Throng." *LAT*, Dec 27, 1910

27. "Big Auto Show Opens Monday." *LAH*, Dec 11, 1910

28. "Unusual Features Promised at Licensed Motor Car Show." *Los Angeles Evening Post-Record*, Dec 17, 1910

29. MCDA minutes, Jan 8, 1913

30. "Los Angeles to Have Automobile Show." *Touring Topics*, Dec 1913

31. "Last Chance to see our Handsome Motor Salon." *LAT*, Jan 10, 1914

32. "Los Angeles Auto Show Will Open Saturday." *Monrovia Daily News*, Oct 9, 1914

33. "Motor Truck Show to Follow Car Exhibits." *LAT*, Oct 18, 1914

34. "Los Angeles to Hold Auto Show." *LAEE*, Jun 19, 1915

35. "Broadway Motor Car Display Will Open Today." *LAEE*, Oct 23, 1915

36. "Maxwell Car Scores Heavily at Show." *Bakersfield Morning Echo*, Oct 31, 1915

37. "Plan Big Auto Show for L.A. This Fall." *The Bulletin* (Pomona CA), Sep 8, 1916

38. "Million Dollar Auto Show At Los Angeles." *The Tribune* (San Luis Obispo CA), Oct 21, 1916

39. The use of special styling add-ons to alter the car's appearance prefigured the important trend of customization that largely originated in Los Angeles and led to hot rods and street rods in the 1930s and beyond. See Gary S. Cross, *Machines of Youth: America's Car Obsession*: 20-27

40. "Auto Show Attendance Passes All Expectations." *LAT*, Oct 30, 1916

41. "Los Angeles Show." *MW*, v.26 n.3, Nov 15, 1916

42. "Great Auto Show Opens to Public." *LAEE*, Oct 28, 1916

43. "Great Auto Show Sure." *LAT,* Dec 3, 1918

44. MCDA, *Report of Eighth Annual Auto Show*, Jan 27, 1919

45. MCDA, *Report of Eighth Annual Auto Show*, Jan 27, 1919

46. MCDA, *Report of Eighth Annual Auto Show*, Jan 27, 1919

47. "Great Motor Show Opens Today." *LAT*, Jan 11, 1919

48. "Creations of Local Motor Fashion Designers Big Hit at Auto Show." *LAT*, Jan 14, 1919

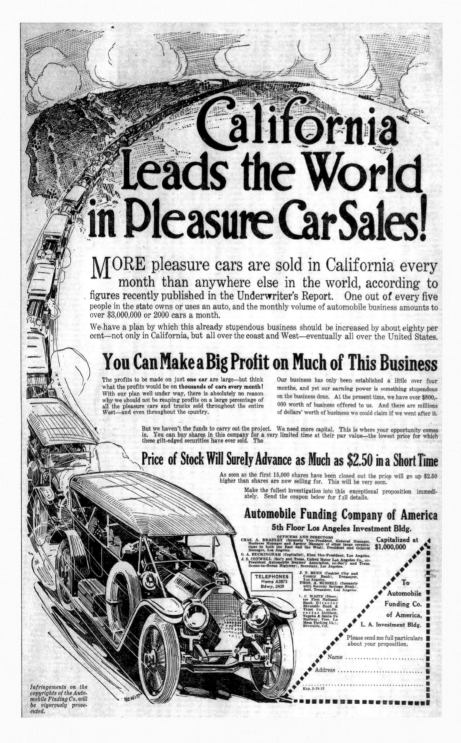

49. MCDA, *Report of Eighth Annual Auto Show*, Jan 27, 1919

50. The Detroit auto show began in 1899 and was sponsored by the sporting goods department of Fletcher Hardware Company and Tri-State Automobile and Sporting Goods Association. The show consisted of automobiles, bicycles, firearms, and fishing tackle. Robert Szudarek, *The First Century of the Detroit Auto Show*: 3

51. "The National Association of Automobile Manufacturers." *Automobile Review*, v.4 n.1, Jan 1901

52. "L.A. Show Will Afford County Dealers Tips." *Santa Ana Register* (Santa Ana CA), Dec 11, 1920

53. "L.A. Show Will Afford County Dealers Tips." *Santa Ana Register* (Santa Ana CA), Dec 11, 1920

54. "Campaign a Huge Success." *LAT*, Apr 10, 1921

55. "'Open Road' Week Huge Success in Los Angeles." *LAEE*, May 10, 1922

56. "Record Attendance Expected at Auto Show." *Long Beach Telegram*, Nov 4, 1923, Nov 10, 1923,

57. Frederick Wagner, "Special Cars Arrive Here For Display." *LAEE*, Mar 10, 1924

58. John W. Swallow, "Colorful Display of 312 Vehicles." *LAEE*, Feb 20, 1926

59. "Why Go To The Auto Show?" *LAEE*, Feb 20, 1926

60. "L.A. Now Third Motor Center." *LAE*, Feb 13, 1927 [ECASB]

61. "Auto Show Bulletin No. 16/29." Sixteenth Automobile Show, Los Angeles, California, Mar 2-11, 1929, Bulletin v.17/29, 20/29, and 21/29

62. "Spectators Flee Auto Show Fire." *New York Times*, Mar 6, 1929

63. "Show Ruins Drawing Card." *LAT*, Mar 7, 1929

64. David Strohl, "The Day the Los Angeles Auto Show Went Up in Flames." Hemmings, Mar 5, 2019

65. "Fire Consumes Relics." *LAT*,
Mar 8, 1929

66. "Motor Distributors Receive Checks
Covering Damages From Fire at
Exposition." *LAEE*, Mar 7, 1929

67. "L.A. Auto Show Again Opened."
LAEE, Mar 7, 1929

68. "Auto Show Spirit Praised." *LAT*,
Mar 8, 1929

69. "Howe, Jack, Exhibit Goes Ahead
Loses But One Day." *LAE*,
Mar 8, 1929 [ECASB]

70. "Two Days More of Auto Show."
LAT, Mar 10, 1929

71. "Film Portrays Auto Show Fire."
LAT, Mar 8, 1929

72. "Auto Show Fire Laid to Wiring."
LAT, Mar 8, 1929

73. A.Y. Tully, "Shootin' Straight."
LAEE, Mar 7, 1929

9: Afterword

1. "You'd Never Guess This City's
Threat." *Daily News* (Los Angeles),
May 6, 1942

2. "You'd Never Guess This City's
Threat…" *Daily News* (Los Angeles),
May 6, 1942

3. "State Official For Pushing Parkway." *Pasadena Post*, Apr 11, 1940

4. "L.A. And Detroit In Production
Tie: In A Way, That Is." *Los Angeles
Evening Citizen News*, Sep 17, 1946

5. "L.A., State Write Golden Chronicle." *Los Angeles Mirror*, Oct 11, 1949

6. "Recreation and Vistas Varied in
California." *Chicago Tribune*,
Oct 21, 1951

7. No headline, *East Whittier Review*,
Nov 20, 1960

8. "Automotive Highlights." *LAT*,
Mar 9, 1952

9. "Automobiles and City Streets."
LAT, Sep 29, 1957

10. "Urge Crash Program for Streets."
Valley Times, Feb 3, 1959

11. "Million Are Expected at L.A.
Exhibit." *LAT*, Dec 31, 1998

AACA Library and Resource Center, Hershey, Pennsylvania: 171, 172.

Author Collection: 104 (bottom), 114, 118 (bottom), 140 (right), 141, 148.

Automobile Club of Southern California Archive: cover, 3.

Robert J. Burdette: from *Greater Los Angeles and Southern California*: 46 (right).

California Historical Society: 97.

California State Library, California Room: 62, 66, 70 (bottom), 118 (top).

Detroit Public Library: National Automotive History Collection 26, 110.

Harvard Business School, Baker Library: 85 (bottom), 89.

Huntington Library, San Marino, California: Parkinson Archive 65, 72 (left); Marquez Collection 158 (right).

J. Eric Lynxwiler Archive: 182, 207, 210.

Leon Dixon Automotive Library: 68, 70 (top), 71, 77 (right), 81, 82.

Library of Congress, Washington DC: 10, 152.

Los Angeles County Museum of Natural History, Seaver Center for Western History Research: 47, 52, 144, 168 (top), 202; General Collection 27, 49 (right), 100, 145, 202; Al Greene Collection 14, 55; Automotive Literature Collection 30 (left); Automotive Photograph Collection 78; C.C. Pierce Collection 143; Del Valle Collection 95; Ephemera Collection 73; Fred Layton Washburn Collection 149; GLANCDA Collection 140 (left); Ralph Hamlin Collection 4, 20, 36, 38, 39, 40, 45, 59, 98, 101, 124, 164, 166, 168, 170, 176; Warren C. Dickerson Collection 22, 146; Miscellaneous Serial File: 199, 203.

Los Angeles Daily News: Aug 13, 1927 211.

Los Angeles Evening Express: Feb 22, 1913 85, Aug 2, 1913 97 (top), Aug 31, 1912 97, Mar 29, 1913 198, Oct 27, 1926 204, May 24, 1913 209.

Los Angeles Evening Post Record: June 15, 1912 197; June 24, 1903 201.

Los Angeles Public Library: Eyre Powell Chamber of Commerce Collection 161; *Herald-Examiner* Collection 16, 24, 28, 49 (left), 51, 136; Security Pacific National Bank Collection 12, 30 (right), 58, 63, 72, 74, 79, 86, 94, 102, 105, 106, 108, 109, 112, 113, 122, 126, 128, 130, 137, 138, 150, 154, 178, 195, 221; Legacy Collection 15; Shades of L.A. Collection 215, Alfred R. Hromatka, Warren & Leora Worthington Collection 104 (top), 118-119.

Los Angeles Times: Nov 30, 1906 120; Dec 17, 1913 158; Jul 27, 1913 207.

Maine Historical Society: 96.

Motor Age: Sep 30, 1915 150.

National Museum of American History, Smithsonian, Division of Home and Community Life: 90, 91, 92, 93.

Out West: February 1913 8, endpapers.

Parkinson Family Archive: 64.

Press Reference Library: *Notables of the Southwest* 1912: 73 (left).

Ralph Hamlin Archive: 23, 41, 48, 50.

Dave Smeds: 121.

Univ. of California Los Angeles (UCLA), Charles E. Young Library, Special Collections: *Los Angeles Times* Photography Collection 60, 76 (right), 177 (left) 179, 222. *Daily News* Negatives Collection 189, 190, 192, 212-213.

Univ. of Southern California (USC) Libraries: "Dick" Whittington Photography Collection 76 (left), 116, 155, 156, 184, 186, 212; California Historical Society Collection 32, 34, 56; Automobile Club of Southern California Collection 162, 216.

Workman and Temple Family Homestead Museum: 6, 54, 103, 159, 177 (right).

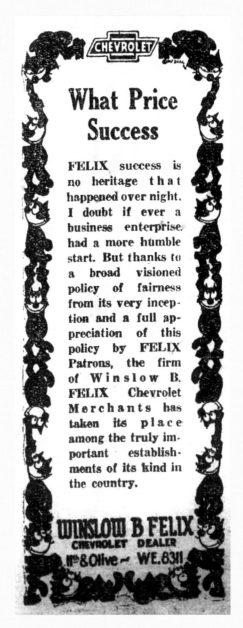

Traffic at Wilshire Boulevard and South Western Avenue, 1930.

BIBLIOGRAPHY

Following is the list of books used to research *Driving Force*. But, in addition to these books, important information came from the newspapers, magazines, diverse publications, and other sources which are cited in the Endnotes to the chapters, starting on page **196**. To conserve space and paper, those sources are not re-listed here. The publications whose names are abbreviated in the key at the beginning of the Endnotes are the publications where information was frequently found, such as *Los Angeles Times*, *Los Angeles Examiner*, *Los Angeles Evening Express*, *Los Angeles Evening Herald*, *Los Angeles Express*, and *Los Angeles Herald*. There was also a wealth of useful information on the early history of auto retailing in a group of weekly, bi-weekly, and monthly trade publications and magazines aimed at automobile enthusiasts, journals that blossomed during this period including: *Automobile*, *Automobile Topics*, *the Horseless Age*, *Motor*, *Motor Age*, and *Motor World*. Particularly important to this research was *Motor West*, a monthly publication that covered the West Coast from its base in Los Angeles.

Breer, Carl; Anthony J. Yanik; and SAE Historical Committee. 1995. *The Birth of Chrysler Corporation and Its Engineering Legacy.* Warrendale Pennsylvania: Society of Automotive Engineers.

Brilliant, Ashleigh. 1964. *The Great Car Craze: How Southern California Collided with the Automobile in the 1920s.* Santa Barbara: Woodbridge Press.

Burdette, Robert J. 1910. *Greater Los Angeles and Southern California: Their Portraits and Personal Memoranda.* Chicago: Lewis Pub.

California, State of. 1960. *Vehicle Code: Official California Vehicle Code Classification.* St. Paul: West.

Canemaker, John. 1991. *Felix: The Twisted Tale of the World's Most Famous Cat.* New York: Pantheon.

Cross, Gary S. 2018. *Machines of Youth: America's Car Obsession.* Chicago: University of Chicago Press.

Davis, J. Allen. 1967. *The Friend to All Motorists: The Story of the Automobile Club of Southern California through 65 Years.* Los Angeles: Automobile Club of Southern California.

Drake, Albert. 1993. *Hot Rodder! : From Lakes to Street, An Oral History.* Portland, Oregon: Flat Out Press.

Epstein, Ralph C. 1972. *The Automobile Industry: Its Economic and Commercial Development.* New York: Arno Press.

Finch, Christopher. 1992. *Highways to Heaven: The Auto Biography of America.* 1st ed. New York: HarperCollins.

Flink, James. 1970. *America Adopts the Automobile, 1895–1910.* Cambridge, Mass.: MIT Press.

Flink, James J. 2001. *The Automobile Age.* Cambridge, Mass.: MIT Press.

Ford, Henry. 1922. *My Life and Work.* Garden City: Doubleday, Page & Co.

Franz, Kathleen. 2005. *Tinkering: Consumers Reinvent the Early Automobile.* Philadel-phia: U. of Pennsylvania Press.

Gelber, Steven M. 2008. *Horse Trading in the Age of Cars: Men in the Marketplace.* Baltimore: Johns Hopkins U. Press.

Georgeano, Nick. 1992. *The American Automobile A Centenary 1893–1993.* New York: Smithmark.

Glasscock, C.B. 1937. *The Gasoline Age: The Story of the Men Who Made It.* Indianapolis, New York: Bobbs Merrill Company.

Grimes, William A. 1926. *Financing Automobile Sales by the Time-Payment Plan.* Chicago: Shaw.

Haverlin, Carl; Carl Grant; and Earle C. Anthony Inc. 1929. *Romance of Transportation and Story of the Packard Building.* Los Angeles: Earle C. Anthony.

Hewitt, Charles M. 1960. *The Development of Automobile Franchises.* Bureau of Business Research, School of Business, Indiana University.

Race at Ascot Speedway, 1913.

Hoffman, Paul G. and James E. Greene. 1929. *Marketing Used Cars*. New York: Harper & Bros.

Hoffman, Paul G. 1939. *Seven Roads to Safety*. New York: Harper & Bros.

Hoffman, Paul G. 1930. *Trends in Motor Car Distribution: Consumer Marketing Series #1*. New York: American Management Association.

Kennedy, E.D. 1941. *The Automobile Industry*. New York: Reynal and Hitchcock.

Longstreet, Stephen. 1952. *A Century on Wheels: The Story of Studebaker: A History*. New York: Henry Holt.

Mead, Rebecca J. 2004. *How the Vote Was Won: Women Suffrage in the Western United States, 1868–1914*. New York: NYU Press.

Musselman, M.M. 1950. *Get a Horse: The Story of the Automobile in America*. New York: Lippincott.

Nelson, Kevin. 2009. *Wheels of Change: From Zero to 600 MPH, The Amazing Story of California and the Automobile*. Berkeley and San Francisco: Heyday Books and California Historical Society.

Newmark, Jacob H. 1915. *Automobile Salesmanship*. Detroit: Automobile Publishing Company.

Olney, Martha L. 1991. *Buy Now, Pay Later: Advertising, Credit, and Consumer Durables in the 1920s*. Chapel Hill: U. of N. Carolina Press.

Powell, Sinclair. 2014. *The Franklin Automobile Company*. Cazenovia, New York: The H.H. Franklin Club, Inc.

Raucher, Alan R. 1986. *Paul G. Hoffman: Architect of Foreign Aid*. Lexington: University Press of Kentucky.

Rubenstein, James M. 2001. *Making and Selling Cars: Innovation and Change in the U.S. Automotive Industry*. Baltimore: Johns Hopkins University.

Scharff, Virginia. 1991. *Taking the Wheel: Women and the Coming of the Motor Age*. New York: The Free Press.

Seltzer, Lawrence H. 1928. *A Financial History of the American Automobile Industry*. Boston: Houghton Mifflin.

Smith, Theodore H. 1941. *The Marketing of Used Automobiles*. Bureau of Business Research, Ohio State University.

Spinella, Art, *et al.*. 1978. *America's Auto Dealer: The Master Merchandisers*. Van Nuys, California: Freed-Crown.

Wilson, Mark A. 2011. *Bernard Maybeck: Architect of Elegance*. 1st ed. Layton, Utah: Gibbs Smith.

◀ Standard Oil service station at West Adams Boulevard and Vermont Avenue, Los Angeles, 1928.

▶ Frank Dillon's Tire Shop on South Olive Street, 1930.

ABOUT THE AUTHORS

DARRYL HOLTER is an adjunct professor in History at USC who has authored books on French coal-mining, Wisconsin labor history, and Woody Guthrie in Los Angeles. He managed several auto dealerships, including Felix Chevrolet, and was the founding chairman of the Figueroa Corridor Business Improvement District.

STEPHEN GEE is an award-winning writer and television producer based in Los Angeles. His other books include *Iconic Vision: John Parkinson, Architect of Los Angeles*; *Los Angeles Central Library: A History of Its Art and Architecture*; and *Los Angeles City Hall: An American Icon*.

DRIVING FORCE
Automobiles and the New American City, 1900–1930

By Darryl Holter with Stephen Gee

Copyright © 2023 by Darryl Holter. All rights reserved.

Design by J. Eric Lynxwiler, Signpost Graphics

10 9 8 7 6 5 4 3 2 1

ISBN 978-1-62640-123-5

Library of Congress Cataloging-in-Publication Data is available.

Published by Angel City Press, www.angelcitypress.com

Printed in Canada

◀ Cars and pedestrians at 5th Street and Broadway.
▶ Motorists escape the city for a drive on Foothill Boulevard, Pasadena, 1918.

PERRY H. GREER, PRESIDENT LOS ANGELES MOTOR CAR DEALERS ASS'N. ONE OF THE MOST ENTHUSIASTIC BOOSTERS FOR GOOD ROADS AND THE MOTOR CAR BUSINES IN SOUTHERN CAL.

(Speech/sign: WE CANNOT BOOST THE AUTOMOBILE SITUATION TOO MUCH)

W. K. COWAN, NESTOR OF THE MOTOR CAR BUSINESS IN SO. CAL.- ONE OF THE ORGANIZERS OF THE DEALERS ASS'N.- WAS ITS FIRST PRESIDENT AND BUILT 1ST GARAGE IN LOS ANGELES IN 1903.

(Sign: VICE PRES. AND MGR OF THE W. K. COWAN COMPANY)

(Paper: I HAVE BOOSTED THE MOTOR INDUSTRY FROM ITS INFANCY- AND SHALL CONTINUE FOR THE GOOD OF ALL - W.K.C.)

RALPH C. HAMLIN, PAST PRES. DEALERS ASS'N PHOENIX ROAD-RACE WINNER, ALL ROUND BIG AUTO BOOSTER AND SELLS SOME FRANKLINS BELIEVE ME.

(Sign: JUST A FEW OF RALPH'S TROPHIES) *(Car: FRANKLIN)*

EARLE Y. BOOTHE THE LIVE SEC'Y OF THE MOTOR CAR DEALERS ASS'N. WHO IS BOOSTIN FOR BETTER LAWS REGULATING TRAFFIC CONDITIONS.

(Sign: NATIONAL AGENCY) *(Paper: PULL HARD FOR BETTER STATE LEGIS-LATION)*

J. S. "POP" CONWELL MGR. UNITED MOTOR-LOS ANGELES CO., DISTRIBUTORS, MAXWELL AND COLUMBIA. "POP" IS THE DEAN OF THE LOS ANGELES DEALERS AND A BIG BOOSTER.

(Signs: I AM A BELIEVER IN HOME RULE UNDER INTELLIGENT DIRECTION AND JUST CO-OPERATION J.S.C.) *(WE WILL HAVE AN OCEAN TO OCEAN HIGHWAY LOS ANGELES TO NEW YORK BY 1915 Pop Conwell)*

William E. Bush, THE PIERCE → MOTOR CARS AND TRUCKS "BILL" IS A PIONEER OF THE MOTOR GAME AND HAS DEVOTED MUCH OF HIS ENERGY TO IT. "LET BILL DO IT"

(Sign: SO. CAL'S SUCCESS? GOOD ROADS! Bill Bush.)

VICE PRES. OF THE DEALERS ASS'N E. ROGER STEARNS PAC. COAST DISTRIBUTOR STODDARD-DAYTON, BAKER ELECTRICS AND FEDERAL TRUCKS. ROGER IS A GOOD SPORT AND SELLS SOME CARS ASK THE COMPETITORS

(Speech: ROGER DIDN'T CATCH ME) *(Label: CATALINA)* *(Sign: TAKE IT FROM AN OLD TIMER-BOOSTING PAYS!)*

CAP. H. D. RYUS, BOOSTING REPRESENTATIVE OF THE BIG OLDSMOBILE, WON 1ST PHOENIX ROAD RACE AND "BALDY" 3 TIMES IN SUCCESSION

(Speech: AIN'T THIS BIG WHEEL A DAISY) *(Wheel: OLDSMOBILE, 43 INCHES)*

DUTTON